The Corporate Startup

How established companies can develop successful innovation ecosystems

Tendayi Viki
Dan Toma
Esther Gons

Management **IMPACT**

The Corporate Startup

Big companies need to innovate or die. The question is how. Companies need a playbook; a process by which they can start the process of transforming their organizations into innovation engines. *The Corporate Startup* is that playbook. It provides a proven methodology — applying Lean Startup principles and more — for building a culture of innovation.

Ben Yoskovitz, Co-Author of *Lean Analytics* and Founding Partner at Highline BETA.

Nothing's harder than creating innovation, and the most valuable creations are exactly those which shrivel under typical corporate management. The authors' approach is to focus on creating an ecosystem that allows innovation to flourish on its own; addressing health of the soil rather than micro-managing the plants. If you want to avoid some of the common traps and give your internal entrepreneurship the best shot, this book will help.

Rob Fitzpatrick, Author of *The Mom Test*.

In a world full of innovation hype and clichés, *The Corporate Startup* manages to provide useful answers and solutions to a complex question — how can corporations innovate faster and better? The book delivers a clear roadmap for creating a strategy, governance structures and implementing an innovation practice. This makes it an absolute must-read for all corporate strategists and innovators and has become "the way we think and talk" about corporate innovation in Copenhagen Fintech.

Thomas Krogh Jensen, CEO at Copenhagen Fintech.

With innovation now a strategic imperative, you are going to need a playbook to help develop practical and scalable approaches to innovation in your company — simply put, you are going to need this book!

Paul Brown, Founder at Rokket Digital.

This book is timely addition to the corporate innovation space. It is a must read for anyone working on innovation in medium-size and large companies. The principles and practices, if well implemented can save a company from the disruption death march.

Tim Deeson, Managing Director at Deeson Group.

In this wonderful book, we have found frameworks and methods that are extremely relevant and helpful in our efforts to structure our open innovation. We are beginning to use Corporate Startup tools and methods to better qualify investment decisions, as well as secure continued board-level understanding and buy-in to the strategy.

Ole Madsen, Senior Vice President at Spar Nord Bank.

The 21st century organization, we're told, needs to be innovative, creative and customer centered. That's all very well if you're a disruptive startup. But what if you're an established organization based on 20th century principles of Taylorism? How do you make your big company as innovative as a small startup? If you want practical advice from people who have been there and done that, there's no better source than this book. Reading this book is like shadowing the authors on a consulting assignment as they coach you on what works and what doesn't.

David Travis, User Experience Consultant and Managing Director of Userfocus.

The authors have clearly spent time in the trenches helping big and small companies transform through applying lean startup principles. This book is full of insightful nuggets you immediately grasp and a simple yet effective framework you can start implementing right away.

Justin Coetsee, Co-Founder at Ignitor.

In this remarkable book, the authors challenge us to take the 'Red Pill' of sustainable innovation: a system of frameworks that work together to generate superior results. If you want to keep yourself in the black, take the authors' 'Red Pill' and follow their advice.

Luke Hohmann, Founder/CEO at Conteneo and Author of *Innovation Games*.

A key reading for leaders that outlines how to effectively innovate for the future and boost growth, while running the core business.

Alex Osterwalder, Co-Author of *Business Model Generation* and *Value Proposition Design* and Co-Founder of Strategyzer.

Lean thinking for business and product development requires the practitioner to strip away misconceptions about how an idea becomes a successful new business. It requires a 're-training' of the brain to suppress those misconceptions and focus on the fastest path to testing the assumptions held about the customer's needs. This book is your 're-training' manual.

Peter Pascale, Vice President of Product Management at Pearson VUE.

Established companies need to innovate or risk losing market share. This book provides a great playbook that managers can use to learn about lean startup methods and apply them within their company. It is a must read for any executive thinking about creating an innovation ecosystem within their business.

Klaus Wagner, CEO at Josera Petfood GmbH & Co. KG.

We have found the Corporate Startup model and the thoughts on the innovation ecosystem very useful in designing our innovation strategy. This book is a must read for all corporate leaders that want to transform their companies to be more innovative.

Erik Kongsvik-Ibsen, Vice President of Strategy and Business Development at Egmont.

The Corporate Startup bridges two worlds that are normally regarded to be quite the opposite. Corporations can learn a lot about startup methodologies and how they apply to their organizations from reading this book. Startup founders should also read it to understand the challenges that large companies face and how to better collaborate with them. I highly recommend this book.

Rune Theill, Co-Founder and CEO at Rockstart Accelerator.

I believe the next wave of entrepreneurship and innovation will belong to the established corporation. *The Corporate Startup* provides a structured and practical approach to help companies make their new business model building machine a reality.

Dr Marc Sniukas, Author of *The Art of Opportunity*.

A book crammed full of real examples and pragmatic (not dogmatic) frameworks for bringing entrepreneurship to corporate dinosaurs. A must read.

Tristan Kromer, Founder at Kromatic and Editor of *The Real Startup Book*.

Tendayi, Dan and Esther are some of the most knowledgeable and engaging members in the startup and corporate innovation community. Not only is their personal knowledge and experience very valuable, I've experienced them to generate profound impact through their engagement with several of our, and others' grassroots initiatives. This book allows anyone in the intrapreneurship field to access that knowledge and create the same impact.

Leon Pals, Chairman at Startup Foundation.

As the role of corporate innovator seems to be getting more complex, what else to wish for than a roadmap that makes things simple and clear? Tendayi, Dan and Esther have done a wonderful job creating exactly such a roadmap with this book, and I'm sure it will support you in getting to your goals, faster.

Hans Balmaekers, Director at Intrapreneurship Conference.

This wonderful book helps companies apply practical and innovative business model development methods using new ways of collaboration, based on an ecosystems approach. *The Corporate Startup* provides a great way of implementing innovation practices for companies to cope in today's hectic and ever changing world.

Corine van Winden, CEO at Global Pets Community.

In my experience the biggest topic that is not covered well for large corporations is the art of managing the innovation process and output. *The Corporate Startup* provides a concrete framework to manage innovation at the strategy, management and practice levels. It connects the topics you likely know such as business model design and lean startup to the bigger corporate picture.

Bob Jansen, Founder at Firmhouse.

This book has helped me, my team and our company's full innovation transformation and I can say it is the most comprehensive guide on corporate innovation to date. The tools and methods described here are helping us on our journey to improve performance and reduce the cost of innovation.

Vegard Hansen, Head of Innovation Ecosystem at Den Norske Bank.

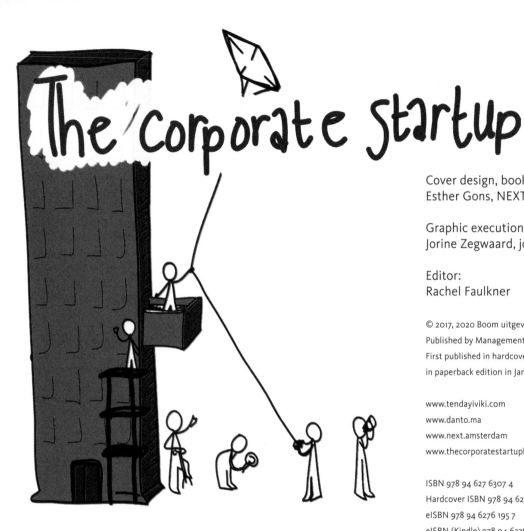

The corporate startup

Cover design, book design and illustrations:
Esther Gons, NEXT.amsterdam

Graphic execution:
Jorine Zegwaard, jorinezegwaard.nl

Editor:
Rachel Faulkner

© 2017, 2020 Boom uitgevers Amsterdam, Tendayi Viki, Dan Toma and Esther Gons
Published by Management Impact, a division of Boom uitgevers Amsterdam
First published in hardcover in April 2017, reprinted in May 2017 and March 2018, first printed
in paperback edition in January 2019, reprinted in March 2019 and October 2020

www.tendayiviki.com
www.danto.ma
www.next.amsterdam
www.thecorporatestartupbook.com

ISBN 978 94 627 6307 4
Hardcover ISBN 978 94 627 6150 6
eISBN 978 94 6276 195 7
eISBN (Kindle) 978 94 6276 196 4

For Elizabeth, Jacob,
Eli and Ben. My reasons.

Tendayi Viki

For having a compass.

Dan Toma

For Anniko and Aaron.
For their future.

Esther Gons

Table of Contents

PART 1

ECOSYSTEM

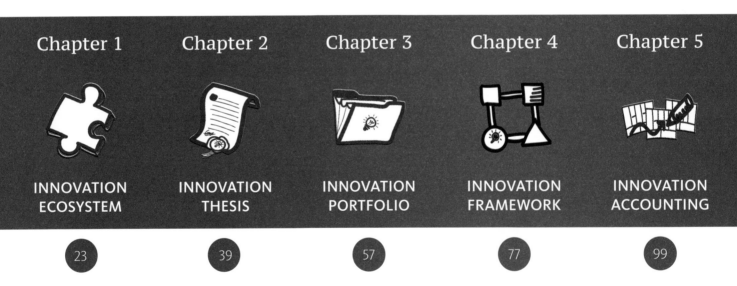

'The basic problem confronting an organization is to engage in sufficient exploitation to ensure its current viability and, at the same time, devote enough energy to exploration to ensure its future viability.'

James G. March, Stanford Professor

Innovation Paradox

In 2015, Microsoft got some of its groove back[1]. But earlier that same year, Microsoft reported its largest-ever quarterly net loss. The loss was the result of a $7.5 billion writedown from the purchase of Nokia's handset unit[2]. The writedown was viewed as another example of Microsoft's struggles in the smartphone business. Nokia's own smartphone struggles are a parallel business story that provides powerful lessons about corporate innovation. It seems that successful established companies often get trapped by their previous success in a manner that limits their capacity to innovate.

We are living in an era where innovation is imperative. It is undeniable that the world around us is changing. Technology and software have transformed business, and continue to do so in more and more dramatic ways. Corporate leadership would have to be in a special kind of denial to overlook how these changes are impacting their businesses. Keeping their heads in the sand is no longer an option. Corporate leaders have to respond. Innovation can no longer be viewed as a sideshow. It is now *the* way to do business in the 21st century and a key driver of sustainable growth.

The challenge of having to respond to change is nothing new. As long ago as 1942, Joseph Schumpeter wrote about *Creative Destruction* as a process that refreshes economies by injecting new blood in the form of innovative new technologies and companies. What is remarkable about our time is the sheer pace of change in social trends, economic factors and technology[3]. The average lifespan of companies is getting shorter. At a churn rate of 75%, it is predicted that the entire S&P 500 index will be replaced by 2027[4]. We have also seen the emergence of startups that quickly become billion dollar companies such as Microsoft, eBay, Google, Amazon, Facebook, Twitter, Dropbox, Uber and Airbnb. Driven by technology, these companies have transformed traditional industries and business models.

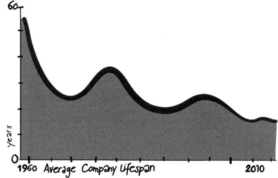

Source: Foster, R. & Kaplan, S. (2011). *Creative Destruction.* New York City: Random House.

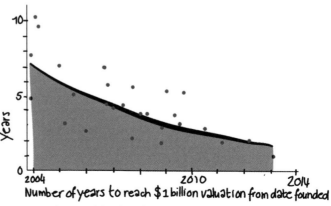

Source: Deloitte Canada (2014). *Age of Disruption: Are Canadian firms prepared?*[5]

11

The Disadvantage of Incumbency

In contrast, traditional long-standing companies appear to be struggling. It seems that being an already successful company can be the Achilles' heel for innovation. In 2007, when Steve Jobs introduced the first iPhone at MacWorld, Steve Ballmer who was then the CEO of Microsoft, was not that impressed. He mockingly declared that:

"There's is no chance that the iPhone is going to get any significant market share. No chance!" [6]

Fast forward to 2014. In an interview with Charlie Rose, Steve Ballmer admitted that one of his greatest regrets from his time as CEO of Microsoft, was not getting in early on the mobile phone hardware business. When Charlie Rose asks Ballmer why Microsoft did not move into the phone business, Ballmer's response is telling:

"When the name of your company is Microsoft and your formula works...
Our formula was working, we were software guys...
So for us it was kind of like a religious transformation." [7]

Nokia was going through its own religious transformation. At one point it was the largest mobile phone company in the world, with more than 50% of the global market share. But Nokia lost in the smartphone battles so badly that by the time Microsoft purchased its mobile phone unit in 2013, it only had 3% of the smartphone market[8]. In a candid interview with INSEAD Olli-Pekka Kallasvuo, the former CEO of Nokia, admitted that:

"It is sometimes difficult in a big successful organization to have the sense of urgency and hunger. No company can defend only. If you have a high market share and you are a market leader, if you start defending you cannot sustain." [9]

Nokia's poor response to the emergence of smartphones is closely connected to Microsoft's historic quarterly net loss. But these two companies were not alone in underestimating the potential disruption that would be caused by smartphones. A similar misjudgment was made by Garmin's CEO Min Kao. During an interview with Forbes in the summer of 2003, he dismissed mobile phones as a commodity business that he would like to avoid[10]. However, as smartphones have gotten better and smarter, Garmin have had to adapt their business model. There is some irony in the fact that Garmin now builds apps for the iPhone and Android.

The comforts of incumbency can indeed be a disadvantage. Leadership teams in successful companies can become 'climate change deniers'. That is to say, they can see the changes happening in the business world, but deny their relevance to the company. This denial is most intractable when the weather is good. In most successful large companies, the focus is on the high revenue

- high profit cash cow products. If the company is currently making large profits from these products, then the hubris that comes with that success can create blind spots. For publicly traded companies, there is further pressure on executives to meet short-term market expectations for returns.

Nokia's former CEO remarks that established companies can only change when they have a charismatic leader or a crisis. We respectfully disagree with this notion. By the time a crisis or a charismatic leader arrives it is often too late to respond. We instead agree with Schumpeter that even in the process of creative destruction, there is always a chance for companies that would otherwise perish to weather the storm and live on "*vigorously and usefully*"[11]. In other words, death is not inevitable. Companies that are able to respond to change can survive and thrive.

Using The Right Lens
In order to survive and thrive, however, established companies have to become clear-eyed about the challenges they are facing. Historically, management teaching has tended to focus on strategy as a method for finding long term competitive advantages. Once a competitive advantage has been found, it becomes the job of managers to devote their energy to protecting it, through good financial management and operational excellence. In contrast, contemporary management thinking recognizes that the idea of a stable and long term competitive advantage is a fallacy. Companies should be managed to quickly exploit current competitive advantages and move on to the next advantage[12].

In order to do this, companies need to use the right management frameworks. It is too simplistic to advise established companies to act like startups. Large companies are not startups, nor should they strive to be. Most established companies we work with complain that the expectation of acting like a startup is unrealistic given that their day-to-day work involves running an already successful and profitable business. Startups can generally focus on one idea without the legacy of an older business. This is the perennial challenge that has always faced established companies; how to engage in sufficient *exploitation* to ensure current viability, while devoting enough energy to *exploration* to ensure future viability[13].

It is important to realize that, even as entrepreneurs have become rockstars, startups still fail a lot. When examined over a period of three or more years, nine out of ten startups fail[14]. Among the entrepreneurs who do succeed, over 90% do so in a business that is different from what they originally planned to do[15]. Most founders rarely get it right at the beginning and have to iterate and pivot their way to success[16]. The Lean Startup movement arose from a need for startups to stop failing so much. The clear message is that being a startup is not about painting colorful walls, using sticky notes, buying bean-bags and setting up foosball tables. In its essence, entrepreneurship is management. And so is innovation!

In one of the great management insights of the 21st century, Steve Blank distinguished *searching* versus *executing* as the key differences between startups and large companies[17]. A startup is a temporary organization whose goal is to *search* for a sustainable and profitable business model. On the other hand, an established company mostly *executes* on a known business model that addresses the known needs of known market segments. This distinction is a powerful metaphor for startups to know where they are on their journey. But for established companies to innovate successfully they have to figure out a way to be *searching while they are executing*. Corporate innovation is a war that is fought on two fronts.

As such, large companies need to stop thinking and acting as if they are single monolithic organizations with one business model. Instead, large companies should take an ecosystem approach to their businesses. Every contemporary company has to be a balanced mix of established cash cow products and new products that are currently searching for profitable business models. This *innovation portfolio*, and the products within it, has to be managed appropriately. The right management tools have to be applied depending on where products are on their innovation journey.

The management practices for creating new products are different from the practices for managing already successful products. Executing on known business models can mostly be managed using traditional accounting methods, cost optimizations and operational effectiveness. Success can be measured using traditional metrics such as profit, return on investment (ROI), accounting rate of return (ARR) and net present value (NPV). In contrast, searching has to be managed using startup methodologies such as design thinking, customer development and experimentation. Success is measured by examining how well the innovation teams are doing in their search for profitable business models (i.e. innovation accounting).

This capacity to *search while executing* is the hallmark of the ambidextrous organization[18]. It is not simply a choice between being in the navy or being a pirate, as Steve Jobs put it. Established companies have to develop processes that allow their innovators to become *pirates in the navy*. This is the innovation paradox.

What Is This Book About?

In this book, we address the questions that underlie the innovation paradox:

- What are the principles for developing a corporate innovation ecosystem?
- If established companies are set up to execute on known business models, then how can they develop startup practices within the same organization?
- What is the role of strategy and how can companies develop and apply an innovation thesis?
- What are the best frameworks to use for innovation portfolio management?
- How can large companies manage their investments in innovation in a manner that is similar to modern startup ecosystems?
- What are the right metrics and KPIs to track for different types of innovation?
- In what ways can large enterprises apply modern startup methodologies such as *Lean Startup, Business Model Design, Customer Development* and *Design Thinking*?
- How can companies begin creating their innovation ecosystems right away?

There are several complexities involved in the innovation process. *The Corporate Startup* provides the principles, methods and tools that companies can use to manage and benefit from these complexities. Each chapter in this book will be focused on the principles and practices of corporate innovation. How these principles and practices come together will be illustrated by examples, innovation activities and case studies. The book has two main parts. Part I outlines the five core principles that established companies can use to build their innovation ecosystems. Part II focuses on how these ecosystems are brought to life through innovation practice.

Is This Book For You?

This book is about developing, managing and sustaining innovation within established companies. The book is mainly targeted at large and medium-sized organizations, although the insights can be useful for small companies and startups too. If you fall into any of the following categories, this book is definitely a must-read for you:

- An executive in an established company that is looking to spark growth through innovation.
- An intrapreneur, innovation manager, product owner or employee looking to apply modern startup methodologies in an established company but facing challenges in terms of where to start and how to do it.
- A management consultant working with established companies to help them with innovation.
- An entrepreneur looking to 'pivot' your career to the enterprise in your quest for even greater challenges, but not knowing what to expect, what challenges you would face in the corporate world and how to manage them.
- A lean innovation and customer development enthusiast and/or practitioner, looking to learn how these methodologies can be implemented within large and medium-sized companies.

Our hope is that, after reading this book, managers and employees will have the knowledge and tools necessary to manage innovation within established companies.

ECOS

ECOSYSTEM
[ek-oh-sis-tuh m, ee-koh-]

A system, or a group of interconnected elements, formed by the interaction of a community of organisms with their environment.
Any system or network of inter-connecting and interacting parts, as in a business.[19]

In order to succeed at innovation, established companies do not have to act like startups. Every startup's aspiration is to become a successful company! So, abandoning business model execution practices and applying searching methods on an already successful business model is a form of waste. We strongly believe that operational excellence is still an important management practice, even in times of rampant disruption. Our cash cow products are how we get the money to invest in innovation.

The challenge comes when companies act as if they are single institutions with a single business model. If they view themselves this way, then the false choice of acting or not acting like a startup becomes 'real'. The best way to innovate is for a large company to view itself as an *innovation ecosystem* with various products, services and business models. A company can then apply the right management tools to products that have validated business models versus those that are still in search mode.

This is how a company becomes an ambidextrous organization that is, in practice, excellent at both *searching* and *executing*. The chapters in this section describe the core principles for building innovation ecosystems.

'Innovation has nothing to do with how many R&D dollars you have... It's about the people you have, how you're led and how much you get it.'

Steve Jobs, Founder and former CEO of Apple

CHAPTER ONE

Innovation Ecosystem

Most senior executives can relate. It usually starts with some startup types within the company telling them scary stories about how startups are coming to eat their lunch. Look at Facebook, Uber, Twitter and Airbnb! Oh, look what happened to Blockbuster, don't let that happen here. Do you know Nokia used to be the largest mobile phone company in the world? Now look at them! We need to innovate like startups! We need to set up an incubator, an accelerator and put more money into R&D.

While there is often agreement that there should be more investment in innovation, the debate is always about where and how those investments should be made. Depending on who they talk to, corporate leaders will often get conflicting advice. Should innovation units be physically separated from the main business, or can innovation be managed within the same company? This is a sensible discussion to have. But much of the advice that leaders get is filled with polemics.

23

Each side takes an extreme view. One commonly cited problem is that traditional managers with MBAs are too stuck in their ways to understand innovation. These managers are also incentivized to behave in a manner that stifles innovation. People cannot get any innovation done within a company that expects a thirty page business case before it funds any idea. Ultimately, such a company will always invest in sure bets; which means that the company always works on the same types of products.

This is indeed a challenge. But it is equally true that setting up separate innovation labs does not guarantee that any successful products will emerge from there. For the most part these are
places where *innovation theater* takes place. Look-a-here! We are doing lean startup, design thinking, customer development, business model canvas and minimum viable products... Sure. Whatever. None of these techniques in themselves represent innovation. The ultimate measure of success is the development of new products with sustainably profitable business models.

Why Innovation Fails

Such polemical debates fail to get at the core of why innovation in established companies succeeds or fails. Ultimately, *innovation* fails when a large company decides to use the same processes it uses to manage its core products to manage its innovation projects. Business planning does not work for innovation. All estimates of ROI, NPV and ARR are fiction. Investments based on such numbers are usually bets made on faith. As already noted, this approach also encourages managers to develop a tendency to invest in 'surebet' products for current markets.

The feeling is that by creating innovation labs, managers can separate innovators from the toxic environment within the company. But these labs fail because companies do not build any management processes around them, allowing innovators to work on whatever they want. There is a common tendency to conflate creativity with innovation[20]. Management sees successful startups coming up with great new products and this motivates managers to pursue the development of similarly cool new shiny products via R&D labs, incubators and accelerators. But creating great new products is *not* innovation.

The investments that are spent on innovation labs often generate poor returns. Strategy & Business, a unit within PricewaterhouseCoopers, has been publishing an annual report of the top 1000 most innovative companies in the world for over twelve years. In that time, they have found that there is no statistically significant relationship between R&D spending and sustained financial performance[21]. This finding applies to total R&D spend, as well as R&D spending as a percentage of revenues[22]. Spending on R&D is not related to growth in sales or profits, increases in market capitalization or shareholder returns[23]. In every annual report that Strategy & Business have published, the top 10 innovative companies are often not the top 10 spenders on R&D.

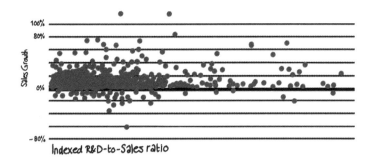

Source: Strategy+Business. The Global Innovation 1000: http://www.strategyand.pwc.com/innovation1000

24

What R&D spending seems to generate is an increase in the number of patents held by a company. However, the number of patents held is not the same as innovation. The US patent office is filled with thousands of patents that have never achieved commercial success. Only a few products from corporate innovation labs will have validated business models, or any alignment with the company's strategic vision. We have seen successful innovators with great products that wither on the vine because there are no managers in the company willing to pick up the products and take them to scale. These products become orphans that are eventually abandoned, thus creating a discouraging and uninspiring environment for future innovators.

We have learned that companies need to put a great process in place in order to manage innovation. Without a clear process, innovators will not get the right level of support. It is hard to succeed when innovation is run as a covert operation that flies under the radar of executives. In that situation, there are often no clear exit criteria for the integration of innovative new products into the main business. There are also no clear career paths for employees working in innovation labs. The truth is that, no matter what you do or where you start, innovative products will always need someone from the main business to make a decision about their future. How those people view the new innovations will ultimately determine those products' mortality rates.

A Corporate Startup Definition Of Innovation

A good place to start developing a management process is by providing a clear definition of what innovation is. Innovation is often simply defined as a novel creation that produces value[24]. From our perspective, the concept of innovation as distinct from creativity involves three important steps. The first step involves the novel and creative ideas that are generated through various methods that trigger insights. The second step is ensuring that our ideas create value for customers and meet their needs. The final step involves finding a sustainable business model. This part of the journey involves ensuring that we can create and deliver value to customers in a way that is sustainably profitable.

This definition lays bare what the role of innovation in any organization should be. It is not to simply create new products and services. New products may be part of the equation but the ultimate outputs of innovation are sustainable business models. A business model is sustainable when our novel creations deliver value to customers (i.e. when we are making stuff people want); and when we are able to create and deliver this value profitably (i.e. we are making some money). Without these two elements, a new product cannot be considered an innovation. It is simply a cool new product. It might be the coolest thing since sliced bread - the most creative product ever made - but if it doesn't deliver value to customers and bring in profits, it is *not* innovation.

These steps make clear that it is the combination of *great new ideas* and *profitable business models* that defines successful innovation. As such, our corporate startup definition of innovation is:

The creation of *new* products and services that deliver *value* to customers, in a manner that is supported by a *sustainable* and *profitable* business model.

Our definition of innovation also provides us with a clear job description for corporate innovators. *Your job is to help your company make money by making products that people want.* The sweet spot is when your creativity meets customer needs and you can make money from serving those needs. It is also important to clarify that not all forms of innovation will be focused on new products or services. It is possible to innovate around internal business processes that are not directly experienced by customers. This form of innovation is not an explicit focus of this book. But, even for these forms of innovation, the delivery of sustainable value is still an important principle.

Red Pill - Blue Pill

From the definition above, it is clear that the only indisputable fact is that innovation should be managed via different processes to those that are used to manage core products. How these processes are instantiated depends on the company, how much management buy-in you have and the innovators' appetite for corporate politics. Sometimes it can be very clear that you will never get full executive endorsement for innovation. The executives are too focused on cash cow products and the best you can hope for is support from a handful of visionary leaders within your business. In these cases, innovators might consider leaving the company for greener pastures.

Alternatively, innovators can start a guerilla movement. A corporate innovation insurgency, so to speak. Tristan Kromer[25], who is a great innovation ecosystem designer, has two recommendations on how innovation ecosystem designers could manage such a movement. First, Tristan suggests that innovators should *lower the costs of innovation*. If they do this successfully, then they will hardly ever need high level budget approvals. The lean startup, design thinking and customer development toolbox provides great methods for lowering the costs of innovation.

Every now and again, innovators will need to surface within the company in order to get investment for their ideas to be taken to scale. It is also possible that things will get to the point where the costs of innovation can no longer be kept low. For this, Tristan recommends that innovation teams find *diplomats*. These are individuals who will do the hard work of corporate politics and smoothing the path for innovation projects. A diplomat is usually someone who is well-connected and respected in the business, who can work outside of normal bureaucratic channels to call in favors and get things done. Without a diplomat, most guerilla projects are dead on arrival.

27

Guerilla movements have been known to succeed, sometimes. Nevertheless, this is our least favored method. We have found that guerilla movements are too difficult. Teams are always watching their backs for unexpected impediments to their work. And if they lose their management sponsor or diplomat, then their innovation efforts are easily placed in jeopardy. So while guerilla tactics can work, they also have a really high mortality rate for product ideas. This is the reason we favor a *full frontal assault* on the company to change its ways of working.

With a full frontal assault, innovators tackle the hard questions upfront. Long-term sustainable innovation is only possible within a supportive ecosystem. As such, it is important to get top level executive and middle manager buy-in. This *aircover* will help in future situations when there is need for support and resources. Regardless of whether the innovation lab is external or part of an internal process, strategic alignment is key. Innovation ecosystems can only be created when we do the hard work of changing and adapting the company's capabilities to ensure that they fully support our chosen innovation approach. The principles for building this innovation ecosystem are the focus of this book.

The Five Principles of a Corporate Innovation Ecosystem

Successful innovation necessitates interactions among multiple actors from multiple parts of a company[26]. In the journey from ideation, product creation, first customer sales, growth and scale, multiple parts of the organization are inevitably involved in innovation. This is why organizational alignment around innovation is critical. Companies need to create an internal process that:

1. Facilitates the serendipity that creates sparks of creative ideation.
2. Captures and tests the outputs of this creative ideation.
3. Transforms ideas into successful products with profitable business models.

This means that organizations need to be designed to create and benefit from serendipity. The goal of this book is to articulate the principles that inform how organizations manage these innovation complexities. We strongly believe that *principles trump tactics*. It is, ultimately, up to each organization to adapt these principles and apply them to its business, strategic goals and context. The five principles for building corporate innovation ecosystems are as follows:

INNOVATION THESIS

We believe that innovation must be part of, and aligned with, the overall strategic goals of the company. This is important when it comes to later transitioning innovation projects into the core product portfolio. Just like venture capital investors have investment theses that specify the types of startups and markets they invest in[27], every large company must have an innovation thesis. An innovation thesis clearly sets out a company's view of the future and the strategic objectives of innovation. For example, an established software company can take the view that driverless cars are the future and they want to get in that market early. Their innovation thesis will be that they invest mostly in new ideas that bet on that future (i.e. software products for driverless vehicles). In this regard, an innovation thesis sets the boundaries or guard rails concerning the innovation projects the company will or will not consider. In addition to this deliberate strategy, the company must also use its innovation process as a source of emergent strategy that is responsive to changes in the market.

INNOVATION PORTFOLIO

To achieve its innovation thesis and strategic goals, an established company should then set itself up as a portfolio of products and services. This portfolio should contain products that cover the whole spectrum of innovation; i.e. those that can be classed as *core*, *adjacent* and *transformational*. The portfolio should have early stage products, as well as mature and established products. A company may also consider having in its portfolio disruptive products that are aimed at lower-end or emerging markets. The goal is to have a balanced portfolio in which the company is managing various business models that are at different stages of their lives. The balance of the product portfolio should be an expression of the company's overall strategy and innovation thesis.

29

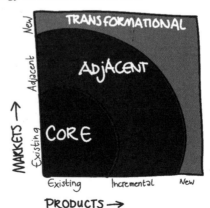

Source: Nagji, B. & Tuff, G. (2012).
'Managing your innovation portfolio.' *Harvard Business Review*, 90(5), 66-74.

INNOVATION FRAMEWORK

In order to execute on its thesis and manage its portfolio of products and services, the company needs a framework for managing the journey from *searching* to *executing*. There are several examples of innovation frameworks; for example Ash Maurya's *Running Lean* framework[28] and Steve Blank's *Investment Readiness* model[29]. At Pearson, Tendayi has been part of a team that has developed the *Lean Product Lifecycle,* which is an award winning innovation management framework[30]. All these frameworks can be synthesized into the three simple steps for innovation; *creating ideas*, *testing ideas* and *scaling ideas*. Every now and again, a company may decide to refresh the business models of its existing products through *renewing ideas*. Having an innovation framework provides a unifying language for the business. Everybody knows what phase each product or business model is in. This then provides the basis for how a company can manage its investment decisions and product development practices.

INNOVATION ACCOUNTING

With an innovation framework in place, the company now needs to make sure they are using the right investment practices and metrics to measure success. Traditional accounting methods are great for managing core products. However, when managing innovation, different sets of tools are needed. We propose that companies should use incremental investing based on the innovation stage of their products. This approach is based on Dave McClure's Moneyball for Startups[31]. We also propose three sets of innovation KPIs that companies should be tracking:

- *Reporting KPIs* focus on product teams, the ideas they are generating, the experiments they are running and the progress they are making from ideation to scale (e.g. assumptions tested and validated).
- *Governance KPIs* focus on helping the company make informed investment decisions based on evidence and innovation stage (e.g. how close are the teams to finding product-market fit).
- *Global KPIs* focus on helping the company examine the overall performance of their investments in innovation in the context of the larger business (e.g. percent of revenue in the last three years).

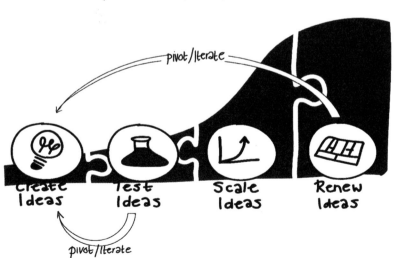

pivot/Iterate

Create Ideas   Test Ideas   Scale Ideas   Renew Ideas

pivot/Iterate

INNOVATION PRACTICE

In addition to correctly managing investments in innovation, the way in which product teams develop their products has to be aligned to the innovation framework. Pearson's Lean Product Lifecycle[32] is accompanied by a great playbook

that provides guidance to product teams as they search or execute on their business models. Adobe's Kickbox provides similar guidance, tools and resources[33]. The core principle for innovation practice is simply that no product can be taken to scale until it has a validated business model. As such, during the search phase the job of innovators is to validate their value hypotheses (i.e. does our product meet customer needs?) and their growth hypotheses (i.e. how will we grow revenues and customer numbers?). This process requires that teams validate both the attractiveness of the product to customers and the potential profitability of the business model. A key part of this innovation practice is the idea of a network or community. Companies have to create and support communities of practices that interact regularly and share lessons on best practice. This ensures that innovation skills are shared and developed as a human capability across the company.

These five principles combine to help create an innovation ecosystem. The first two principles (thesis and portfolio) focus on innovation strategy, the next two principles (framework and accounting) focus on innovation management and the last principle is where rubber meets the road and the company begins interacting with customers and validating business models. Most innovation labs have tended to just focus on this last part (innovation practice). But the truth is that without a supportive ecosystem in place, products coming out of innovation labs will have high mortality rates. This is why applying all five principles is important.

As you can see, these elements are interconnected; each representing a *create-test-learn* loop of its own. To the extent that strategy informs investment decisions, the success of these decisions in turn informs strategy. To the extent that investment decisions impact innovation practice, innovation practice produces learnings that inform investment decisions and, in-turn, inform strategy. This is an innovation ecosystem at work. Each interconnected piece is responding to data from the other pieces. Such a holistic approach allows companies to innovate like startups, without having to act like startups. We will now describe each principle in detail in the following chapters.

31

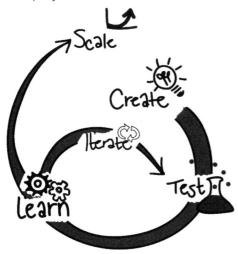

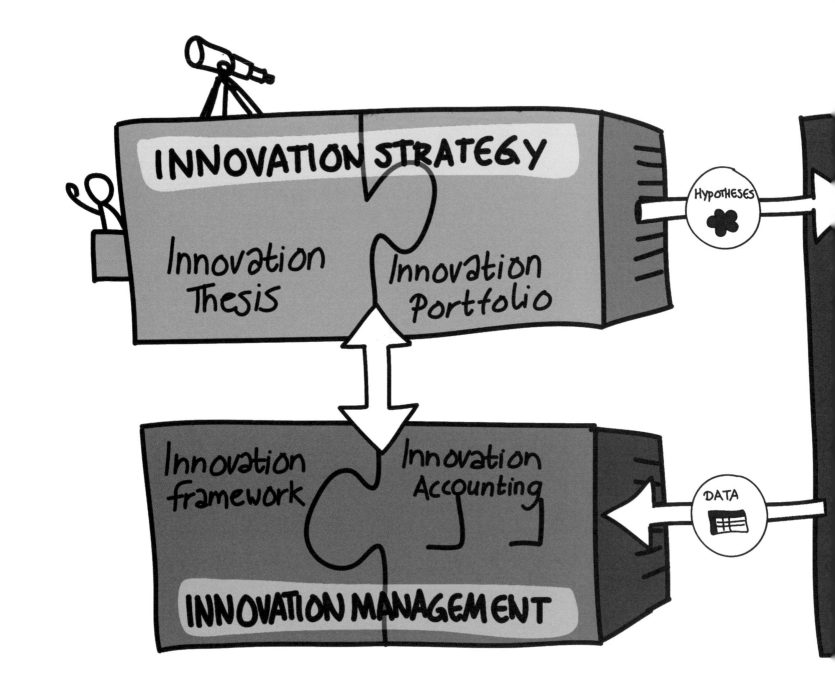

CONVERSATIONS ON INNOVATION
Tristan Kromer

LEAN STARTUP COACH AND ADVISOR

Tristan Kromer is a thought leader in the lean innovation space. He coaches startups and intrapreneurs on adopting Lean Startup principles and putting them into practice. He has worked with companies as early stage as $0 revenue to larger enterprises with over $12 billion in revenue. Tristan is also an expert at developing innovation ecosystems within established companies. He has developed an innovation ecosystem model (a.k.a. 'the ecosystem sandwich'), which he uses as a framework when he advises and consults with companies.

CS: IN YOUR THINKING, WHAT IS AN INNOVATION ECOSYSTEM?

TK: An innovation ecosystem is to an innovator what the savannah is to a lion. It's the environment that intrapreneurs work within. The ecosystem is composed of individuals, organizations, and resources that generate new ways of creating value. Intrapreneurs and entrepreneurs rely on certain inputs in order to be able to create new business models and value streams. These inputs range from things like human capital (or skills) to tools (such as 3D printers) to financial capital and co-founders.

CS: WHY DO COMPANIES NEED TO CREATE AN ECOSYSTEM? ARE INDIVIDUAL CAPABILITIES NOT ENOUGH ON THEIR OWN?

TK: Individuals tend to move to the most favorable environment just as deer might abandon a drought stricken area. If a company can't create an innovative environment for intrapreneurs, they may quickly find the intrapreneurs have quit to build their own startups and only the bureaucrats are left. Then the company's pipeline of new products and revenue dries up completely! The goal of an innovation ecosystem is to have an equilibrium where innovation is a constant output and not fluctuating wildly or collapsing entirely.

CS: PLEASE TALK US THROUGH YOUR INNOVATION ECOSYSTEM MODEL AND HOW THE DIFFERENT ELEMENTS JOIN TOGETHER?

TK: In the middle of the 'sandwich' is where all the action is. There are a lot of specific elements here that allow us to manipulate a company's ecosystem. For example, if the company is lacking certain *Skills*, we can do skill training workshops. If the company is mired in red tape, we can provide *Tools* to help cut through that and expedite innovation processes.

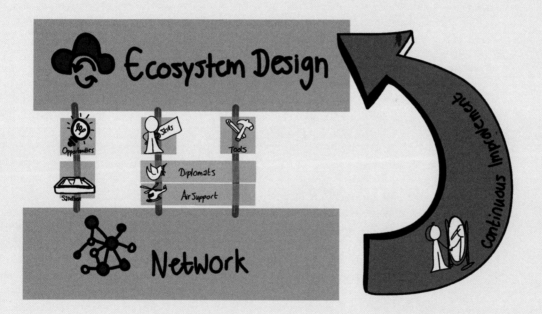

The top and bottom hold the ecosystem together. At the top is the *Ecosystem Design* itself, meaning that someone needs to be actively monitoring and improving the ecosystem as part of a larger vision. Without that, the innovation funnel tends to get bottlenecked due to uncoordinated improvements. For example, increasing innovation by sponsoring company hackathons can be great. But if all the focus is on that first stage of generating ideas, then employees may be discouraged when none of those ideas are subsequently sponsored. *Ecosystem Design* helps systematically build the level of innovation at every stage by balancing efforts to improve the ecosystem in a coherent strategy.

At the bottom, the *Network* allows for peer-to-peer learning within the organization. Without a stable network of intrapreneurs, the company may train teams that work on a project, but then are disbanded and the skills atrophy and disappear. So companies wind up in a cycle of constant workshops with no long term impact. With a network, knowledge is retained and passed on from intrapreneur to intrapreneur.

Lastly, the Network needs to be feeding observations and insights back to the Design level so that the entire ecosystem is being continually improved! A lot of companies lack this and stick with a four-year one shot transformation program which ultimately does not deliver the promised benefit.

CS: CAN YOU DIG IN A BIT MORE INTO THIS MIDDLE PART OF THE 'SANDWICH'?
TK: The middle can be divided into three phases. The first step is just to generate ideas. Intrapreneurial activity in an ecosystem is the result of Opportunities divided by Fear. *Opportunities* are created by intrapreneurs with free time to be creative and pursue innovative projects (or even think of them). The *Opportunities* will also improve if intrapreneurs can interact with teammates from different disciplines to find spontaneous collisions of ideas that may inspire something novel. Fear of failure, embarrassment, or financial pressures inhibit idea generation. If there is a lot of fear, we can address this by providing a *Sandbox* for intrapreneurs to play in (e.g. an incubator or 20% innovation time). A sandbox is meant to protect the intrapreneur from the company and allow them to make a mess without being blamed. This reduces the debilitating fear that can prevent intrapreneurs from even proposing a project.

In the second phase, projects must get around the *create-test-learn* loop at least once. The major obstacle here may be a lack of *Skills*. For example, a team may lack a designer they need to build a landing page. We can either create a team with a complete skill set or provide training for small gaps. Alternatively, innovation teams can also rely on *Diplomats* who know how to move between silos to get things done. These people can barter and call in favors to borrow some time from the design department to help with the landing page. Similarly, getting *Air Support* and getting funding for innovation projects would allow the team to hire a contract designer. *Air Support* is usually from a business sponsor who provides resources and also some political cover from other stakeholders.

In the last phase, innovation projects have to continue around the create-test-learn loop at speed. A major and common obstacle to innovation is red tape and bureaucracy which can be solved with better *Tools & Processes*. For example, if a team is not allowed to use the 3D printer that another department owns due to some arcane regulation that has existed for twenty years, this restriction can be removed. Again, Diplomats can help hack around these regulations and Air Support could allow the team to buy their own 3D printer.

CS: THE CONCEPTS OF DIPLOMATS AND AIR SUPPORT ARE VERY INTERESTING. IF YOU HAVE ONE DO YOU NEED THE OTHER?

TK: I don't think you absolutely must have both, but the healthiest and most stable innovation ecosystems seem to have both Diplomats and Air Support. Sometimes the roles are even served by the same person at first. Diplomats are perhaps more useful when just getting started. Typically, you don't need a lot of money when just getting an initial idea off the ground. You need favors. There's always someone in the company who manages to wheel and deal favors to get things done. Having someone who can talk to the legal department outside of official company process and get approval to launch a small pilot of five customers is going to be a lot more valuable to an early stage project than a wad of cash.

CS: IF I AM WORKING IN A LARGE COMPANY AND WANTING TO SET UP AN ECOSYSTEM TOMORROW, WHERE SHOULD I START?

TK: Always start with discovery. Your intrapreneurs have problems. What are they? What is stopping an intrapreneur from proposing a new project? From building a team? Is there red tape in the way? Is there a network where intrapreneurs can learn from one another? Discovering the problems is a much better bet than jumping into a solution like, "let's run a hackathon!" There's nothing worse than a hackathon where a hundred great ideas are created and all of them are orphaned. Maybe the real problem wasn't coming up with ideas, it was finding a business sponsor to fund them.

37

'Innovate before you need to...
the urgency of innovation
and the ability to innovate
are inversely related.'

Scott D. Anthony, Managing Partner of Innosight[34]

CHAPTER TWO

Innovation Thesis

When Kodak went into bankruptcy in January 2012[35], it was not only an economic tragedy for one of the great companies of the last century, it was devastating for the city of Rochester, New York, where the company was based[36]. Kodak was once a household brand whose dominance in the photographic film business was unparalleled. The phrase "Kodak moment" came to epitomize the cultural relevance of the brand. At its height, Kodak's market share of the photographic film market was more than 80% in the US and about 50% globally. It employed over 60 000 citizens of Rochester, the majority of whom became unemployed when the company collapsed[37].

Kodak was a *juggernaut* of a company; but the tragedy of its collapse runs deeper. It is not that the company could not have saved itself by responding to change. The tragedy is that Kodak invented the change that eventually killed it. A Kodak engineer, Steven J. Sasson, invented the first digital camera in 1975. In an interview with *the New York Times*, Sasson describes how Kodak's management reacted to his camera:

"It was filmless photography, so management's reaction was: 'that's cute — but don't tell anyone about it'."[38]

At that time, Kodak was focused on maintaining the large profits it was making from its sales of photographic film. However, as digital cameras grew in popularity, Kodachrome, the photographic film that was Kodak's cash cow, was discontinued in 2006 after 74 years of production. Kodak had not failed to imagine a new future. It had failed to capitalize on the imagination and inventiveness of its scientists. In fact, Kodak had a bigger treasure trove of about 7000 patents which it had not been properly exploiting to develop new products and business models. As it has emerged from bankruptcy, it has started to do more with these patents[39] (i.e. developing technology in digital imaging and touch screens[40]).

Kodak is not the only company that has gone through this cycle of near death and then a slow revival. BlackBerry struggled for years and is slowly making a comeback as a software company[41]. Nokia now runs a profitable network equipment and software business[42]. TomTom and Garmin are now succeeding by providing mapping technologies for marine, aviation and automotive companies[43]. The 'roll your eyes' question for us is why these companies were unable to do some of this innovation during the good times when they were still profit making.

39

Death and Taxes

Is Nokia's former CEO right? Do companies need a crisis before they start to respond to change? Is it necessary for companies to experience a near collapse before they start innovating? Is creative destruction, like death and taxes, inevitable? One of the questions we often get asked is why we care so much about the survival of large companies. Our responses is that the economic impact of large company failure is often felt more widely than the failure of startups. Rochester, New York is a case in point. But even more important to us is the fact that the failure of many of these companies is mostly unnecessary. Given their resources, we feel that well established companies are poised to be the largest beneficiaries of the lean startup movement.

Most discussions about large company failures highlight how these companies failed to adapt to changes in their environment. Yes. True. Indeed. We couldn't agree more. But what does failing to adapt actually mean in practical terms? It is not possible for a juggernaut of a company to simply change on a dime every time a shift happens in the business environment? The size of the company and its built-in processes make this impossible. To be adaptive, the capacity to change has to already be in place within the company's DNA. The company has to be strategically designed to be changing, in advance of that change becoming necessary for survival.

In *The Innovator's Dilemma*[44], Clayton Christensen distinguishes between *human capabilities*, which are the skills, knowledge and abilities of the people that work in a company; and *organizational capabilities*, which are the structures, processes and culture of the company. When developing human capabilities, companies often train and coach their product teams on new innovation methods such as design thinking, lean startup and business model design. In our experience, developing human capabilities is not enough. A company needs to develop its structures and processes to match the innovation practices it is teaching its people.

In fact, *organizational capabilities* trump *human capabilities* any day. A team that has been trained to design business models and run experiments cannot apply these skills within an organization that values business planning and financial projections before it invests in new ideas. Unless you use guerilla tactics, knowing how to iterate is not effective when your managers expect you to deliver new products according to the roadmap in the plan; on time and on budget. As such, a good place to start when building an innovation ecosystem is organizational capabilities. This chapter focuses on how we approach strategy. We believe that how a company views and develops its innovation strategy can support its long term survival or be its Achilles' heel.

Strategic Innovation Management

Strategy has traditionally been defined as a company's coordinated efforts to use its *core competencies* to gain a *competitive advantage*[45]. A company is considered to have a competitive advantage when it implements a strategy that its competitors find too hard or too costly to imitate. Companies are expected to invest enormous resources to protect this competitive advantage. This view of strategy is flawed because companies can only protect long term competitive advantages in stable business environments[46]. Furthermore, the practices that are needed to protect current advantages often run counter to those that are necessary for innovation.

One of the counterintuitive lessons from *The Innovator's Dilemma* is that the companies that get disrupted are 'well run companies' with excellent conventional management practices[47]. As such, strategy can no longer be defined as the singular exploitation of core competencies to maximize gains. We now need *ambidextrous organizations* that are excellent at searching while executing[48]. *Strategic innovation management* is defined as the ability of a company to compete in mature markets with mature technologies where operational efficiency and incremental improvements are the main ways to do business; while exploring new markets with new technologies where agility and experimentation are paramount[49].

Researchers O'Reilly and Tushman have examined ambidextrous organizations in several companies including IBM, Cisco, Misys, USA Today and Ciba Vision[50]. The key lesson from their research is that companies need separate processes for managing innovation versus core business. At the same time, companies need tight integration and buy-in at the senior executive level. An ambidextrous company needs a senior management team that is comfortable with the paradox of maintaining multiple strategic agendas, using different success criteria for different products and sharing resources between currently profitable cash cow products and future facing products.

41

Putting It All Together - An Innovation Thesis

It is difficult to achieve executive alignment without a compelling strategic narrative. There has to be a clear strategy for executives to rally around. This strategic narrative explains and justifies why financially successful business units should share resources with new, up and coming business units or innovation labs. Without a common strategic vision and shared values, it is difficult to maintain organizational ambidexterity in the long term. The ideas that emerge from innovation labs can quickly become orphans that the core business will not to take to scale.

It is also important to stress that companies should not be investing in every new idea that their employees come up with. Not all ideas are created equal. Rita McGrath argues quite strongly against the notion of 'letting a thousand flowers bloom' and then hoping to find something that works. According to McGrath, there *is* such a thing as a *bad* idea[51]. Throwing stuff on the wall and seeing what sticks is *not* strategy. Just setting up an innovation lab and asking entrepreneurs to come up with some cool stuff can be quite paralyzing. In contrast, setting strategic boundaries can have quite a liberating effect on innovators[52].

If we pause and think about it, startups operate within a bigger economic ecosystem. Part of that ecosystem are the investors who put up their money to help these new companies succeed. Similarly, large established companies also have their own micro-economies. Ideas that are generated by employees, are invested in and developed within this micro-economy. As such, key lessons can be learned from how venture capitalists operate and make investment decisions within startup ecosystems. Venture capitalists and other investors will receive funding requests from startups working on all kinds of products and services. If they are not disciplined about their investment process they will end up investing in a myriad of unconnected business ideas. This *opportunistic* type of investing is a method some investors use, but it is not a highly recommended approach.

Most venture capital investors develop an *investment thesis*, which is essentially their point of view on the world. The dictionary definition of a thesis is *a statement or a proposition that is to be supported or proven*. An investment thesis states an investor's beliefs about where the world is going in a particular arena within the next five to ten years. This can be in terms of trends in technology, socio-economics, population changes, individual needs, legal and political changes, macroeconomics and market developments. This assessment is followed by clear hypotheses about how the firm thinks new companies can take advantage and benefit from these trends. On this basis, investors can then state the types of ideas, arenas and startups they are willing to invest in. A thesis can also include the types of founders, teams and lifecycle stages of products investors are willing put money into (e.g. seed funding).

According to Pedro Torres-Picon, a thesis is made up of two parts; 1) a clear articulation of a unique perspective of where the world is going and what sort of startups will succeed in that world; 2) a clear articulation of the types of ideas that a firm feels best suited to invest in[53]. In its investment thesis, the firm also makes clear the types of ideas it will *not* be investing

in. Torres-Picon refers to this as the firm's *anti-thesis*. The clarity of what you will *not* invest in is just as important as knowing what you will invest in. At the end of this process, a venture capital firm produces a clear statement, which usually fits on one page, of its investment thesis.

Dave McClure published a wonderful post in 2010 outlining his investment thesis for five hundred Startups, the startup accelerator he co-founded[54]. We will adapt and develop his notion of *Moneyball for Startups* in Chapter 5, showing how established companies can use it to make investment decisions. Another good example of an investment thesis is the one developed by Union Square Ventures, the firm co-founded by Fred Morris. In summary, their thesis can be described as follows:

"We invest in large networks of engaged users, differentiated by user experience, and defensible though network effects."

More details underlying this thesis and the types of companies they invest in, such as Twitter, Tumblr, Etsy and SoundCloud, can be found on their blog[55]. Suffice it to say that this investment thesis makes clear how Union Square Ventures think their chosen arena is evolving, along with the types of businesses they will and *will not* invest in.

In a similar fashion, we believe that an established company should develop an *innovation thesis*. To create a compelling strategic narrative, organizations can use the worksheets in the innovation activity to answer some of the following questions:

- **What are our current business models and core products?**
- **Which products/services within our current business are facing decline?**
- **What are the emerging trends within society, the economy and technology?**
- **What future technologies are still in their infancy and may affect our industry in the long-term?**
- **Which new markets do we want to enter and grow in?**
- **Within these trends, what are the threats and opportunities for our business models?**
- **Are there new competitors from within or outside our industry?**
- **How do we expect innovation to help us respond to important emerging trends?**
- **Which arenas should we be exploring in order to find the next set of business models that can sustain our company?**
- **Which arenas are we going to play in and what sort of things are we going to invest in?**
- **Which arenas are we *not* going to play in and what sort of things are we *not* going to invest in?**
- **What are the expected outcomes from implementing our innovation process? What will success look like?**

At the end of this process, a clear strategic narrative that fits on a single page must emerge. Management must be able to articulate, in clear terms, where they think their industry or arena is going and how they plan to use innovation to keep up. Then they have to state clearly the types of ideas they will invest in so as to execute and test the thesis. These ideas can include core, adjacent and transformational innovation. The statement must also clarify what the company will *not* be investing in. This innovation thesis will then form the guard rails for future investment decision-making.

There is no prescriptive way to develop a thesis. Companies must feel free to change and adapt our worksheets to their circumstances. But once a company develops their innovation thesis, they must stick to it as much as possible. A thesis will evolve over time, but companies should try as much as possible to avoid investing in ideas that are totally outside their thesis. Fred Wilson differentiates thesis-based investing from theme-based investing[56]. With theme-based investing, companies simply invest in ideas that fall within a narrow or broad theme (e.g. farming or mobile). While this is a better approach than opportunistic investing, it often results in bucket filling because there are no extra criteria for choosing ideas within a theme.

Thesis-based investing provides much more clarity about exactly what we will and will not invest in; and why. An innovation thesis is also powerful in other ways. Within the company, it can serve as an inspirational framework for ideation. It communicates to people what they should be ideating around. Rather than random instructions to come up with cool ideas, people understand that our company wants to get ahead of these specific trends or solve these sets of customer problems. A thesis brings discipline which ultimately makes the company a better investor. The company will develop domain expertise and over time it will get better at understanding what works and doesn't work within its chosen arenas.

An innovation thesis also provides a good guide for success metrics. Since we know what we are expecting from innovation, it becomes easier to measure whether we have failed or succeeded[57]. This clarity allows the company to use data to revise the thesis where necessary. The ultimate benefit of having an innovation thesis is that it provides a great narrative for both management and employees to rally around. Without such buy-in, it is difficult to succeed at innovation. In Chapter 1, we noted that one of the challenges innovation labs face is gaining executive support. Rather than treat the innovation lab as an island away from the core, an innovation thesis helps to connect the lab to the future of the main business.

Deliberately Emergent Strategy

Fred Wilson notes that thesis-based investing brings the highest levels of returns when compared to thematic-based or opportunistic investing[58]. However, these returns are only possible if the investment thesis is correct. If the thesis is wrong, this approach can lead to pretty large losses. So as much as we think companies should stick to their innovation thesis when investing, it is also important to know when to evolve your thesis. It is not possible for a company to be entirely correct at the beginning. You will make some wrong calls, the markets will change and evolve; and you will learn new things. This is why it is called a thesis and not a law!

45

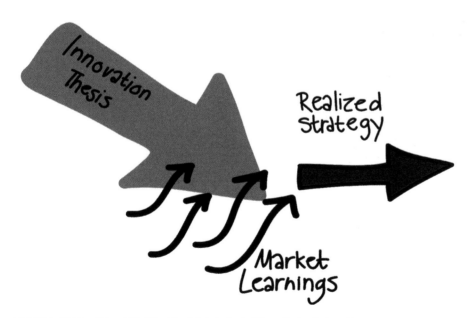

Adapted from Mintzberg, H. (1994). 'The fall and rise of strategic planning.' *Harvard Business Review*, 72(1), 107-114.

The approach we recommend is a combination of deliberate strategy based on vision and emergent strategy based on learnings from the market. In a turbulent business environment, emergent strategy is highly adaptive as it allows managers to respond to an ever-changing landscape[59]. It is important to view our innovation thesis as a set of hypotheses about the world and what works. The goal is to test these via our innovation portfolio and use any lessons learned to refine our thesis.

As we will note in later chapters, within the company's innovation portfolio those business units working on innovation projects will be constantly testing their business models with customers within the market. These ongoing tests will lead to the ongoing refinement of those specific business models. On a quarterly, biannual or annual basis management must also review the lessons emerging from their innovation projects and refine the innovation thesis accordingly. In Chapter 5, we will describe the KPIs that can be used to evaluate the success of innovation and evolve the thesis.

A look at the complete view of our framework shows a series of *create-test-learn* loops that ultimately lead back to an evolution of the innovation thesis.

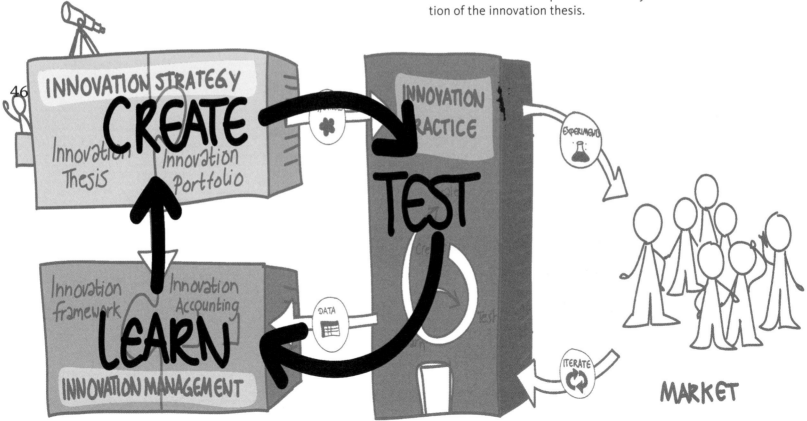

As an ongoing process of examining a company's strategy, the experiments and customer conversations being conducted in innovation projects will provide useful feedback as to the potential success of any particular strategic direction. Just as an example, senior executives may first propose that the company should compete on cost-leadership with a new product in a certain market. But through customer engagement, teams in the innovation team may discover a specific form of differentiation that creates more value for the company. Since strategic conversations are integrated at the top management level, it is possible for these learnings to be quickly taken up and used to adapt the proposed innovation strategy.

The End of Boom and Bust

Gordon Brown, the former Chancellor of the Exchequer in the United Kingdom - the Robin to Tony Blair's Batman - was famed for declaring that his prudence at the Treasury had brought an end to the previous cycles of "boom and bust" economics[60]. The 2008 economic crisis proved him wrong in a pretty dramatic fashion. At the risk of tempting fate and facing similar ridicule, we believe that the methodologies described in this book will bring an end to the boom and bust cycle most businesses go through when faced with disruption. We do not believe that a decline after success is an inevitable part of doing business. There is no need to become a comeback kid, as long as companies don't get settled in their success and start using strategy as a way to protect their competitive advantage.

47

Instead, strategy should be viewed as a process for managing mature business units through operational excellence, while at the same time exploring new opportunities and new markets (i.e. *searching while executing*). The exploration work can then be guided by an innovation thesis that provides the rationale for innovation and makes clear what ideas the company will invest in. An end to boom and bust economics will then come to fruition if the company instantiates their innovation thesis through an ecosystem that has a balanced portfolio of products and services. How to build this portfolio is the focus of the next chapter.

Innovation Activity: Seven Steps to Creating Your Innovation Thesis

In our work with companies we have developed a methodology to help them develop their innovation thesis. We gather ten to twelve top executives within the business for a full-day or two-day workshop. The length of the workshops depends on the complexity of the business.

The main requirement for the workshop is a cross-functional team of the top executives. This must include all the top decision makers across operations, finance, marketing, heads of business units and the CEO. It is also possible to develop business unit or division specific innovation theses and the executives from the relevant division would be involved in the process.

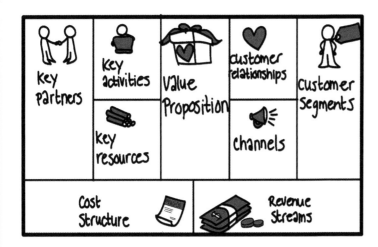

Source: Osterwalder, A. & Pigneur, Y. (2010). *Business Model Generation*. New York City: John Wiley & Sons.

Step 1 - Pre-Workshop:

Prior to the main workshop, we host a half-day pre-workshop in which we map the company's main business model. If the company has more than one business model, we map several models and then converge on the main business models it uses. The point of this workshop is not to map business models on a product-by-product basis, but rather to map the general approach that the company takes when doing business in its core markets. We use Osterwalder's Business Model Canvas[61] for these workshops.

Step 2 - Research:

At the end of the workshop, we give the executives A4 sized copies of the business environment canvas. They are then given two to three weeks to work with their teams and do the research necessary to be able to complete the categories on the business environment canvas (e.g. key trends). They are also encouraged to make a first pass at completing the environment canvas with their teams.

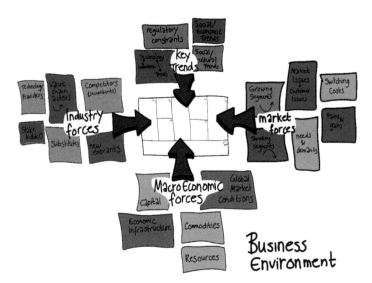

Business Environment

Source: Osterwalder, A., & Pigneur, Y. (2010). *Business Model Generation*. New York: John Wiley & Sons.

Step 3 - Workshop:

After the research period, we then reconvene the team of executives for a full day's workshop. During this workshop we collaboratively map the key trends, market forces, industry forces and macro-economic forces impacting their business model(s).

Step 4 - Review:

After mapping their business environment, we then have the executive's review their initial business model in terms of how adaptive it is to the business environment they have mapped. The point of the task is to identify key gaps and potential problem areas. The identified gaps are articulated and captured on a separate document.

Step 5 - Options:

After identifying gaps, we then work with the executives to consider how these gaps may be dealt with. The goal of this exercise is to create innovation options. These can range from changes to their current business model, introducing new products into adjacent markets or coming up with transformational ideas. The point is not for the executives to come up with specific product or service ideas (but this can happen). Instead, their role is to identify the types of ideas, markets, industries and arenas in which they would like innovation to happen. In other words, they will be defining how they expect innovation to help with the gaps and challenges identified in Step 4.

Step 6 - Thesis:

After deciding how they would like to use innovation to help with closing the gaps in their portfolio, they can then start working on their innovation thesis. First, they complete the innovation thesis worksheet. We then show them examples of investment theses from various venture capital firms. As they work on their theses we make sure that they are focused on providing a clear strategic narrative about how the world is changing, how they expect to use innovation to benefit or take advantage of these changes, and specifics about the types of ideas and teams they will invest in. We also help them articulate what they will not invest in.

Step 7 - Iterate:

After completing their first drafts, we adjourn for the day. They then have the task to share the thesis with their teams, get feedback and iterate on the thesis. The final versions of the thesis are then shared with the rest of the company.

Innovation Thesis Worksheet

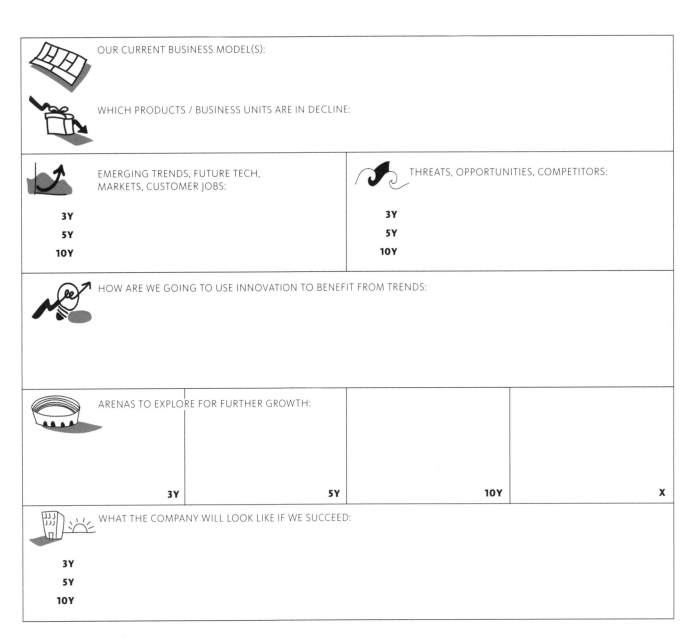

OUR CURRENT BUSINESS MODEL(S):

WHICH PRODUCTS / BUSINESS UNITS ARE IN DECLINE:

EMERGING TRENDS, FUTURE TECH, MARKETS, CUSTOMER JOBS:

3Y

5Y

10Y

THREATS, OPPORTUNITIES, COMPETITORS:

3Y

5Y

10Y

HOW ARE WE GOING TO USE INNOVATION TO BENEFIT FROM TRENDS:

ARENAS TO EXPLORE FOR FURTHER GROWTH:

3Y   5Y   10Y   X

WHAT THE COMPANY WILL LOOK LIKE IF WE SUCCEED:

3Y

5Y

10Y

Thesis Statement

Vision of the future We believe that the future will be...

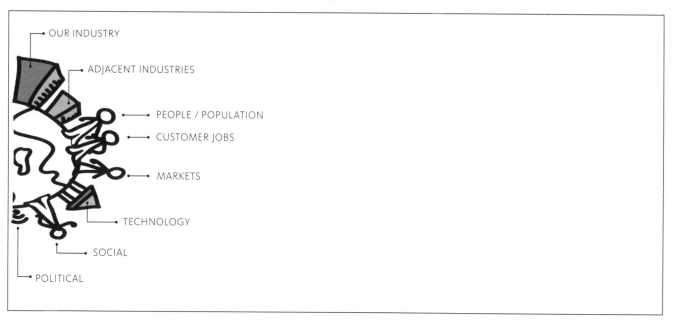

OUR INDUSTRY

ADJACENT INDUSTRIES

PEOPLE / POPULATION

CUSTOMER JOBS

MARKETS

TECHNOLOGY

SOCIAL

POLITICAL

Innovation Thesis We believe that our company can benefit from current trends by investing in...

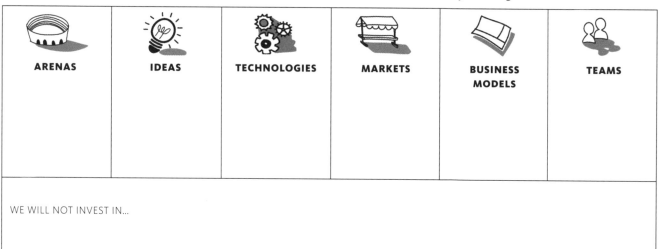

ARENAS	IDEAS	TECHNOLOGIES	MARKETS	BUSINESS MODELS	TEAMS

WE WILL NOT INVEST IN...

CONVERSATIONS ON INNOVATION
Ole Madsen

SVP COMMUNICATION AND BUSINESS DEVELOPMENT AT SPAR NORD BANK

Spar Nord is a Danish bank based in North Jutland, Denmark. Fifteen years ago the bank implemented a Local Strategy which was aimed at growing and winning market share beyond their base in North Jutland. This strategy was focused on giving their local banks decision-making autonomy and room for manoeuvre. The strategy was such a success that, even through the financial crisis, Spar Nord experienced fifteen years of uninterrupted growth and profits. However, there are emerging trends that are currently changing the banking market. So even though the bank is currently doing well, they have also started developing new strategies with a view to dealing with these emerging trends.

CS: PLEASE DESCRIBE FOR US YOUR ROLE IN SPA NORD AND WHAT YOU DO?
OM: That's always a tough question. The formal answer would be that I am a part of the bank's management group. And that my areas of responsibility include strategy development and M&A, business development and digital innovation, corporate communication, investor relations, marketing and customer service. I guess, I am the person whose role it is to ensure that we adopt a holistic view of the business and that creativity is applied to the parts of the business where creativity is called for.

**CS: SPAR NORD HAS BEEN VERY SUCCESSFUL OVER THE PAST TWO DECADES.
HOW HAS THE LOCAL STRATEGY HELPED WITH THAT SUCCESS?**

OM: The simple idea behind the *Local Strategy* has been to empower people in the customer facing units much more than most of our competitors tend to do. And to explicitly state that we want our team members to play an active role in the local community. This has been a strong asset in the effort to attract people with the right entrepreneurial spirit and subsequently to attract customers in all the cities where we have set up new branches. Of course, the flip side of a strategy where you give decision-making power to many people across the organization, can be problems achieving the desired economies of scale and the cost efficiencies that investors expect. But in general, we have been able to achieve a growth and sales performance that has more than made up for our cost intensive way of doing business.

**CS: WITH SUCCESS THAT THE BANK HAS ALREADY HAD,
WHY NOT JUST CONTINUE WITH THE LOCAL STRATEGY?**

OM: It has to do with the seismic shifts we see occurring in customers' behavior and expectations - to a large extent driven by the rapid development and adoption of new technology. On one hand, our customers are still remarkably satisfied with our personal and down-to-earth approach to banking. On the other hand, customers' transactions and day-to-day service needs are now handled much better in digital channels than in the physical branches. Furthermore, we now have access to a wealth of data that - if applied intelligently - should make us able to "know" our customers even better. This opens up an immense potential for providing insight-driven advice and thereby to grow our business. One of the key challenges in making that happen is that working with data and interacting with customers on digital platforms, calls for a somewhat more uniform way of doing things. So we still want the same local empowerment but with a little less anarchy in the work processes.

**CS: WHAT MADE YOUR BANK DECIDE TO DEVELOP A NEW STRATEGIC APPROACH?
WHAT KEY TRENDS HAVE YOU BEEN NOTICING IN THE BANKING MARKET?**

OM: First of all, we felt that the changes in our operating environment were of such dimensions that we had to question some of the key assumptions, we had held for the past fifteen years. Therefore, we did a lot a qualitative and quantitative research in customer behavior, technology adoption and the like. The first two trends, we decided to focus on when developing our new strategy were digitization and the changes in customer behavior digitization leads to. Furthermore, we had to focus on the challenges in our operating environment that stem from the low growth in the general economy and from the massive regulatory burden that has been imposed on banks following the financial crisis.

CS: ON THE BASIS OF THOSE TRENDS, WHAT IS THE NEW EMERGING VISION OR STRATEGIC DIRECTION FOR THE BANK?

OM: From our research, we learned that customers - even the so-called digital natives - still value personal interaction when they need advice on matters of a more substantial nature. For example, when buying a house or setting up a pension plan. On the other hand, we learned that local engagement and traditional brick and mortar banking is becoming much less important, whereas state-of-the-art digital solutions are becoming more and more important. This led us to a strategic ambition and a value proposition where we want to sustain and leverage the virtues of personal banking with face-to-face contact in physical branches, and at the same time use new digital opportunities to become even more personal and relevant instead of just viewing digitization as a means of rationalization. This is what we have called "*the personal bank in a digital world*".

CS: TO DELIVER ON THAT VISION, WHAT HAVE YOU IDENTIFIED AS THE KEY MUST-WIN BATTLES.

OM: We have identified three key areas, which we have named "*top-notch personal advice and service*", "*local ownership and strong central support*" and "*digitization the Spar Nord way*". Among the concrete initiatives, some of the most important are designing our customer engagement, training our team members in great customer service, redecorating our physical branches and implementing state-of-the-art CRM. In addition to that, we will launch a number of digital innovation projects in areas we find relevant.

CS: WHAT DIFFERENT INNOVATION APPROACHES ARE SPAR NORD IMPLEMENTING IN ORDER TO DELIVER ON THE VISION AND MUST-WINS?

OM: Fundamentally, we believe in open innovation. Instead of hiring in two hundred people and setting up a separate innovation entity, we want to open our platform to third party innovation. This includes getting the core banking systems ready for integration and getting all the legal requirements in place. So basically, what we want to do, is to share our strategic ambition about becoming "*the personal bank in a digital world*" with anyone - be it innovative start-ups or more established players - who are able to contribute. More concretely, what we do is enter into various types of collaborations, make corporate venture investments and host so-called incubator and accelerator programs.

54

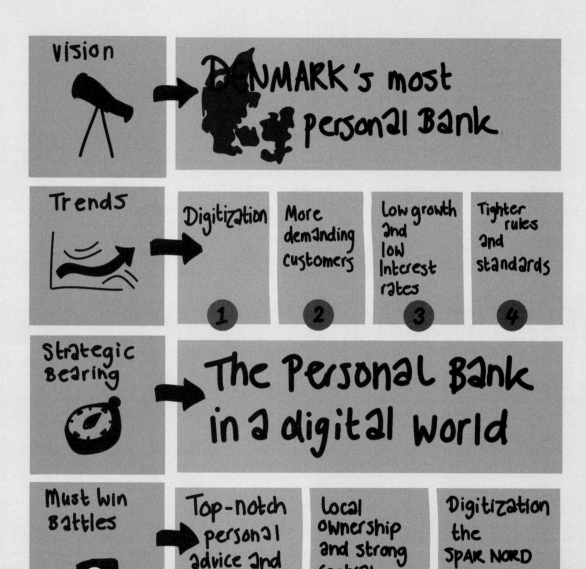

Vision → DENMARK's most personal Bank

Trends →

1. Digitization
2. More demanding customers
3. Low growth and low Interest rates
4. Tighter rules and standards

Strategic Bearing → The Personal Bank in a digital World

Must win Battles 1 →

1. Top-notch personal advice and service
2. Local ownership and strong central support
3. Digitization the SPAR NORD way

'No company can defend only.
If you have a high market share
and you are a market leader,
if you start defending
you cannot sustain.'

Olli-Pekka Kallasvuo, Former CEO of Nokia

CHAPTER THREE

Innovation Portfolio

Much has been written about the changing landscape in the business of education[62]. The publishing industry, from books to magazines and newspapers, has been slowly getting disrupted by digital technologies that are slowly rendering the printing press obsolete[63]. Between 2010-2015, there was a significant increase in investments in the EdTech space which grew over 503% during that period. However, these investments slowed down significantly in 2016[64]. During that same period there have been discussions about the rise of startups that are disrupting education, and whether they are here to stay[65].

The education business provides a great cautionary note to large incumbent companies about what disruption might look like while it is happening. What managers have to realize is that it is not badly run companies that end up getting disrupted, but well run companies that are making sensible management decisions, given their business and where they are in their lifecycle. Disruption also occurs because the disruptors often look like they don't know what they are doing. The current 'chaos' in the EdTech industry and the significant reduction in venture capital investments may give incumbents a false sense of comfort. This comfort will lead incumbent companies to continue to make strategic decisions about protecting their current competitive advantages. This is not only wrong, it is dangerous.

57

Disrupting Class
In early 2016, *Inc. Magazine* published the top 50 fastest growing education companies as part of their annual ranking of the Top 5000 fastest growing companies[66]. The growth rates of the new education companies were fascinating, with some companies growing by as much as 1552%. Even the slowest growing education company still had an impressive 87% growth rate. The average growth rate across the companies was 301%. But these growth rates are not where we will find the hidden gems of disruption. The secret to disruption is hiding in the revenue numbers that the companies posted.

The fastest growing company on the Inc. list, *Capture Education*, only posted revenues of $2.1 million. The highest revenue numbers were posted by *Curriculum Associates* at $83.5 million. In fact, 37 of the top 50 companies all had revenue of less than $10 million. These small revenue numbers are where the danger lies for large incumbent companies. When you are multi-billion-dollar juggernaut, why should you care about a little startup somewhere that has only $2.1 million in revenue? If a large company added this revenue to its bottom line, this would not provide the growth rates that they require to meet their obligations to shareholders.

This takes us to Christensen's second principle of disruption: *small (emerging) markets don't solve the growth needs of large companies*[67]. While a $20 million dollar company needs to find only $2 million in new revenue to grow 10%; a $5 billion dollar company needs a whopping $500 million in new revenue to grow at a similar rate. As such, it makes management sense to dismiss $2 million dollar ideas because they will not meet the short term growth needs of a large company. It gets even worse when the ideas are transformational innovations that take a long time to generate revenue. These longer horizons do not play well within quarterly market dynamics. It appears to make more sense to pursue reliable sources of short-term large revenues. Such management decisions are made with the best intentions. But that is also how disruption happens.

Corporate executives often wait to enter emerging markets until they are large enough for their growth needs. They will also wait until some of the startups are successful enough to acquire. This strategy might work. But startups always have the option not to sell. And some of them will create better and better technologies; they will keep growing and taking away market share from large incumbents. At some point, the incumbents will wake up and realize they have lost even their

best customers to these upstarts. It is clear that large companies need to get into some these nascent markets early. What they need is a strategic framework for how to do that. Providing this portfolio framework is the goal of this chapter.

The Innovation Portfolio

While large companies are not startups, they also need to stop thinking and acting as if they are a single monolithic institution with one business model. To develop an innovation ecosystem, they need to view themselves as portfolios of products and services. A good place to start is by developing an innovation thesis because this sets out the company's innovation ambitions. The distinction between *searching* and *executing* also provides a powerful lens for building an innovation portfolio. The company can use this lens to assess which of its products have validated business models and are mostly in execution mode; versus new products that are still searching for profitable business models. At any point in time, a company needs to have a mix of products that are searching and products that are executing.

The aspiration is to use the innovation thesis we developed in Chapter 2 to inspire a balanced portfolio of products so that when shifts happen, the company is already engaged in a systematic process of searching for new advantages. If a company has put in place an innovation thesis and a balanced portfolio before a crisis arrives, they are better placed to respond, adapt and cope. Kodak were relatively lucky to have their patents. But they only started actively developing products from these patents after their bankruptcy crisis. Strategic portfolio management means that you build an innovation portfolio ahead of time as an ongoing part of doing business.

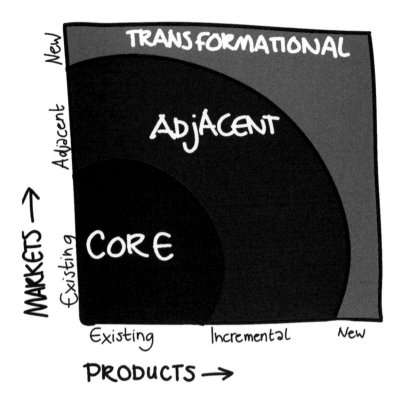

Source: Nagji, B. & Tuff, G. (2012). 'Managing your innovation portfolio.' *Harvard Business Review*, 90(5), 66-74.

But how can a company actively build an innovation portfolio? There are frameworks that can help us put this idea on a more rigorous footing. One of our favorites is Nagji and Tuff's Innovation Ambition Matrix[68], which provides a method for companies to build balanced portfolios. Their framework is an adaptation of Ansoff's Matrix[69] and is based on two main dimensions; *products* (new products *versus* existing products) and *markets* (new markets *versus* existing markets). Rather than use the binary distinctions that Ansoff uses in his matrix, Nagji and Tuff use a range of values. On the basis of the above two dimensions they distinguish three main types of innovation which are: core, adjacent and transformational.

- With *core innovation,* company efforts focus on making incremental changes to existing products for existing customers. This can be in the form of new packaging, small redesigns of products or improvements in service. The important point here is that these innovations draw on assets the company already has in place and customers that they already understand well. These are the typical optimizations that most large companies are very good at.
- With *adjacent innovation* the company takes something it currently does well and applies it to new markets or to the development of new products and services for current markets. The point here is that the company is drawing on existing capabilities and putting them to new uses. Entering adjacent markets or developing new products using current capabilities can be a stretch; but it is not typically out of reach for many large companies.
- In contrast, *transformational innovation* focuses on creating new offerings for new markets. Here, the company often has to develop new capabilities, products or services, while simultaneously testing these new offerings in new markets. This process is the most difficult for large companies to do while they are running their core business. The risks involved and the long horizons for seeing returns are something large companies may not have an appetite for.

59

The Innovation Ambition matrix is similar to the three horizons framework from McKinsey. Featured in the seminal book *The Alchemy of Growth*[70], this framework provides a lens through which companies can manage for future growth without hurting current profitability:

- *Horizon One (H1)* represents the core businesses and products that are currently providing profits and cash flow. This is similar to core innovation since the focus is on optimizing the performance of the current business models in order to maximize revenue, profits and returns.
- *Horizon Two (H2)* focuses on emerging opportunities that are likely to generate sustainable profits in the near future. Similar to adjacent innovation, the products and services may require some investment but the levels of risk are no longer as substantial. This is because H2 products are often H1 products being taken to new markets, or validated H3 products being taken to scale. Investment in growing these opportunities will very likely generate substantial new revenues for the company.
- *Horizon Three (H3)* focuses on ground-breaking ideas that may result in profitable growth in the future. These are the 'crazy plays' that are bets on future trends, emerging technologies and emerging markets. This is similar to transformational innovation in that the company is thinking about new products for new markets. As such, they could invest in research and development, innovation labs or even take stakes in emerging startups.

The point of these frameworks is to illustrate how an established company should view or examine its portfolio of products. It is important that a company has products that cover the three horizons and the three types of innovation. If a company's portfolio only has core products, then that company is not geared up to be adaptive to changes in its environment. But before we proceed to a discussion about what balanced portfolios look like, we would like to first examine Christensen's notion of disruptive innovation and how it relates to the frameworks we have presented so far.

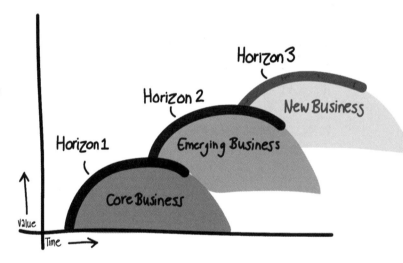

Source: Bahgai, M., Coley, S. & White, D. (1999). *The Alchemy of Growth*. London: Orion Business.

Disruptive Innovation

Disruptive innovation, as distinct from sustaining innovation, was first introduced by Clayton Christensen[71]. Since then, the term 'disruption' has been commonly used to describe any situation in which a large incumbent company is replaced by a startup. However, it is important to highlight that the *sustaining innovation* versus *disruptive innovation* distinction is different from the three types of innovation we have described above. There are two main types of disruptive innovation that can impact incumbent large companies.

The first type of disruption is referred to as *low-end foothold* disruption. This describes a situation in which new smaller companies enter markets by first targeting overlooked lower-end segments and delivering products with more suitable functionality, often at cheaper prices[72]. This happens because large companies tend to focus on their most profitable custom-ers by providing ever-improving products and services; while paying less attention to their least profitable or low-end customers. In doing this, they end up with products that provide functionality that is well beyond the affordability and needs of the lower end of the market. This opens up an opportunity for new entrants to enter the market at the low-end.

The second type of disruption is referred to as *new-market foothold* disruption. In this situation, new entrants start by focusing on new or emerging market segments that are currently too small for large companies to pay attention to or care about. This often happens through a focus on non-consumption (i.e. they successfully turn non-consumers into consumers). The technology serving these nascent and low-end markets is often still rudimentary and not to the standard that mainstream customers would appreciate.

61

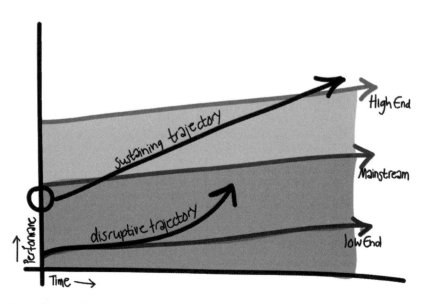

Source: Christensen, C. (2013). *The Innovator's Dilemma.* Boston: Harvard Business Review Press.

The EdTech space we described at the beginning of this chapter is a good example of an emerging but still relatively small market compared to traditional schools and universities. Another example is the Apple 1, which was very rudimentary but also targeted an emerging market of personal computer enthusiasts. This market was so nascent that executives at HP, where Steve Wozniak worked, passed up a chance to build the computer five times because they did not feel that ordinary people would ever have a need for computers[73].

In the meantime, large incumbent companies continue to focus on improving their current products and services for their most profitable customers. This activity is what Christensen refers to as *sustaining innovation*. These business decisions make short-term sense in terms of revenues and profits, but in the long-term they also create the challenges we identified at the beginning of this chapter. This is because, while large companies are focusing on meeting the needs of their most profitable customers, the new entrants continue to improve their products and start to move upmarket.

As the new entrants move further upmarket, they have the advantage that they can preserve their lower cost-structures and the customers that made them successful at the lower end of the market. Eventually the new entrants will start delivering product performance that attracts the more profitable customers of the large incumbent companies. When the customers of the large incumbent companies start buying the new entrant's product and services, disruption is said to have occurred[74]. This illustrates that disruption is a process, not a sudden event. The process can happen quickly or take years, but understanding how it happens can help companies as they think about how to manage the three horizons of innovation.

Highlighting the distinction between disruptive innovation and the other types of innovation is not merely theoretical nit-picking. We feel that in order to develop a balanced portfolio, large companies need not only to consider the three horizons of innovation; they also need to be conscious of how much of their work is focused on low-end and nascent markets. The lower profits and higher risks in these markets may lead large companies to ignore or avoid them, even as they are working across the three horizons of innovation. A focus on disruption directs managers to think counterintuitively and look for markets in places they would not normally look[75].

A Balanced Portfolio

Understanding the different types of innovation is also important because it has practical effects on how managers view their role with regards to their product portfolio. These distinctions provide companies with a language and taxonomy that they can use in a consistent way within the company. Using the same language means that managers and teams can easily communicate about products and services, where they sit within the portfolio and what needs to happen with them. In addition to this, the goal of these innovation frameworks is to help companies create a portfolio of products, services and business models that is balanced.

A balanced portfolio is one in which a company has products and services that cover all three horizons of innovation. We strongly recommend that companies should manage all three horizons at the same time. If the management of horizons is done in a linear fashion, the company might end up facing a crisis before they even get to the second horizon! The only way to guarantee that the company is being run with a short-term, medium-term and long-term view, is to manage the three horizons concurrently. Nagji and Tuff propose a "magic formula" of 70-20-10 that companies can use to balance their portfolios. As shown below, they recommend that companies should invest 70% of their resources into core innovation, 20% into adjacent innovation and 10% into transformational innovation.

63

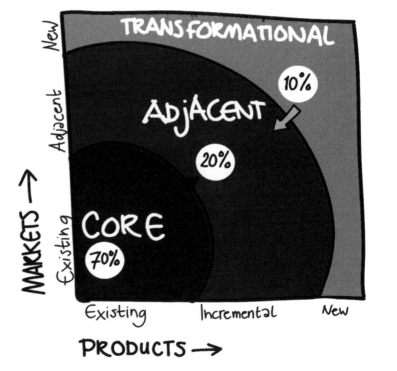

Source: Nagji, B. & Tuff, G. (2012). 'Managing your innovation portfolio.' *Harvard Business Review*, 90(5), 66-74.

This magic formula is not uniform across industries. It can change on the basis of industry norms. For example, Nagji and Tuff identify the ratio for consumer goods companies as 80–18–2; whereas the ratio for mid-stage technology firms in 45–40–15. Even with these norms in place, a company can decide its own ratios based on its strategic goals and innovation thesis. The point is to make explicit what your innovation ambitions are. Without explicit decisions, it becomes hard to be consistent about creating a balanced portfolio. And yet, having such a portfolio is key for a company to move from competitive advantage to competitive advantage over time.

Google is Alphabet + Facebook Ten Year Horizon

Google is an impressive company when it comes to building an innovation portfolio. Over the years, Google has expanded the range of its products to go beyond just the search engine and advertising which is a massive cash cow product. Based on an innovation thesis of betting on technical insights, Google has launched or acquired a wide range of products and services including Gmail, Google Maps, Google News, iGoogle, YouTube and Android[76]. The company has even bet on physical products by acquiring Motorola, working on self-driving cars and launching Google Glass. Not all of Google's bets have succeeded (e.g. Google Wave), but they have a had quite a few phenomenal successes.

Google's innovation ecosystem was made explicit when it transformed itself into the holding company Alphabet on August 10th, 2015[77]. Alphabet became the parent company to Google and various other divisions including Nest Labs (smart home products), Google Fiber (high speed internet) and Google Ventures (growth stage investing[78]). Looking at the new structure it is clear that the rest of Alphabet represents bets on the industries of the future, whereas Google is the part of the business that pays the bills for now. This aspiration is clear in the statement below from Larry Page's letter to the market at the launching of Alphabet:

64

"We've long believed that over time companies tend to get comfortable doing the same thing, just making incremental changes. But in the technology industry, where revolutionary ideas drive the next big growth areas, you need to be a bit uncomfortable to stay relevant."[79]

Larry Page, CEO Alphabet Inc.

Facebook 10 year Roadmap

Just like Google, Facebook is also building its innovation portfolio. At the F8 conference in April 2016, Facebook's CEO Mark Zuckerberg announced the company's ten-year roadmap. The roadmap was divided into three sections, which represent the three horizons of innovation. The first three year are focused on improving Facebook as an ecosystem; the five-year horizon is focused on strengthening products such as WhatsApp and Instagram; and the ten year horizon includes technologies such as artificial intelligence and virtual reality[80]. This third horizon is a bet on emerging technologies in nascent markets. If this roadmap is well executed, it will move Facebook away from an exclusive focus on its core product (i.e. the social network); and allow it to move into the future in a sustainable way.

Mind the Disruptors

In building an innovation ecosystem, management must be mindful of disruptive innovation emerging from the low-end or emerging markets. What the company must resist at all costs is the natural reaction to walk away from apparent low profit margins and revenues. An established company should try as much as it can to 'disrupt' itself. A great example of this is Intel's creation of the Celeron processor. As a highly innovative company, Intel has historically pushed the envelope in designing faster and better processors for computers and other devices (e.g. Intel Core i7-4770K). After meeting with Clayton Christensen, Andy Grove who was at the time CEO of Intel, concluded that in addition to the pursuit of better and faster processors, Intel should also create their own low-end products. This gave birth to the highly successful low-end Intel Celeron processor[81].

An innovation portfolio is not balanced until it covers the three types of innovation, while considering disruptive innovation. How a company does this will be determined by market conditions, future trends, its strategy and innovation thesis. There are frames of reference that the company can use. For example, when considering adjacent innovation, a clear option is to develop versions of current core products that can be taken into low-end markets. In contrast, when considering transformational innovation a company can examine emerging technologies and nascent markets. This is how the three horizons and disruptive innovation can intersect.

Managing The Portfolio

It is no longer an option for an established business in the 21st century to ignore the balanced portfolio. Creating and maintaining a balanced portfolio is now *Management 101*; it is now the job of every executive in a large established company. Our innovation thesis comes from an analysis of the world and tells us where we need to go. An analysis of our portfolio tells us whether we have what we need to get there. It is then important to have detailed conversations about what the right portfolio mix should be (see innovation activity). If portfolio mix decisions are made without an innovation thesis, you are likely to have a hotchpotch of product ideas in your portfolio that are not strategically aligned.

This is not to say that companies should not have investments dedicated to 'playing with off-script ideas' in terms of strategy. It is hard to be exact when predicting the future. So this should be allowed. Our argument is that all these decisions should be made consciously and then managed appropriately. We have already proposed that the three horizons of innovation have to be managed simultaneously. It is also important to recognize that adjacent and transformational innovation should not be farmed out to low-level managers within the business. Executives can view their jobs as being to run and manage the core business. Innovation, as a 'nice to have', can then be done by the startup types in jeans and t-shirts. In our experience, innovation needs top-level executive attention. It is the only way to ensure that the innovation horizons are not starved of budget and resources; which is often the instinctive tendency of companies, especially during times of crisis[82].

67

Companies also need to recognize that they cannot manage the innovation using the same methods that they use to manage their core products. Adjacent and transformational innovation should be managed differently from core products. This is both in terms of product development practice and investment decision-making. Taking core product management practices and applying them to innovation is one of the reasons why innovation fails within large companies. Innovation product development practice should be done using startup methods that include experiments and iterations. Investments should be done incrementally via multiple small bets with a view to the innovation stage at which that product is. These practices are the focus of the next two chapters.

Innovation Activity: Mind the Gap

In order to build a balanced portfolio, a company has to make clear its innovation ambitions. How does it plan to deliver on its innovation thesis? What ratios across the three types of innovation is it trying to achieve? How will it allocate resources to the three horizons? The innovation thesis developed in Chapter 2 forms a good basis for this work. However, the company also needs to do the hard work of analyzing their current portfolio. Knowing where we stand today provides a benchmark from which management decisions can then be made.

Step 1 - Set the Target:

In a half-day workshop or meeting, we work with executives to apply their innovation thesis and prior analysis of their business environment to set what they think is a well balanced portfolio for their company. This work involves setting targets around the combination of the three types of innovation and the products, markets or business models that may be used to achieve our goals. To set our target, we can also analyze competitor portfolios or follow recommended standards for our industry (e.g. 70-20-10). It is important to note that this target setting is not a one-off exercise. This target will have to be looked at and revised annually, in order to make sure that we are meeting our strategic objectives and responding to any changes in our environment. So managers should not spend too much time debating the target.

The point is to set an ambition that allows the company to get started. So using the worksheet below, or a redesigned version of our own, we can set the percentage of the overall portfolio for each type of innovation, as well as the products, markets or business models we should be aiming for. At the end of the meeting, we should know where we want to go as a company, in terms of portfolio balance targets, products and business models.

Step 2 - Review Current Portfolio Against Target:

After setting our target, the real question is whether we currently have what it takes in our portfolio to get to where we want to go. It is, therefore, important for management to know what the current balance is in their portfolio. To do this work, management can appoint analysts to review their current portfolio of products, services and business models. Using the definition of the three types of innovation noted above (i.e. existing versus new products; existing versus new markets), the analysts will be able to inform the company what the current balance of the portfolio is. Using the sheet below they can look at each of the three types of innovation and analyze how many products within our portfolio are of each type? Of these products, how many are in-sync or out-of-sync with our overall strategy as a company? What percentage of our products are future facing and aligned with our innovation thesis?

Analysis can also be done on the amount of resources being invest in each type of innovation. These can then be mapped against the target balance using a table as shown below:

	Target Investment	Current Investment
Core Innovation H1	70%	85%
Adjacent Innovation H2	20%	10%
Transformational Innovation H3	10%	5%

Step 3 - Analyze the Gap:

After the portfolio analysis, we then reconvene management for another half-day workshop to analyze and review the gaps in their portfolio. This meeting is a deep dive review of how investment decisions have been made so far. Where do the gaps lie for each type of innovation? Where are divergences between investment decisions and strategy happening? How big are the gaps? Are the gaps similar across all business units? What have we been over-investing or under-investing in?

Step 4 - Make Investment Plans:

After identifying gaps, executives need to then make explicit decisions about what they are going to do to redress the balance. What specific investments are they going to make? What areas of the innovation thesis are those investments going to be focused on? What sacred cows are they willing to kill? Our advice is to make small incremental steps. If the gap between the target and current state is large, then an annual plan for incrementally reducing the gap should be made. A large and immediate shift in investment practice may not yield the expected returns. It also limits the capacity for learning and course correction.

In addition to this work, management have to set aside and protect the investment resources needed to build a balanced portfolio. In fact, management bonuses and incentives should be connected to how well they are meeting their balanced portfolio targets. At 3M, they manage their portfolio via stretch goals. This means that 25%-30% of all revenue must be from products launched within the last four years. Bonuses are then aligned to how well managers are hitting their stretch goals. Similar incentives could be used to drive managers to meet their balanced portfolio goals.

Step 5 - Revise Thesis:

After making the investment plan, it might make sense to revise the innovation thesis. In some cases, the thesis might have to be more aggressive in its ambitions than initially stated. Management then have the task to share the thesis, portfolio and investment plans with their teams and get feedback. More importantly, management must explain their decisions to the business, communicate appropriately and socialize their thinking.

	Target	Current	Year 1	Year 2	Year 3
Core Innovation (H1)	70%	85%	80%	75%	70%
Adjacent Innovation (H2)	20%	10%	15%	17%	20%
Transformational Innovation (H3)	10%	5%	5%	8%	10%

Target Portfolio Worksheet

 OUR INNOVATION THESIS:

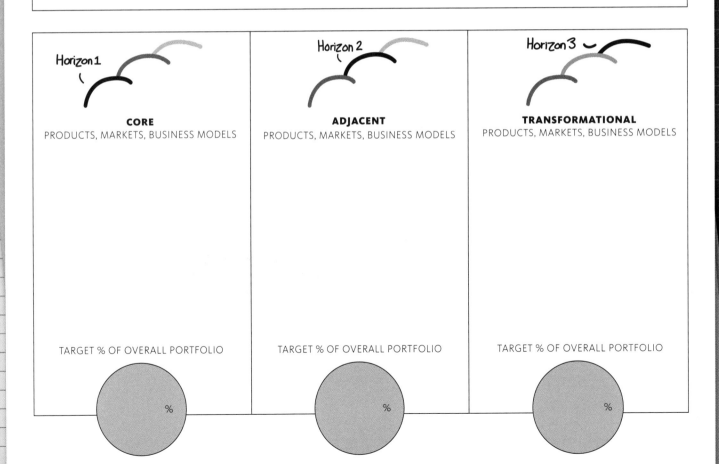

Horizon 1	**Horizon 2**	**Horizon 3**
CORE	**ADJACENT**	**TRANSFORMATIONAL**
PRODUCTS, MARKETS, BUSINESS MODELS	PRODUCTS, MARKETS, BUSINESS MODELS	PRODUCTS, MARKETS, BUSINESS MODELS
TARGET % OF OVERALL PORTFOLIO	TARGET % OF OVERALL PORTFOLIO	TARGET % OF OVERALL PORTFOLIO
%	%	%

Portfolio Analysis Worksheet

OUR INNOVATION THESIS:

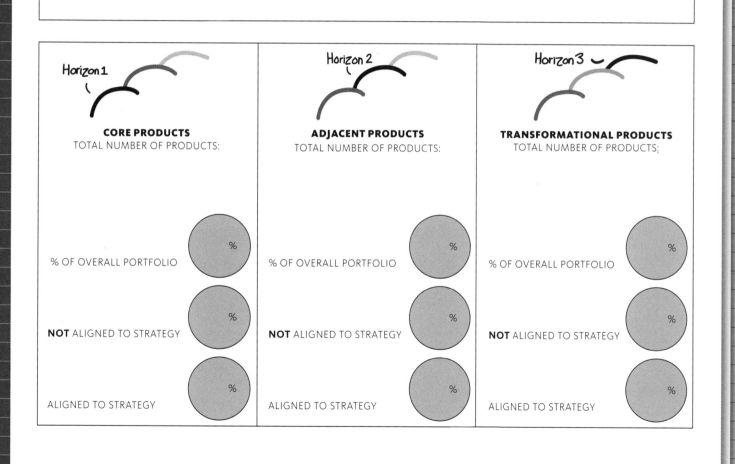

Horizon 1

CORE PRODUCTS
TOTAL NUMBER OF PRODUCTS:

% OF OVERALL PORTFOLIO   %

NOT ALIGNED TO STRATEGY   %

ALIGNED TO STRATEGY   %

Horizon 2

ADJACENT PRODUCTS
TOTAL NUMBER OF PRODUCTS:

% OF OVERALL PORTFOLIO   %

NOT ALIGNED TO STRATEGY   %

ALIGNED TO STRATEGY   %

Horizon 3

TRANSFORMATIONAL PRODUCTS
TOTAL NUMBER OF PRODUCTS:

% OF OVERALL PORTFOLIO   %

NOT ALIGNED TO STRATEGY   %

ALIGNED TO STRATEGY   %

CONVERSATIONS ON INNOVATION
Aaron Eden

CO-FOUNDER AND COO AT MOVES THE NEEDLE

Aaron Eden is a co-founder & Chief Operating Officer at Moves the Needle. For more than twenty years, Aaron has utilized his passion for innovation, entrepreneurship and customer empathy to launch multiple successful businesses and turbo-charge product teams in industries ranging from information technology, real estate, education, entertainment and management consulting. Previously, Aaron worked as a product manager in multiple product and functions during his time at Intuit, Inc. with specific focus on helping senior leaders apply Lean Startup principles. He created and rolled out a series of Lean Innovation workshops inside of Intuit. In the first year alone, after working with over a hundred teams, the insights and startups from the workshop accounted for hundreds of millions in new revenue.

CS: CAN YOU TELL OUR READERS ABOUT THE "100 STARTUPS IN 100 DAYS PROGRAM"?
AE: *Problem* - Teams inside Intuit were applying Design Thinking pretty consistently, but in many cases were still not able to make a rapid business impact.

Insight - I observed startup teams applying Lean Startup in my local eco-system and launching businesses in a matter of days.

Solution - Combine Design Thinking and Lean Startup for Intuit teams.

How - We conducted two pilot events in San Diego and Mountain View. These events went well enough that we decided to increase the scale. Myself and Ben Blank, who is Innovation and Transformational Change Leader at Intuit, used the initial business impact stories to convince one of the senior leaders to cover our travel costs to put ten teams at ten different locations through a two day Lean StartIN workshop over the course of ten weeks. Hence 100 Startups in 100 Days was born.

We convinced local site leadership at the ten sites to let us speak in their staff meetings and promoted the event that would be coming to their site soon. We put together blog posts, email promotions, slides for local TV displays, wall fliers, etc. Effectively we ran all the marketing for each site with support of any early adopters we could identify at each local site.

CS: HOW WERE THE IDEAS GENERATED? AND HOW WERE THEY ALIGNED WITH GLOBAL STRATEGY?
AE: Ideas were generated through Intuit Idea Jams and sourced from our idea management platform called Brainstorm. Teams came to each Lean StartIN event pre-formed and with an idea to work on for the two days.

Most ideas were loosely aligned with global strategy, but were not required to be. Additionally, we had lots of teams with internal innovations (new IVR features, HR training programs, finance operations innovations, etc).

Keep in mind that with Lean innovation the idea that you begin with is never the idea you end with. The topic of the idea should not be weighted heavily. This is magnified if your organization is less mature from an innovation perspective. If you're early in the journey then getting out the door with any idea can be a huge win for most organizations. While I am downplaying the importance of how ideas are generated, this is an important question because executives will always want to ensure this is happening. The problem is that unless they are extremely enlightened and have lived this previously, it will be extremely hard to convince them of this fact.

CS: WHAT WAS THE IMPACT OF THE PROGRAM?
AE: We trained almost five hundred Intuit employees and leaders, and generated hundreds of millions of dollars of revenue for Intuit. We also boosted employee engagement scores by over 7% (we heard stories of employees and leaders being promoted as a result of being able to outperform their peers) and increased Net Promoter Scores (NPS) across multiple product lines. Ben and myself received a Leadership Award from the CEO of Intuit, Brad Smith.

Additionally, as we interviewed everyone that went through the program we discovered a few surprises. First, we found that there were a handful of employees that had left Intuit to go work for startups. They described situations where they would go back to their core work and their boss would not allow them to apply what they had learned during the Lean StartIN. We quickly understood that we could not only focus on employees. We would need to re-shape how the managers led as well.

73

Second, we found that annual employee survey scores around questions like: "My organization innovates effectively" dropped significantly. We had created a situation where individuals were empowered to work differently, but didn't necessarily understand how to spread Lean Innovation in their department. We would need to quickly support these employees and ensure that they didn't revert back to old behaviors. Based on these insights, I would recommend that organizations trying to utilize something like 100 Startups in 100 Days, ensure that you have the environment the employees will return to set up so that they will be supported when they return, or you will have a huge mess to clean up.

CS: WHAT ACTIONS WERE BEING TAKEN TO MAKE THE PROGRAM SUSTAINABLE?

AE: We followed up with as many employees as possible to understand what got in their way afterward. Many stories were related to managers not being supportive of employees applying what had learnt in their daily work. About five months afterward I moved into a new role in leadership development to tackle to issue head-on. Additionally, many local sites started hosting their own Lean StartINs on a quarterly basis as the methods taught were integrated into the HR on-boarding programs and rotational development programs.

CS: IN GENERAL WHEN IT COMES TO CAPABILITY BUILDING, IN YOUR OPINION, SHOULD THIS HAPPEN BOTTOM-UP OR TOP-DOWN?

AE: It really depends on the maturity level and culture of the organization. In most situations leadership won't be supportive until you have proof that Lean Innovation works in their own company. If this is the case, you'll need to start bottom-up to create data and insights to be able to even get the buy-in from leadership. If you are fortunate enough to have leadership support then starting top-down can work. Either way, you have to build capabilities at all levels of the organization for transformation of the culture to occur and lean innovation to stick.

I have helped multiple organizations solve this problem using a network of Innovation Champions that are certified in all parts of the organization. The ICs are closest to the employees and leadership that need capability building and can speak the language of the local team which increases their chances of making an impact in those teams. It's simple in theory, but extremely difficult to get right as every company's culture is different and you cannot use a one-size-fits all structure.

CS: HOW AND TO WHAT EXTENT SHOULD, SO CALLED, SUPPORT DEPARTMENTS (EG: COMPLIANCE, COMMUNICATION, ETC.) BE INVOLVED IN INNOVATION CAPACITY BUILDING?

AE: All support functions should be completely involved. If support functions are not involved then innovation and product teams will only be able to move as fast as the slowest support function. Getting supporting functions to behave like product teams has a significant impact on current products and ensures that the support functions know how to support innovation teams for new products and services. For example, a large insurance company we were working with recently had a couple of four-person teams going through our accelerator program. They ran into issues where they were required by the compliance team to document tons of details about every customer they interacted with in a centralized database. As you can imagine this slowed the team down significantly. We quickly started working with the compliance team to support them in creation of parallel innovation policies for the team to adhere to.

CS: WHAT CAN YOU TELL OUR READERS ABOUT THE CONCEPT OF 'LEAN LEADERSHIP' AND ITS IMPORTANCE?

AE: Lean leadership is critical to ensuring organizations can be ambidextrous (handling both search and execution in the same company). On execution focused projects, leaders are paid for being right, get promoted by saying no and compensated for playing it safe. Decisions are made based on the HIPPO (The highest paid person's opinion). Behaving this way is how big, successful companies became big and successful. On search focused projects, leaders are paid for learning what works, get promoted by saying "let's learn together" and compensated for being bold. Decisions are made based on data and insights generated by interacting with customers directly. This requires significant humility, ability to mentor teams and a willingness of leaders to put their own ideas through the same rigorous Lean Innovation process that every other idea goes through.

For example, from an IT team we worked with: The team was working on overhauling an internal ticketing system which employees used to request help from the IT team. After an experiment the team got into a heated debate about the placement and coloring of a couple of key interface elements. As most teams would do, they brought the issue to their manager to make the decision. The manager had been through a few days of training on Lean Innovation and knew he could not make the decision for the team.
He asked: "How can the customer help you make the decision?"

The team quickly designed an experiment that allowed them to determine which version of the user interface worked better for their customers. When I discussed this with the manager he noted that it was extremely empowering for him to not need to make that decision. He could focus his time and energy on the team rather than making product and design decisions and breaking up team debates through hierarchy.

'There is a wide difference between completing an invention and putting the manufactured article on the market.'

Thomas Alva Edison

CHAPTER FOUR

Innovation Framework

On January 24th, 1984, Apple launched the Macintosh Computer.[83] That historic day is now the stuff of legend. It was the first time a computer had a graphical user interface (GUI). This heralded the end of the MS DOS era, meaning that people who were not an expert in text based operating commands could now use a personal computer easily. The Macintosh also featured a mouse, which for that era, was a revolutionary new innovation. Except that it wasn't. Steve Jobs and Apple had not invented the GUI or the mouse. That honor belonged to Xerox PARC, the innovation arm of Xerox Corporation. So why was it Apple and not Xerox that was launching a product in 1984 and benefiting from PARC's great inventions?[84] The answer to that question lies in the fact that invention is not enough. In order to innovate successfully, companies need frameworks that help them take their inventions from ideas to commercial successes.

The Great Inventor

Back in 1970, Xerox Corporation set up a research arm on Coyote Hill Road in Palo Alto, California. Xerox PARC (i.e. Palo Alto Research Center) was given the mandate to invent the technologies of the future. PARC assembled great scientists, engineers and programmers who rose to the challenge of inventing the future of computing. PARC researchers invented technologies that were so widely successful, we take them for granted today. The Ethernet, a prototype of the modern PC, the graphical user interface, a commercial version of the mouse, page description languages and laser printers were all invented at PARC. Despite all these technological advancements, Xerox was not able to capitalize on the market potential of the product research that was getting done at PARC.

It was in December 1979, that Steve Jobs made his first visit to Xerox PARC. As part of a deal that allowed Xerox to buy one hundred thousand shares of Apple, Jobs was given permission to see the inventions that PARC engineers were working on.

Ever the visionary, Jobs was blown away by what he saw at PARC. The commercial value of the technology was clear to

him. Larry Tesler, who conducted the demonstration of PARC's personal computer, the Xerox Alto, is quoted as stating that:

"Jobs was pacing around the room, acting up the whole time. He was very excited. Then, when he began seeing the things I could do on screen, he watched for about a minute and started jumping around the room, shouting: 'Why aren't you doing anything with this? This is the greatest thing. This is revolutionary!'" [85]

And revolutionary it was. While the Xerox Alto was a commercial flop, Apple's Macintosh was a legendary success that kickstarted a personal computing revolution. Xerox's failure to commercialize its own inventions was partly due to the disconnect between those ideas and its core business making copiers. Executives within the main business were disparagingly referred to as "toner heads" because of their failure to see the value in new inventions that were not directly related to copying or printing. Xerox is perhaps another example of how companies can get trapped in their current success within certain product categories or markets.

In Chapter 1, we argued that companies need to design their internal processes to engage in three key activities; 1. *facilitating the serendipity that creates sparks of creative ideation among employees*, 2. *capturing and testing the outputs of this creative ideation*, and 3. *transforming creative ideas into successful products and services*. Interestingly, in the case of the Macintosh, these key activities appear to have happened in three different organizations:

"The mouse was conceived by the computer scientist Douglas Engelbart, developed by Xerox PARC, and made marketable by Apple."

Malcolm Gladwell

A critique of Xerox PARC would be that it failed at executing the final activity (i.e. commercialization), which is the step at which Apple succeeded. This final activity is key to taking innovation beyond creativity. The aim of this book is to help organizations manage all three activities successfully within their companies.

Why Business Models Matter

The Xerox story also speaks to the debate about whether innovation should be based within or outside the company. Xerox had the foresight to set up PARC as an external innovation lab that was geographically located far away from the main business. Most large companies never go that far. PARC had the best minds working on inventing the future. What PARC's story shows is that no matter where products are invented, business models are important.

John Seely Brown, former Chief Scientist and Director at Xerox PARC, highlights this point in the statement below:

"Not everything we start ends up fitting with our business later on. Many of the ideas we work on here involve a paradigm shift in order to deliver value. So sometimes we must work particularly hard to find the 'architecture of revenues'. At Xerox there has been a growing appreciation for the struggle to create a value proposition [from] our research output, and for the fact that this struggle is as valuable as inventing the technology itself." [86]

Seely Brown's notion of finding the 'architecture of revenues' lies at the heart of what turns R&D labs from hotbeds of creativity and invention, into hubs of innovation. *Business models* are the connector between new technologies and commercial success. Business models provide the platform on which inventions benefit both customers and companies; customers by delivering value and companies by delivering profit. This is well illustrated by Steve Jobs, who inspired his teams at Apple to enhance PARC's inventions in a way that delivered value to customers, with a product that could be manufactured in a cost efficient manner.

In the seminal book *Business Model Generation*, Alexander Osterwalder and colleagues defined business models as "... *the rationale of how a company creates, delivers and captures value*". They identify nine key blocks that constitute most

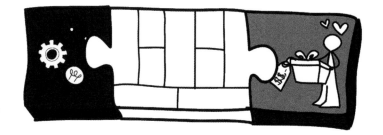

business models. These blocks are *value propositions, customer segments, customer relationships, channels, key partners, key activities, key resources, revenue streams* and *cost structures.* [87] Together, these nine blocks are important for the success of any product idea or invention. Innovators have to solve for each element of their business model in order to be successful. Solutions to this business model riddle are what we *search* for during the innovation process.

BUSINESS MODEL CANVAS

Source: Osterwalder, A. & Pigneur, Y. (2010). *Business Model Generation.* New York City: John Wiley & Sons.

The Waterfall and The Silo

It seems unfair to lecture established companies on the importance of business models. After all, they became successful by figuring out a profitable business model that led to high growth and success. But what often happens as established companies grow, is that they kill the entrepreneurial spirit that was responsible for their initial success. Over time these companies become deliberately slow moving and bureaucratic.[88] They develop siloed specialist departments such as sales, finance and marketing. The people that work in these departments collaborate via memos and hand-offs. The annual budgeting cycle is long and tedious. Every new project within the company requires a business case with five year projections of profits and ROI.

These management practices permeate and calcify within the company's culture via four key elements: the people that work in the company, the structures that are created for them to work within, the processes they use to deliver value and the KPIs against which their work is measured. In such a context, innovation is managed via traditional waterfall methodologies. First, there is some form of ideation (e.g. idea competitions). After this, the teams with the chosen ideas are expected to complete an extensive business case before receiving budget. If they succeed at getting their budget, the teams then create product roadmaps and spend months in product development as they navigate the silos of their company. After a while, they will launch their product, marketing will begin and it is only then that customers get to see it.

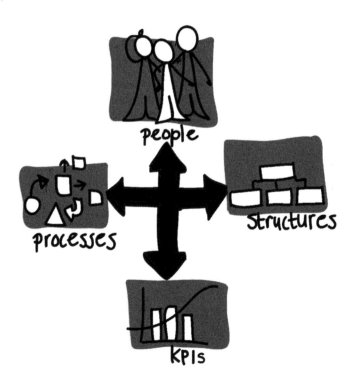

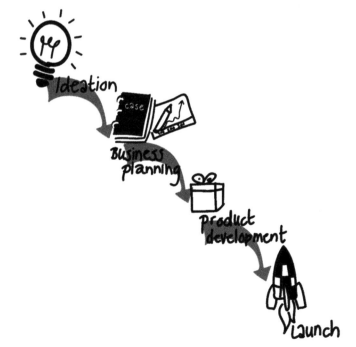

The challenge really starts when companies make the leap from ideation to business planning. In such practice, anyone with an innovative idea has to make a financial case as to why that idea might succeed. Transformational innovation is about imagining the future. The proposed business models are often different from the company's current models. As such, management will not have seen the projected financials play out in reality before. Since they are making decisions without actual evidence of success, it is hard for them to judge the potential of the transformational idea. They have to make the choice to 'believe' what the innovators are saying, or invest in product ideas that are more familiar to them.

"The moment that you put H2 or H3 next to a 'run the business project', it's going to be a clear loser, because you can't predict ROI, you have no idea what the market size is. Everything about it is an unfair test." [89]

Craig Wirkus, Innovation Program Manager at Cisco

This was the challenge for the 'toner heads' at Xerox. As managers, they were not being unreasonable. They just did not see or understand the opportunities that were being presented to them. Steve Jobs on the other hand, understood the market opportunity well. He had already launched three versions of a personal computer (Apple I, Apple II & Apple III). He knew the markets, the customers and their needs. When he saw the technology at PARC it was clear to him how this would work and benefit customers. Steve Jobs was not a magician or a prophet. In fact, the first three versions of Apple computers could be viewed as unintended minimum viable products that tested the market for the eventual launch of the Macintosh. As the early Apple computers succeeded, they allowed Steve Jobs and Apple to learn about the market.

Business Plan or Just Do It: A False Choice for Innovation

We strongly believe that it is possible for innovators to provide executives and other decision makers with similar market knowledge. But this can only happen if they are given the opportunity to test their ideas before they take them to scale. The challenge here lies within the choices that innovators have traditionally faced when asking executives to make investment decisions on innovation. The first choice that innovators have faced is to write the twenty to thirty page business cases. The assumption here is that innovation is a linear process that can be planned; and if we build our products according the plan, the customers will buy them. This is not always true, of course.

Given the difficulties they have faced with business planning, innovators in established companies then make a second choice that is also flawed. They begin to argue, with some success, that because innovation is a non-linear process, it should not be managed. Instead, they should be given investment dollars and left to just get on with it. This *Just Do It* camp bases its argument on the notion that innovation needs visionaries who are passionate about their ideas. While we fully accept this as true, we reject the idea that a passionate visionary cannot be part of a clear innovation management process. Vision and management are not mutually exclusive.

81

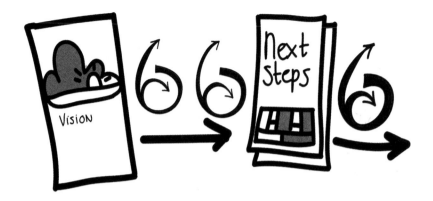

All investment decisions about innovation involve spending money. Therefore, management have the right to make informed decisions. This is not a crazy notion. It is just that until now, management have been using the wrong tools to inform their decision making (i.e. business plans). The advent of lean startup provides us with a set of methods we can use to treat innovation as management. Both vision and planning become part of the process. We capture the innovator's vision as a set of assumptions to be tested. We then test the vision with customers using experiments. As we iterate towards success, the role of management is to track how well teams are doing at aligning the innovator's vision with a profitable business model.

A key principle for innovation management is the idea that only validated business models are taken to scale. So for new ideas, business model validation is what management should be investing in. Small investments in testing ideas, help to achieve both the need for innovators to work on creative new products and the need for executives to make more informed decisions. Rather than base decisions on fictional business plans, we can invest in new ideas using frameworks that expect product teams to create learnings based on data. These lessons learned then help management to get comfortable with investing more resources in the new ideas. In essence, managers

become like Steve Jobs when he first visited Xerox PARC. They can now make inspired decisions based on validated customer insights.

The Innovation Journey

Google X was set up as a research lab by Google to pursue moonshots. These are crazy ideas such as driverless cars, that are high risk bets, but revolutionary if they became successful. Now renamed X under the new Alphabet setup, this R&D lab is also tasked with transforming those moonshots into successful businesses. The clear effort here is to avoid making the mistake of previous R&D labs such as Bell Labs and PARC that focused almost exclusively on invention. As part of their process, X have instituted an intermediate step called The Foundry.[90] This step is focused on helping the innovators within X to test their ideas in the market and find successful business models (i.e. sustainable costs and revenue models).

The Foundry process at Google X is a great example of recognition that new product development follows an innovation lifecycle. Between ideation and sustainable profits, there are intermediate steps that have to be managed. These intermediate steps mostly focus on searching for a great business model and taking it to scale. Indeed, another way to conceptualize the three horizons (H1, H2 & H3) is to view them as stages on an innovation journey. H1 products are mature products that are currently generating revenue and profits. H3 products are the inspiring moonshots that are still in R&D mode. H2 can sometimes have products that are enhancements to H1 business models. What is more critical to innovation is the fact that H2 is, for the most part, the holding stage for products that have successfully exited H3 and are now seen as potentially viable businesses. Without a proper management process to take them to scale, these potentially great products can fail.

Geoffrey Moore, author of *Crossing the Chasm*, highlights the importance of managing the H2 horizon appropriately. In an article for *Harvard Business Review*, he notes that investment management decisions for H1 products are relatively easy to make, because these products are currently generating revenue. As such, profit and growth can be managed using traditional management practices. H3 product ideas are often viewed as long-term R&D projects, so these do not come under early pressure from management to generate profit levels similar to H1 products. Moore refers to H1 as the *battleground* for profit and H3 as the *playground* for invention.[91]

In contrast, once an H3 product is moved to H2 there appears to be an immediate expectation that this product will now deliver H1 levels of revenue, growth and profits. Out of the playground, and straight to the battleground. There has to be a middle ground! An innovation lifecycle approach recognizes that before any product reaches sufficient maturity to enter H1, there are a series of stages it must pass through. Each of these stages has different expectations for the products, which also means that products in the different innovation stages should be managed differently. What is important is company alignment around a core philosophy that only products with validated business models are taken to scale.

83

The Innovation Lifecycle

At the heart of the innovation lifecycle are two broad stages; *searching* and *executing*. Execution happens when we have found a profitable and sustainable business model. Prior to that, innovators must search for this profitable business model. Searching requires them to identify and mitigate certain risks. Steve Blank makes the distinction between *technical risk* and *market risk*.[92] Technical risk concerns the question of whether we are capable of making the product at all (i.e. can it be done?). Can the technology be made to work? In contrast, market risk is mostly about whether customers will buy and use the product (i.e. should it be done?). Even if the technology works, will we ever make money with it?

Innovators have to solve for both technical and market risk. Within R&D labs, companies have traditionally focused on technical risk. However, market risk questions are just as important. We want to know early in our process whether the product should be created at all. In this regard, Eric Ries makes the distinction between *value hypotheses* and *growth hypotheses*.[93] With value hypotheses, innovators are testing whether the product serves genuine customer needs. In contrast, growth hypotheses focus on how customers will find and buy the product; and also how the product will grow market share and profits. Resolving for these two hypotheses is key to successful innovation.

Steve Blank's Customer Development Process describes four steps in the innovation lifecycle. The first two steps represent the searching phase and the last two steps are the execution phase. During *customer discovery*, the innovator's vision is captured and turned into business model hypotheses. These hypotheses are then tested during *customer validation*. After this, scaling can begin with *customer creation* as the team builds user-demand and drives sales to grow the product. During the last stage (*company building*), the team completes the transition from a startup to a core product or company executing on a validated business model.

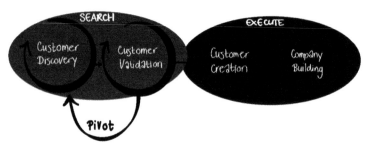

Source: Blank, S. & Dorf, B. (2012). *The Startup Owner's Manual.* California: K&S Ranch.

In the book *Running Lean*, Ash Maurya describes the innovation lifecycle as three stages of a startup.[94] Combining the work of Ries and Blank, Maurya describes how startups can navigate the innovation lifecycle by asking and answering three sets of important questions:

1. *Problem - Solution Fit*: Do we have a problem worth solving? Do customers have a real need for the product? Are we working on a solution that meets customer needs? Will customers pay for the solution?
2. *Product - Market Fit*: Have we built something people want? Are we achieving traction in the market? Have we found the right channels to reach customers and deliver value? How well are we signing up customers and retaining them? Can we create and deliver the product with the right costs and margins? Are customers paying for the product? And is our revenue model sustainable?
3. *Scale*: How do we accelerate growth? Have we found the right growth engines? How fast are we growing beyond the early adopters of our product? How quickly are we adding and retaining new customers? How fast are we growing revenues? Have we reached break even or profitability?

Maurya proposes that product teams should focus on resolving the first two stages of the lifecycle before they take their product to scale. He argues that teams should experiment, iterate and pivot before they achieve product-market fit; and then scale after they have achieved product-market fit.

Adapted from Maurya, A. (2012). *Running Lean*. Sebastopol: O'Reilly.

At Pearson, the Lean Product Lifecycle (aka Lean PLC) applies the concepts of Maurya, Ries and Blank to a corporate environment. There are six stages within this framework; *idea, explore, validate, grow, sustain* and *retire*.[95] The first three stages are focused on searching for sustainable business models; whereas the last three stages are focused on executing validated business models. During the *idea* stage, teams are expected to articulate their product idea with clear hypotheses about customer needs and alignment to company strategy.

In the *explore* stage, teams get out of the building and focus on confirming customer needs, developing the business model, and understanding the critical features that the product must have. During the *validate* stage, teams start building the solution beginning with the minimum viable product. They also test other aspects of the business model including market demand, revenue models and channels. The point is to get to product-market fit by the end of the *validate* stage, and prepare to scale the product.

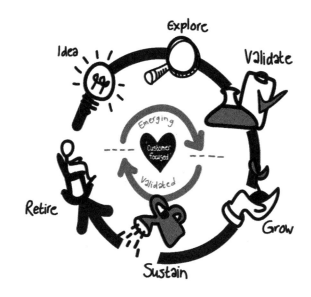

Source: Viki, T., Strong, C. & Kresojevic, S. (2017). *The Lean Product Lifecycle*. London: Pearson

During *grow*, teams take their product to scale by increasing customer numbers, revenues and market share. In the *sustain* stage, the product has matured and the focus turns to exploitation by maintaining revenues, profitability and customer satisfaction. Teams work on optimizing operations while reducing costs. In the end, every product reaches the end of its lifecycle and must be retired. During *retire*, a product is moved out of the portfolio quickly, while ensuring that customers are not inconvenienced.

85

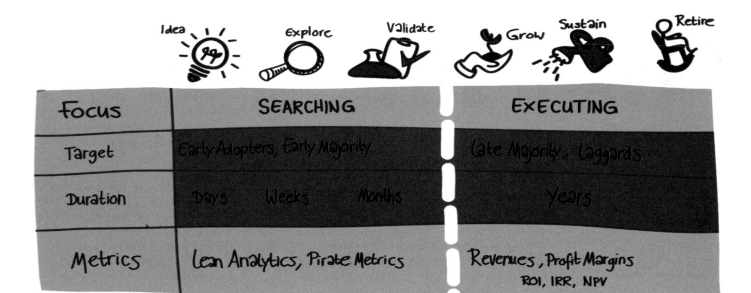

Focus	SEARCHING			EXECUTING
Target	Early Adopters, Early Majority			Late Majority, Laggards
Duration	Days	Weeks	Months	Years
Metrics	Lean Analytics, Pirate Metrics			Revenues, Profit Margins ROI, IRR, NPV

Source: Viki, T., Strong, C. & Kresojevic, S. (2017). *The Lean Product Lifecycle.* London: Pearson

According to Sonja Kresojevic, Pearson's former SVP of Product Lifecycle, the Lean PLC informs both product development best practice and investment governance. This ensures that product teams are working on the right things at the right time. For example, in order to move from the *idea* stage to the *explore* stage, no business plans are needed, teams just need to state the key hypotheses they plan on testing and how much they think this will cost. To move from *explore* to *validate*, no business plans are needed either. Teams just need to confirm that they have validated customer needs and then indicate how much they need to build a minimum viable product and test the rest of their business model. The long-term financial projections that make up a typical business case only show up when teams are ready to move from *validate* to *grow*. At this point, these financial projections make sense because they are based on validated learning.

This is the power of a framework based on the innovation lifecycle. It allows innovators to work on great new ideas and managers to make informed investment decisions. One of the reasons innovations fail is premature scaling. This is when a product is taken to scale before the business model is validated. Having an innovation framework provides a unifying language for the business that helps to prevent premature scaling. Everybody knows what phase each product or business model is in. There is no jumping from ideation to execution. This approach provides the basis of how a company can manage its portfolio, investment decisions and product development practices in a unified and consistent way.

The Corporate Startup Framework: Putting it all together

A review of the frameworks described above led us to the conclusion that they can all be synthesized into the three simple stages for innovation; *creating ideas*, *testing ideas* and *scaling ideas*. After scaling is complete, the innovation process has succeeded and businesses can enjoy the benefits of exploiting their successful products. But every now and again, the company should refresh the business models of its existing products by *renewing ideas*. When this happens, the newly revised business models would then go through testing and iterating before they are again taken to scale.

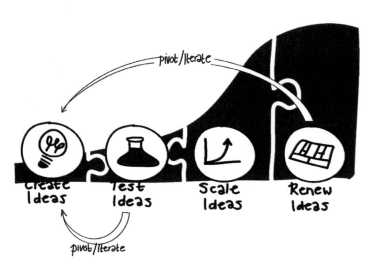

Within each of the four innovation stages, there are three sub-stages that represent key steps. Each of our stages is presented as a chapter in Part II of this book. In those chapters, each stage will be described in greater detail. For purposes of the current chapter, a brief summary of each stage and its sub-stages will be provided.

It is also important to note that our framework, as well as the others, is described in a linear fashion for storytelling purposes only. In practice, innovation is a nonlinear process and can start at any point within the framework. It is also possible to go back and forth between innovation stages as we iterate our way towards success.

The goal is simply to make sure that we are testing key questions around creating customer value and building sustainably profitable business models.

CREATING IDEAS

This is one part of the innovation process that the frameworks presented above have tended to ignore. These frameworks mostly begin with the assumption that the idea is already present and all that is left to do is test it. However, creativity and ideation are the basis for any innovation process to succeed. The design thinking process developed by Tim Brown and colleagues at IDEO provides great frameworks and tools for ideation.[96] To generate great ideas, organizations need to break down the silos of specialist departments and create cross-functional teams. The mixing together of different disciplines provides a context in which creativity can flourish. This was the practice at Bell Labs, which resulted in the invention of some of the great technological breakthroughs of the last century, including the discovery of silicon.[97]

A company must also stay connected to its customers in order to develop deep empathy and understanding of their needs. In addition to customers, companies must also pay attention to changes and trends in their business environment. This allows the business to keep a pulse on shifts and trends in socio-economics, technology, startups and competitors. A future focus on trends helps the company imagine a future in which current products may be disrupted and this helps with developing an innovation thesis. All of this knowledge should be part of daily conversations within the business, across silos and within

87

management teams. This provides a good basis for developing a point of view about customers and markets, which in turn informs ideation.

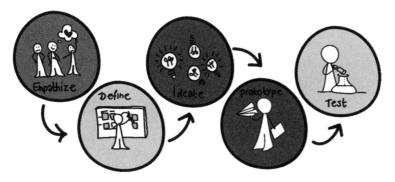

Adapted from Brown, T. (2009). *Change by Design.*New York City: Harper Collins.

In an environment rich with insights and collaboration, ideas can come from everywhere (i.e. *idea generation*). Individual employees can have lightbulb moments based on insights. Companies can organize ideation sessions that are focused on tackling specific challenges. There can also be open calls for ideas via competitions, with winning ideas getting investment for testing, iterating and potentially taking to scale. Companies can also invest in innovation by setting up R&D labs to develop technologies of the future and work on moonshots. All of these activities can become rich sources of *idea generation*.

When a number of ideas are being generated, companies need to create a platform on which these ideas can be captured. The next step in the process would be evaluating and selecting a few ideas to work on (i.e. *idea selection*). Decisions on ideas to work on can be made using our innovation thesis and balanced portfolio goals. Finally, all selected ideas must be examined for their underlying assumptions (i.e. *idea review*). Reviewing our ideas and identifying risky assumptions helps prepare for the next big innovation stage (i.e. *testing ideas*).

All ideas that are generated must be captured and kept on an open platform. The decisions about whether or not to invest in any idea must also be recorded and tagged for future innovators to look at. Even ideas that end up failing in the market must be logged and kept on this platform. Ideas must not get lost in company conversations. Capturing ideas is key because it is often the case that insights generated today only begin to make commercial sense when they are considered by another team in the future. This is the asynchronous nature of creativity and innovation. But once the company decides to work on an idea, it is important to make sure that we do not take the idea to scale prematurely, before we have tested it.

TESTING IDEAS

Once we start working on an idea, our initial work is to test it for market viability. First, we need to test whether customers have the needs or problems we are assuming they have (i.e. *problem exploration*). This answers the important question of why customers would ever buy our product. What jobs-to-be-done arise in their lives that would cause them to go out and buy our product? Second, we need to test that the solution we are creating satisfies customer needs in a manner that they are willing to pay for (i.e. *solution validation*). We can start with minimum viable versions of our product and use these to iterate our way to success.

Testing customer needs and our proposed solution are such an important part of innovation that it is surprising how much innovation teams tend to ignore these two critical steps. Jessica Livingston is co-founder of Y-Combinator, the famous accelerator that has invested in over a thousand startups, including Dropbox and Airbnb. In a speech at the Female Founders Conference, Livingston provided the attendees with a list of how to make sure your startup does not fail. Number one on the list was making something people want. Livingston notes that:

"Nothing else you do will matter if you are not making something people want. You can be the best spokesperson, the best fundraiser, the best programmer, but if you aren't building a product that satisfies a real need, you'll never succeed." [98]

The same principle applies to corporate innovation. If the company is making something nobody wants, their innovations will not succeed. After validating customer needs and our proposed solution, we can then turn our attention to validating the remaining parts of our business model (i.e. *business model validation*). This final sub-stage involves testing our channels, customer relationships, key partners, costs and revenue models. We know we are creating a product people want. The only remaining question is whether we can create and deliver the product profitably. If the answer to this question is positive, then we have a working business model and we are ready to take the product to scale.

SCALING IDEAS

The processes of scaling innovative ideas with new business models can be difficult. When they enter their growth phase, they often come under pressure to grow fast enough to meet expectations and transition to the core product portfolio (i.e. H1). It is often assumed that large companies possess the resources and expertise needed to take products to scale. After all, they have done it successfully before. Nevertheless, the resources and expertise that were used to grow their previously successful products, may not apply to the current crop of new ideas. These new products and their business models may have different growth engines. As such, before any product is taken to scale, it is important to understand the growth engine that the new product will use to scale. Eric Ries describes three main growth engines any product can use:

89

1. *The Sticky Engine:* This engine focuses mostly on customer retention. If the rate at which the product acquires new customers is greater than the rate at which customers abandon the product, then scale will be achieved.
2. *The Viral Engine:* This engine depends on customers doing the vast amount of marketing. This can be via word-of-mouth, network marketing or as a side-effect of people using the product.
3. *The Paid Engine:* This engine relies on paid marketing, advertising or a sales force to drive the growth of the product. The principle here is that the cost of customer acquisition must be less than the financial value that the customers bring over their lifetime using the product.

What we have learned with some surprise is that a lot of established companies do not have the lexicon to describe their growth engines; despite the fact that they are running an already successful business! This creates the risk that successful companies will try to sell new products via the same channels and sales methods they have always used. The point of testing our ideas is for the market to tell us what the right channels and growth engines are. If we learn that the best way to scale a product is different for what we have traditionally done, it is critical that the company develops the capacity and knowledge to manage this new growth engine.

Once we identify our engine of growth, our first job is to *tune the engine.* The focus here is on optimizing the engine and making sure that it is working well. In order to tune our engine, we need to make sure we are tracking the right metrics. It is also important to recognize here that all metrics are not created equal. The ultimate measure of success will be whether we are able to create value and deliver it profitably. For example, if we have a very low customer churn rate, but each customer we get does not provide us with sufficient revenue to cover our costs, then our product will still fail. As such, the ultimate measure of whether our growth engine has been successfully optimized, is reaching break even or profitability.

Once we are satisfied that our growth engines are working, we can now *accelerate growth.* The company can pour resources and energy into grabbing as much of the market share as possible. This is analogous to pouring rocket fuel into a well designed rocket. As we reach the peak of growth within our market share, the final stage of scaling an idea is *exploitation.* During this phase, the company optimizes costs and focuses on exploiting their successful business model as much as possible; before renewing the idea or moving on to other opportunities.

RENEWING IDEAS

After achieving scale, a company will be exploiting its new found success and milking those cash cows! One of the things that companies should avoid at all costs is complacency. A large part of our work is about reminding companies that business  models have a tendency to expire as business environments change and shift. Every company should keep its ear to the ground and its eyes on the horizon. It should always monitor emerging trends and threats. Every quarter, a company should run an exercise during which teams map some of their successful business models against the current business environment and review whether the business models are still viable in the face of emerging trends (i.e. *business model analysis*).

Companies should not just monitor trends in their environment. The second sub-stage is to actively figure out ways to respond (i.e. *business model redesign*). Business models can be renewed in a number of ways. New revenue models can be explored, new channels to reach customers can be created, new customer segments can be targeted and new technologies that reduce the cost of value creation can be acquired. However, once we have decided to redesign our business model, the final sub-stage is to review the new model for any assumptions that need to be tested (i.e. *business model review*). Our newly revised business model should not be taken to scale without testing.

The Adoption Cycle

Our innovation framework maps well to the adoption cycle developed by Everett Rogers in 1962.[99] Rogers was interested in how new ideas and technologies spread through cultures. He identified five innovation adoption categories. *Innovators* are willing to take risks and adopt technologies that may ultimately fail. *Early adopters* also adopt technologies early. But they are more discerning than innovators in their adoption choices. The *early majority* will adopt an innovation after a significantly longer time than innovators and early adopters. They wait to see if the new technology works. In fact, Geoffrey Moore describes the distance between early adopters and the early majority market as a chasm.[100] The *late majority* are more skeptical and adopt an innovation only after the average customer has done it. *Laggards* are the last group to adopt an innovation. These individuals typically have an aversion to change.

Within our innovation framework, companies should create and test ideas with innovators and early adopters (also referred to as earlyvangelists).[101] These are the people that are happy to take risks with early versions of your product and give you feedback. There is also less brand and reputational risk for a company if we start working with early adopters before we target the main market. After testing, products can then be taken to scale via the early majority. This is a chance to test our growth engines and traction metrics. When the late majority start using our product we have achieved scale. This might be the time to think about renewing our business model. It is not wise to carry on with exploitation until we have all laggards using our product. We want to keep our business model fresh and ahead of potential disruptors.

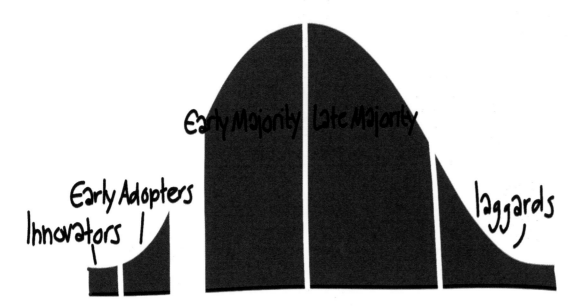

Source: Moore, G. A. (1999). *Crossing the Chasm.* New York City: Harper Business.

Epilogue:
Innovation Framework and Innovation Portfolio

An interesting aspect of having an innovation framework is that it adds an extra dimension to how we analyze and manage our innovation portfolio. Beyond the three types of innovation (core, adjacent and transformational), we can also map our products in terms of where they are on their innovation journey. In this mapping, there will be a lot of core products that are already at scale and a lot of transformational ideas that

are at still being created and tested. Nevertheless, mapping our portfolio across these two dimensions allows a company to not only get a sense of how balanced the portfolio is, but also where products are on their innovation journey. This mapping is a form of innovation accounting which is the focus of our next chapter.

	Create Ideas			Test Ideas			Scale Ideas			Renew Ideas		
	Generate	Select	Review	Problem	Solution	Business	Tune	Accelerate	Exploit	Analyze	Redesign	Review
Core Innovation H₁												
Adjacent Innovation H₂												
Transformational Innovation H₃												

93

Innovation Activity: Map Your Product

One of the great things about having an innovation framework, is the fact that you can use it to map any product in terms of where it is on its innovation journey. This is particularly useful for large companies who are often attempting to institute an innovation framework when they already have a portfolio of products in place. Among those products will be several innovation projects that are at different stages of their lives. Some will have solutions already built and others will not. Some will have already been launched in the market; while other will still be ideas on the backs of napkins.

An innovation framework provides guiding principles for developing a series of questions that can be used to assess where a product is along its journey. These questions can be viewed as a hierarchy that focuses on idea generation, idea selection, idea review, problem exploration, solution validation, business model validation, tuning growth engines, accelerating growth, exploitation and business model renewal. The assessment can also be done using various metrics such as customer numbers, revenues and profits.

Mapping a product along its innovation journey not only helps with knowing where we are, it also helps with making decisions about what to do next. For example, if we have built a solution but have not yet validated customer needs, we know that this is the next most important thing for us to do. We have developed the assessment below to help teams map each of their products. The ability of the product teams to answer each of these questions and present supporting evidence can be useful in understanding where they are on their journey. Use our questions as guidance only. Feel free to adapt and develop your own questions as necessary:

Innovation Stage Mapping Survey

1.	Product Name:			
2.	Product Owner:			
3.	Business Unit:			
4.	Is this a new idea that has just been generated?		YES	NO
5.	Is your product core, adjacent or transformational innovation?			
6.	Does the idea align with our innovation thesis?		YES	NO
7.	Have you reviewed your idea and captured key assumptions?		YES	NO
8.	Have you tested and validated customer needs?		YES	NO
9.	What customer needs does your product solve?			
10.	What are the customer jobs to be done?			
11.	Have you tested and validated the solution with customers?		YES	NO
12.	Does your solution meet their needs/solve their problems?		YES	NO
13.	Do you have customers currently using the product?		YES	NO
14.	What feedback are customers giving you about the product?			
15.	Do you have paying customers?		YES	NO
16.	Have you figured out the channels you are going to use to reach customers?		YES	NO
17.	Have you identified your growth engines?		YES	NO
18.	What are your key growth metrics? Are they showing growth?		YES	NO
19.	Has your product reached break even or profitability?			
20.	How well are you growing customer numbers, revenues and profits?			
	a. Customers			%
	b. Revenue			%
	c. Profits			%
21.	Would you consider your product a mature product in the market?		YES	NO
22.	Have your growth rates slowed down significantly over the last four quarters?		YES	NO
23.	Are you facing significant pressure from competitors or important changes in your business environment?		YES	NO
24.	Have you redesigned your business model?		YES	NO
24.	Have you identified risky assumptions in the renewed model that need testing?		YES	NO

Key:

- Questions 4, 5, 6 and 7 are about creating ideas
- Questions 8, 9 and 10 are about testing ideas (*problem exploration*)
- Questions 11, 12 and 13 are about testing ideas (*solution validation*)
- Questions 14, 15 and 16 are about testing ideas (*business model validation*)
- Questions 17, 18, 19 and 20 are about scaling ideas.
- Questions 21, 22, 23, 24 and 25 are about renewing ideas.

Sonja Kresojevic

SVP PRODUCT LIFECYCLE AT PEARSON

Sonja Kresojevic is a senior executive with over twenty years of global experience building products and driving agile and lean transformation for companies in the media, publishing and education sectors. More recently she was a Senior Vice President in the Chief Product Office at Pearson, where she led the implementation of the Global Product Lifecycle, an award-winning innovation program focused on transforming product portfolio investment management and delivering a faster and more entrepreneurial focused organization.

CS: A LOT OF COMPANIES HAVE TRIED TO BRING THE LEAN STARTUP INTO THE ENTERPRISE, WHY DO YOU THINK THEY STRUGGLE?

SK: I think a lot of companies struggle because they don't understand the scale of the challenge and all the different aspects that are involved with bringing lean startup into the enterprise, and they often focus on just one of the aspects, mostly skills training and ignore the rest. There is no focus on how they manage strategy, apply a portfolio approach to products, change their investment process whilst changing the culture through strong communities. So they will bring in consultants, trainers and coaches that will teach the teams how to run experiments, build minimum viable products and design innovative business models. This skills training is important and the workshops can be really inspiring. The problem is that when these teams return to their day to day work, they are still part of a company that uses traditional methods to manage innovation. Also, we have seen a lot of companies failing to connect lean startup to key business outcomes. It's not that companies need lean startup per se. What they need is a methodology to respond to disruption, and changes in how they nurture innovation and growth. Lean startup is just one of the modern management approaches we all need to utilize.

CS: HOW DOES THE LEAN PRODUCT LIFECYCLE GO BEYOND JUST PRODUCT DEVELOPMENT PRACTICE?

SK: Lean Product Lifecycle focuses a lot on improving product development practice and nurtures the right behaviors that differ from stage to stage. But it also goes beyond just the best practice and defines the investment criteria that are appropriate for each lifecycle stage. These criteria are different during the search stages (i.e. Idea to Validate) versus the execution stages (i.e. Grow to Retire). The Lean PLC also provides a new lense companies can use to assess their portfolio investment distribution across the stages. This gives them a clear indication in terms of health of the portfolio. The Lean PLC also significantly improves the strategic planning process. The Lean PLC helps companies look at the distribution of investments across the six stages and three horizons and provides a mechanism for management to react throughout the year when things don't go according to the plan.

CS: WHY IS SUCH INVESTMENT GOVERNANCE IMPORTANT?

SK: The main reason why most products fail is premature scaling and premature large investments based on fictional business cases with no real evidence of product market fit. Investment governance provides a framework that prevents premature scaling by requiring teams to hit certain milestones before they are allowed to take their product to scale. Investment governance also eliminates waste because investments are done incrementally. There are no big-bang large investments upfront. At the beginning of the process, small investments are made to allow the teams to explore customer needs and build minimum viable products. As the teams show success and traction, larger investments are then made. This also allows the investment board to stop failing projects early before too much money is spent. At Pearson, we implemented a budget limit of £50K for the Explore stage and £250K for the Validate stage. So the maximum loss if a project fails after validation is £300K. This allows the company to make multiple bets and test which ideas will work before taking any one idea to scale.

CS: IF I AM IN A LARGE COMPANY AND WOULD LIKE TO IMPLEMENT THE LEAN PLC, WHAT IS THE MOST CRITICAL FACTOR I SHOULD CONSIDER FOR SUCCESS?

SK: Get executive Aircover. One thing we learned early at Pearson is that doesn't matter how much the product teams love lean startup methods, if there is no executive buy-in it is hard to implement any innovation process. So try as much as possible to get executive buy-in early. And make sure its genuine buy-in and not just a lip-service commitment to transformation. Also be prepared for a multi-year journey in which you will have to transform the whole organization. At Pearson, we used our PLC approach to manage the transformation program which meant going through the early stages, using validated learnings to adapt our own approach, pivot and react to what we were learning. It is really important to make sure that you are bringing the whole organization on the journey with you. So be consistent in sharing your learnings with management and product teams.

'Everybody is a genius.
But if you judge a fish by its
ability to climb a tree,
it will live its whole life
believing that it is stupid.'

Albert Einstein

CHAPTER FIVE

Innovation Accounting

In Greek mythology, Procrustes was a blacksmith and bandit from Attica. He was notorious for owning a house by the side of the road where he offered hospitality to strangers. The strangers were offered a great meal and then invited to rest in a very special bed, whose length Procrustes claimed exactly matched whoever lay in it. What the guests did not realize was that it was not the bed that had an adjustable length. Instead, Procrustes used to force the guests to fit the length of the bed by chopping of their limbs if they were too long, or stretching them on a rack if they were too short. One can imagine the immense relief of the occasional guest that had the good fortune to fit exactly the length of the bed!

Over the years, the term *Procrustean* has been used to describe frameworks or systems that enforce conformity without taking into consideration natural variations. The way most large companies manage innovation could be regarded as Procrustean. In fact it is fair to say that every established company has its own management instincts. These have been honed by its history, traditions and culture; fanned by the flames of its previous successes. These instincts are reflected in how the company runs its business; what types of people get investment, what types of ideas get invested in, what types of success get rewarded and celebrated; and even more importantly, what employees need to do to get someone in the company to invest in their ideas.

These management instincts are the company's antibodies to ideas and practices it considers harmful. Unfortunately, these instincts also create Procrustean beds that act as antibodies to innovation. Large companies have traditionally used business plans to make investment decisions. They have then measured and tracked the success of their investments using traditional financial metrics, such as return on investment (ROI) and accounting rate of return (ARR). These practices are often uniformly applied to core products, as well as products that are adjacent and transformational innovations. This one-size-fits-all approach to management and decision making can crush innovative new ideas before they even get a chance to be tested.

At the moment, the instinct in most companies is to panic when they are asked to invest in an idea that does not have a five year business case:

Oh No! Where Is Your Business Case?!

However, there are currently very few companies that panic about the possibility of investing in a business case that is yet to be tested and validated with customers. Very few executive boards have ever said to innovators:

Oh No! Where Is Your Validated Business Model?!

But why are we being so negative about business planning? A lot of companies have been successful using this process. Despite this success, our experiences have left us with a very strong understanding that business planning does not work for innovation. At the beginning, the majority of innovative new ideas will be mostly based on assumptions. Traditional business planning takes these assumptions and pretends that they are already true. The reality is that innovation is a process that involves several false starts and failures. Such a process cannot be rigidly 'planned' in advance, and any business investment process that pretends it can, is setting the company up for failure.

In fact, once an investment decision is made, we have found that most product teams begin to act as if their untested business models are canonical truths. Tendayi was once in a meeting where he was trying to convince a team to test their business model. In response to this suggestion they kept saying they did not need to do that because their business plan was valid. After they had repeated this several times, Tendayi asked them to explain what they meant when they said that their 'business plan was valid'. They responded that their business plan was valid because it had been approved for investment by the board. He had to remind them that business models are only valid if they have been tested with real customers in the market place. An investment decision is not a blessing from the pope!

Most corporate investment boards will make their decisions based on financial numbers. These long-term projections are meant to show management that they are going to make a lot of money on their investments (a.k.a. ROI). However, if we look at the formula for calculating ROI, we can clearly see the problem with this approach for new ideas. To calculate ROI, you need data on the total revenue the product will make and total costs of creating the product. For new product ideas, the honest answer to these questions is usually "we don't know". But if a company requires these numbers in order to make a decision, then innovators are going to make them up. The ritual board meetings that follow, serve to further institutionalize these falsehoods by having executives evaluate the numbers as if they are real!

Innovation can struggle because projects with the highest levels of ROI are often the ones that leverage a company's existing assets. This is because the marginal costs of creating more outputs using the same assets, tends to go down over time (i.e. marginal cost theory).[102] In contrast, transformational innovation may require the creation of new assets and capabilities. As such, in any competition for resources based on ROI, projects that leverage current assets will often look better. This problem is further exacerbated if the company is listed on the stock market. Financial market valuations such as return on net assets (RONA) tend to reward companies that increase net income, while reducing the number of fixed assets employed to create that income.

$$ROI = \frac{Total\ Revenue - Total\ Cost}{Total\ Cost} \times 100$$

Using financial metrics to make investment decisions in new ideas, can result in companies deciding to work on the same types of products they have always worked on. Tendayi once ran a workshop with a pet food company that had brought him in to help them develop transformational ideas. At the end of a great ideation session, it was time to decide the top three ideas we were going to work on. The two owners of the business and the CEO were going to make the decision. At the top of their list of criteria was a question of how quickly an idea could be brought to life using current assets. As expected from such criteria, the final three ideas chosen were very similar to current products. It took one brave employee to complain that they had not come to a lean innovation workshop to spend all day working on ideas that were so similar to what they do every day. It was only then that the leadership realized the flaw in their decision making process and rectified it.

Financial metrics not only ensure that companies keep investing in the same types of products they have always worked on, they can also result in companies destroying their own internal capabilities to innovate. A great example is Dell, whose pursuit of RONA led them to outsource most of their capabilities to ASUS. Christensen and colleagues refer to the Dell-ASUS story as a Greek tragedy.[103] At the beginning, Dell outsourced the manufacturing of circuits and motherboards to ASUS. Later, they started outsourcing their supply chain management and computer design work. Every time Dell outsourced its capabilities to ASUS, its RONA numbers went up. They were making more money with fewer assets, which pleased the markets. The problem then occurred when ASUS decided to launch its own computers. This move was a blow to Dell, who no longer had the capabilities to respond quickly, because they had outsourced them to a company that then decided to become a competitor.

Innovation Accounting

In order to build successful innovation ecosystems, companies should avoid relying exclusively on traditional accounting methods to manage innovation. Investment decisions on brand new ideas can be made using a combination of strategic goals, an innovation thesis and balanced portfolio goals. *Innovation accounting* can then be used to manage the development of the new products and business models. The term innovation accounting was coined by Eric Ries in the book *The Lean Startup*.[104] Our goal with this chapter is to develop the concept further and articulate how it can be applied within large companies.

At its heart, innovation accounting is about managing three key activities:

1. Making investment decisions on different products at different points in their innovation journey and ensuring that we are investing appropriate amounts.
2. Tracking and measuring the success of specific innovation projects, which informs executive decisions to keep investing in certain products versus others.
3. Assessing the impact that innovation is having on the business as whole, to see whether the company is meeting its innovation goals and portfolio targets.

This means that innovation accounting has to be done at different levels of granularity. These levels are represented in our

innovation ecosystem. Innovation accounting applies to a team measuring and tracking the success of a single experiment to test a specific hypothesis. As teams do this work via *innovation practice*, the data they are gathering informs executives and managers trying to make decisions on whether to double-down investments in particular projects. As investment decisions are made via this *innovation management* process, the data and learnings can be used to inform *innovation strategy* as the board evaluates the net-contribution of investments in innovation within the company's overall product portfolio.

Within our model, there are three types of key performance indicators (or KPIs) each company should be tracking for innovation. *Reporting KPIs* are connected to innovation practice. These focus on product teams, the ideas they are generating, the experiments they are running and the progress they are making from ideation to scale. *Governance KPIs* are connected to innovation management. The focus here is on helping the company make informed investment decisions based on evidence and innovation stage. *Global KPIs* are connected to innovation strategy. The focus here is on helping the company examine the overall performance of their investments in innovation in the context of the larger business.

Within each of these KPIs we can also make a distinction between *activity metrics* and *impact metrics*.[105] *Activity metrics* focus on how busy the company has been with innovation. They measure the level of innovation activity going on (e.g. number of new products launched, number of experiments run, ideas prototyped). In contrast, *impact metrics* measure the tangible results that are emerging from this innovation activity. Revenue and profits are the ultimate measure of impact. The distinction between activity and impact is similar to Eric Ries' distinction between *vanity metrics* and *actionable metrics*. In our experience, innovation labs have had a tendency to track activity metrics. This might be fine during the early days of innovation investments, but over time all innovation projects must demonstrate impact.

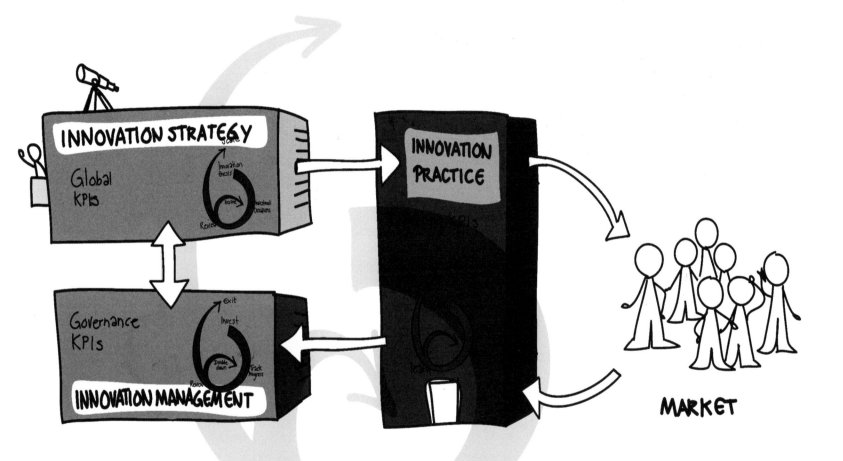

Incremental Investing

Innovation accounting is also fundamentally connected to the innovation framework we presented in Chapter 4. This is because our innovation framework tells us where a product is on its innovation journey. Knowing a product's innovation stage informs how we should be investing in it and what metrics to use to track its progress. For example, if a product is still in the problem exploration or solution validation stages, then we should not be using revenues or profits as measures of progress. Instead, the focus should be on whether the team has gathered sufficient evidence that customers have a real need that they will pay to be solved.

An innovation framework also informs how we make investment decisions. Most business plans with three to five year projections often result in large investments being made upfront in untested ideas. We have met teams who were three years into a project, had spent millions building their product, but still had no market traction and no idea what customer needs their product was actually serving. With an innovation framework, we can use innovation accounting to measure progress and make *incremental investments*.

In 2010, Dave McClure published a post in which he described the investment method he uses at the startup accelerator he co-founded, *500 Startups*. He called the process *Moneyball for Startups*.[106] The basic investment principles he outlined in the article involve making small investments before product-market fit and then doubling-down after. According to McClure, this process is analogous to card reading at a blackjack table. The small initial investments allow an investor to learn if the product idea has potential before they make further investments. This is quite different from making one large investment based on a business plan.

Within corporate environments, our innovation framework provides guidelines and benchmarks that can be used to invest and measure success. Since the early stages of an innovation journey are mostly about testing the market and potential solutions, small amounts of money can be invested. As ideas start to show traction, companies can then make larger investments to get to product-market fit and then take the product to scale. Within our model, we recommend spending between $5k-$25K on generating, selecting and reviewing ideas. To test ideas, we recommend spending less than $150K on problem exploration and solution validation to get to problem-solution fit. After that, we recommend spending between $150k-$500K building the product, testing marketing channels, costs, revenue models and distribution channels to get to product-market fit.

After achieving product-market fit, the company can then decide the amount of investment needed to take the product to scale (e.g. $500K-$2M). Other decisions can also be made at this point; such as selling the business unit making the product or spinning it out as an independent entity. It is important to note that our recommended investment amounts are not fixed in stone. Specific amounts for each innovation stage can be different depending on the company and industry. For example, manufacturing companies may need to spend more on R&D, whereas software companies may only need to spend a

few thousand dollars getting out of the building and talking to customers. In any case, incremental investing provides companies with a chance to invest in testing product ideas before they are taken to scale. This is powerful because it provides companies with a method to track progress and stop investments in failing projects before too much money is spent.

We will now turn our attention to outlining the key metrics and KPIs that can be used to track progress, make investment decisions and manage an innovation portfolio. We will make the distinction between *reporting KPIs*, *governance KPIs* and *global KPIs*. We will also make the distinction between activity and impact metrics. Although we are going to propose specific metrics for each type of innovation accounting, it is also important to note that some metrics may be used for more than one type of accounting. As such, there may be some overlap and repetition. Furthermore, our list of metrics is not exhaustive; what we describe is for illustrative purposes only. Companies can come up with different metrics that better suit their context.

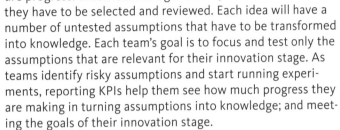

REPORTING KPIs

As product teams are doing their work, reporting KPIs help them track and measure progress. When ideas are generated, they have to be selected and reviewed. Each idea will have a number of untested assumptions that have to be transformed into knowledge. Each team's goal is to focus and test only the assumptions that are relevant for their innovation stage. As teams identify risky assumptions and start running experiments, reporting KPIs help them see how much progress they are making in turning assumptions into knowledge; and meeting the goals of their innovation stage.

Activity metrics for teams can include the number of ideas generated, the number of ideas selected, the number of ideas reviewed and the number of assumptions identified for testing. Once the teams start running experiments they can track the number of experiments being run, the number of customer conversations taking place, the number of customer observations and the number of usability tests. When the team begins testing solution ideas, they can track the number of prototypes or minimum viable products (MVP) built and the number of customers exposed to each prototype or MVP. If the team is using design sprints and hackathons, they can also track the number of these events they have run, the number of people who participated and the number of prototypes/MVPs that were created during each design sprint.

These activity metrics are great for tracking the level of activity that teams are having. However, they do not tell us how much progress the teams are actually making. For that we need impact metrics such as the number of assumptions validated. Indeed, for each team, before beginning any experiment they should set minimum success or fail criteria. These criteria set the benchmark for how the team will know whether their assumptions are supported by the evidence. At the end of each experiment, the team should analyze the lessons learned and

make decisions about what to do next. This process of analyzing experimental evidence and decision making, is innovation accounting at its most granular level. It is based on the *create-test-learn* loop shown below.[107] The combined outcomes from each experiment inform the team how well they are doing in terms of validating the assumptions they had before they began testing their idea.

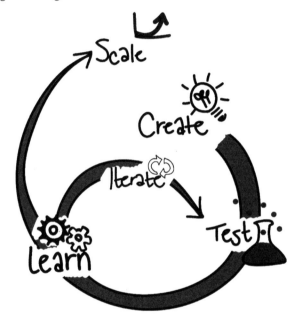

In addition to the outcomes of a single experiment, product teams can also track success using metrics that are connected to the potential success of their product in the market. Are we acquiring new customers at a high enough rate? Are our customer having a great experience with our product? Is our product meeting their needs? Are we retaining customers or getting repeat business from them? Are customers willing to pay for our product? Is what they are paying enough for us to cover our costs and make a profit? Are customers happy to refer us to other people? These business metrics refer to key steps in a customer's journey through acquisition, activation, retention, revenue and referral. Dave McClure calls these *Pirate Metrics*,[108] because if you put together the first letter of each step it spells AARRR... me hearties!

All impact metrics are not equally important at every innovation stage. Depending on the business model, innovators must focus on the metrics that matter for their innovation stage. During the early stages, confirming customer needs and validating the solution are key impact metrics. To carry on working on the product, our data needs to tell us that we are on the right track here. In later stages, showing traction, revenues and profits is key. This is where metrics such as customer churn rates, cost of customer acquisition and customer lifetime value are important.

Other key impact metrics include *cost-per-learning*, which measures the average cost of testing each assumption and gaining insights or knowledge. The *cost-per-learning* metric can also be measured in terms of time, such that teams are tracking the average *time-cost-per-learning*. The aim is to reduce the time and costs of going through a single *create-test-learn* loop. Teams that can move fast often run more experiments within the limited time and investment dollars they have. This can also be referred to as *learning velocity* (i.e. the number of assumptions teams can test over a given time).

In the end, the ultimate goal for any product team is to move between innovation stages. We want to achieve problem-solution fit and product-market fit quickly, so we can move to scaling our idea. As such, beyond measuring how quickly teams are completing single experiments or testing specific assumptions, we are also interested in their *validation velocity*. This measures how quickly and at what cost teams are moving from one innovation stage to another. Movement between innovation stages is the ultimate measure of progress for any innovation team.

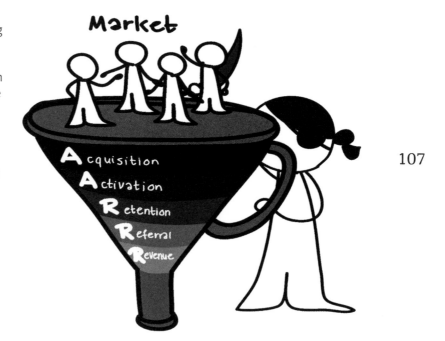

107

ACTIVITY METRICS	IMPACT METRICS
number of ideas generated	risky assumptions identified
number of ideas chosen	hypotheses developed
number of assumptions	minimum fail criteria set
number of experiments	experiment results
number of customer conversations	cohort analysis
number of customer interviews	decisions made (pivot, persevere, retest)
number of customer observations	pirate metrics *(acquisition, activation, retention, revenue, referral)*
number of prototypes developed	customer lifetime value
number of MVPs built	cost-per-learning
number of hackathons held	time-cost-per-learning
umber of design sprints	learning velocity
	validation velocity

GOVERNANCE KPIs

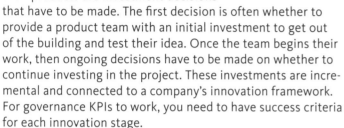

Connected to the product team's day to day work of testing their ideas and building their products are investment decisions that have to be made. The first decision is often whether to provide a product team with an initial investment to get out of the building and test their idea. Once the team begins their work, then ongoing decisions have to be made on whether to continue investing in the project. These investments are incremental and connected to a company's innovation framework. For governance KPIs to work, you need to have success criteria for each innovation stage.

As teams navigate the innovation stages, there is a version of the *create-test-learn* loop that is connected to investment decision making. This involves investing the appropriate amount of money for the innovation stage, tracking progress via the team's reporting KPIs, and reviewing the team's progress at a decision making investment board. At that point it also involves making the decision to double-down investment, move the team to the next innovation stage or stop the project entirely. This is innovation accounting at the innovation management layer of an ecosystem.

Companies have the choice to place their decision gates at the end of main stages within our framework (i.e. *create ideas, test ideas, scale ideas, renew ideas*). They can also choose to place the decision gates at the end of each sub-stage (e.g. *test ideas: problem exploration, solution validation, business model*). This how the Lean Product Lifecycle at Pearson works. A combination of both approaches can also be adopted, with teams getting their total investment runway at the main stage gates (e.g. *test ideas*), but having an on-going progress review that is connected to the sub-stages. The choice of how to govern and where to place the decision gates will be informed by the number of decisions that have to be made and also how often decision makers can feasibly meet.

The first types of activity metrics we can track for governance KPIs, are simply the number of products we have in our innovation pipeline and the number of products at each innovation stage. We can also track metrics connected to decision making, such as the number of ideas submitted for investment decisions, the number of decisions we have made, the number of products moving between each innovation stage every quarter or year and the average amount of money being invested in products at each innovation stage. These metrics provide some visibility of the investment decisions we are making as a company.

However, the main work of innovation management is ensuring that investments are being made in products that are aligned with our strategic goals, and have the greatest chance of success. Governance KPIs allow us to assess both strategic alignment and progress toward success as we make each decision. Innovations succeed when teams find a sustainable business model by reducing their assumptions compared to knowledge. In the early stages of innovation, teams will have more assumptions than knowledge. As they navigate the innovation stages, the closer this *assumption-to-knowledge*[109]ratio gets to 1, the more confident we can be of success.

A company's innovation stage-gate criteria should assess how well teams are testing their assumptions and reducing their assumption-to-knowledge ratio. The teams should also be testing the right assumptions for their innovation lifecycle stage. The table below shows the basic minimum success criteria that an investment board can use when making decisions about a team moving between innovation stages. Each criterion listed in that table is an exit criterion to move to the next stage. More detailed and refined questions can be developed depending on the company's context, but these represent the main criteria for investment decision making.

Innovation Stage Success Criteria

CREATE IDEAS	GENERATE	Are our ideas aligned to our company's strategic goals and innovation thesis?
	SELECT	Does this idea help us meet our goals for achieving a balanced portfolio?
	REVIEW	Has the team identified their risky assumptions and made clear plans to test them?
TEST IDEAS	PROBLEM	Has the team validated customer needs and identified the customer job to be done?
	SOLUTION	Has the team tested their solution with customers, and found that the solution meets their needs and they are willing to pay for it?
	BUSINESS	Has the team found a sustainable way to create their product, the right channel to deliver it to customers and the right price point for profitability?
SCALING IDEAS	TUNE	Has the team identified and optimized their engine to grow customer numbers, revenues and profits?
	ACCELERATE	How fast is the team growing customer numbers, revenues and profits and is the growth rate improving?
	EXPLOIT	As growth rates have slowed down, how well is the team optimizing costs and operational efficiencies?
RENEW IDEAS	ANALYZE	Has the team successfully analyzed their business environment for key trends and threats relevant to their business model?
	REDESIGN	Has the team redesigned their business model in a manner that makes it adaptive to the changes in the business environment?
	REVIEW	Has the team identified the risky assumptions in their revised model and made clear plans to test them?

Beyond investment decision making, other impact metrics include a measure of the proportion of our product ideas that achieve problem-solution fit and product-market fit. *Validation velocity* is also a key impact metric for governance KPIs (i.e. how quickly and at what cost teams are moving from one innovation stage to another). Other impact metrics include the number of validated business models at the end of each quarter or year, the returns on product development expense and any process improvements that happened when innovation projects were launched successfully.

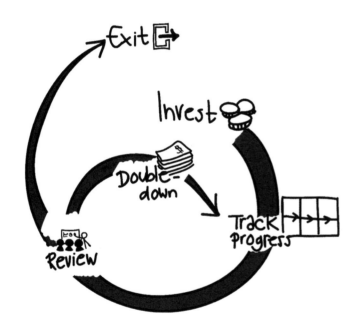

ACTIVITY METRICS	IMPACT METRICS
number of products in pipeline	assumption-to-knowledge ratio
number of products per innovation stage	stage-gate criteria
number of ideas submitted	% of products at problem-solution fit
number of decisions made	% of products at product-market fit
number of products moving stages	% of products at scale
average amount spent per stage	number of validated business models
	validation velocity
	returns on product dev. expense
	process improvement metrics

GLOBAL KPIs

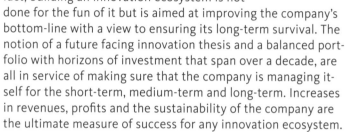

We have presented several cases throughout this book about corporations that failed to innovate and then struggled to survive. In fact, building an innovation ecosystem is not done for the fun of it but is aimed at improving the company's bottom-line with a view to ensuring its long-term survival. The notion of a future facing innovation thesis and a balanced portfolio with horizons of investment that span over a decade, are all in service of making sure that the company is managing itself for the short-term, medium-term and long-term. Increases in revenues, profits and the sustainability of the company are the ultimate measure of success for any innovation ecosystem.

Global KPIs measure how well our investments in innovation are contributing to the overall health of the company. Underlying our innovation strategy is a *create-test-learn* loop that begins with our innovation thesis. Our thesis is effectively a series of strategic hypotheses about the future and how our company can succeed in it. The strategic hypotheses are tested by the investments we make in our innovation portfolio. The success or failure of these investments informs us of how good our innovation thesis is. A review of these lessons learned informs how we iterate and improve our thesis. This is innovation accounting at the strategic level.

The activity metrics for global KPIs mostly focus on the product portfolio and the types of products in it. In this regard, a company can track metrics such as the number of products by type of innovation (i.e. core, adjacent and transformational) and number of products at each innovation stage. We can also measure and track the percentage of products that are aligned with our innovation thesis versus those that are not. Other global innovation activity that can be tracked includes the number of patent filings, startups partnerships, academic collaborations and the proportion of products built using lean methods.

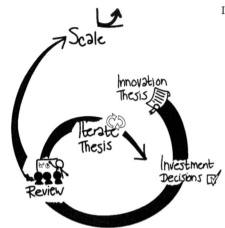

In Part II of this book, we will examine how a company can leverage the innovation ecosystem to change its innovation culture. At this point, it is suffice to say that we can measure the overall cultural impact of our innovation activity in the company by tracking the number of employees that have received innovation training (e.g. lean startup or business model design), the number of investment boards that have been set up and are making decisions, the number of innovation coaches trained, the number of innovation events held (e.g. meetups and hackathons), the number of external speakers invited and the number of external events that have been hosted, spoken or attended.

In terms of impact metrics, the ultimate measure of our ecosystem is *innovation contribution*. This is the percentage of revenue coming from products launched within a certain period (e.g. three to five years). For many years, 3M has managed its innovation process by setting 'stretch goals' for its management teams. In 1977, this stretch goal was 25% and was raised to 30% in the 1990s.[110] In a similar way, other companies can set stretch goals and then track them via measuring innovation contribution. The great thing about stretch goals is that they also have the capability to change management culture, especially when they are tied to incentives and rewards.

113

Connected to revenue are *cost savings*. Some innovation projects can result in process improvements whose impact can be measured via total cost savings or reductions. This is an important KPI that is connected to measurable improvements in profits. Other global KPIs include *innovation conversion*, which is a measure of the percentage of our old customers that are switching to our new products. We can also measure how well our new products are doing at *gaining market share* in areas we view as strategically important for our business (e.g. number of new customer segments entered and growth rates within those segments, increased shelf space, increased share of wallet or an increased distribution footprint). We can also measure the number of patents successfully granted and the number of new business models successfully launched. Another great measure of innovation success is overall improvements in *customer satisfaction* (e.g. measured by net promoter score or usability testing).

114

ACTIVITY METRICS	IMPACT METRICS
number of products by type of innovation *(core, adjacent, transformational)*	innovation contribution
number of products per innovation stage	cost savings
% of products aligned to innovation thesis	innovation conversion
number of patent filings	new product market share
startup partnerships	new segment market share
academic collaborations	increased shelf space
number of products built using lean	increased share of wallet
number of employees trained	increased distribution footprint
number of investment boards	number of patents granted
number of innovation coaches	new business models taken to scale
number of innovation events	customer satisfaction *(net promoter score, usability testing)*

Conclusion

Global, governance and reporting KPIs combine to provide a robust toolbox for innovation accounting. Those who have wondered what they would ever do without business plans and how they could ever measure progress for innovation, may now feel overwhelmed by their options. Although we have presented a number of metrics here, it is important to note that companies do not have to measure them all. They must select a few key metrics that are connected to their strategic goals, business models and product types. What's more important is to use the metrics not only to measure progress but to make decisions. If product teams or executives cannot make decisions based on a metric then it is probably a vanity metric. Product teams should be making decisions about what to do next after each experiment. Investment boards should use evidence to make decisions on whether to increase investment, move a product from one innovation stage to another or stop the project entirely. Finally, corporate leaders should review the overall impact of their investments in innovation on the company as a whole, to make decisions on whether their innovation strategy is working.

Craig Wirkus & Harvey Wade

INNOVATION PROGRAM MANAGERS AT CISCO

Cisco Systems is a multinational American technology conglomerate with over 70 000 employees. Headquartered in San Jose, California, Cisco had over 49 billion dollars in revenue in 2016. Even as a large successful company, Cisco understands that the only way to remain relevant is to continually innovate. So the company has been empowering its employees to continuously push the innovation envelope. This has resulted in the creation of a really interesting ecosystem, with investment boards that manage investments in new ideas.

CS: IS EVERYONE ALLOWED TO GENERATE IDEAS?
CW & HW: Pretty much so but with a twist - they need to validate their own ideas before they will get funding to scale.

CS: DO THE PEOPLE THAT GENERATED THE IDEA GO THROUGH A VALIDATION-DISCOVERY DRIVEN PROCESS BEFORE THEY ACTUALLY ASK FOR FUNDING?
CW & HW: Yes. The idea is to have them list out the problem they are trying to solve, the customers they are solving it for and the rank sorted assumptions that need to be true in order for the solution to be viable - before they actually apply for funding. There is no emphasis on the solution at this stage since the teams are going to pivot away from the initial idea anyway. We use an Implementation Readiness Level (similar to Steve Blank's Investment Readiness Level) and ensure that the idea is congruent with strategy.

CS: AFTER THEY'VE DONE THE INITIAL VALIDATION THEY WILL GO LOOK FOR BUDGET. WHERE DO THEY GO TO GET INVESTMENT?

CW & HW: They go to either the business line lead or an innovation funding board if appropriate. One of the things we are now trying to institutionalize when funding an idea for incubation is to, through a funding board, include enough funding to backfill that position while that person is incubating the H2 or H3 idea. By supporting the manager of the employee incubating the new venture we can help ensure that the RTB isn't impacted by the innovation work. It increases the odds of the new venture being successful as well by allowing the intrapreneur to dedicate more time to the incubation project.

CS: WHAT IS AN INNOVATION FUNDING BOARD?

CW & HW: The innovation funding boards are designed to handle H2 and H3 innovations (reference to the Three Horizons model). What they have innovation teams do first and foremost is try to 'kill' their own ideas before they even enter the funding round. And after they are ready to enter the funding round, they have to complete some due diligence using methodologies like Discovery Driven Planning and Lean Startup. The goal is to only let the great ideas through. And this can only happen if the teams quickly identify the critical assumptions quickly do customer validation and ultimately find product/market fit.

CS: HOW MANY FUNDING BOARDS ARE THERE IN THE COMPANY?

CW & HW: Being a global company we have quite a few. Each funding board is responsible for a business domain; take for example Internet of Things, Security or Cloud.

CS: HOW DO THESE FUNDING BOARDS TAKE DECISIONS?

CW & HW: They look for validated progress over 'PowerPoint wizardry', they are looking to see if the teams that applied are developing their idea through validated customer learning, iterating on prototypes etc. The innovation funding boards are there to make sure that the ideas that go through are congruent with their strategy and fit in their portfolios.

CS: IS THERE A PARTICULAR MANDATE THESE FUNDING BOARDS HAVE?

CW & HW: Each board has their own objectives and scope of control but our goal is to normalize the vernacular and distribute best practices across the organization. Ideally they are de-risking the new ventures by using small tranches of funding and using Lean Startup to ensure that the built ventures are successful in the market place. By culling the ones that aren't early stage funds can be redirected to more fruitful endeavors.

CS: WHAT HAPPENS IF AN IDEA SCALES?

CW & HW: There is no one-size-fits-all, it really depends on the nature of the idea, the importance of the founder and what's already in the portfolio. The goal though is to maximize the impact of an implemented idea by ensuring it gets deployed fully or even replicated to other business areas or customers.

CS: IT'S CLEAR THAT YOU HAVE MULTIPLE INNOVATIVE PROJECTS RUNNING AT THE SAME TIME. HOW DO YOU MAKE SURE CROSS-POLLINATION HAPPENS AND HOW DO YOU ENSURE THAT KNOWLEDGE AND LEARNING TRAVEL HORIZONTALLY WITHIN THE ORGANIZATION?

CW & HW: The company is interconnected on different levels such as: roles, levels, geographies – we aim for transparency and as much cross-pollination as possible. Some of this is done through sharing what's in each others portfolios', networking between groups. There's also a lot of emphasis on founder teams having cross-representation across functions and business units. Leveraging the same platforms and best practices is another way we are trying to do it. What we can improve on, from what I have visibility into, will be to have a single repository with all the strategic priorities, all the portfolios of incubation projects and all of the funding boards. Basically having everything more easily discoverable.

117

Putting It All Together

An innovation ecosystem always comes full circle. We began articulating our model by describing the innovation thesis in Chapter 2. The very last sentence of Chapter 5 again makes reference to the innovation thesis in connection to innovation accounting. What this shows is the interconnected nature of the ecosystem. At its most granular level are product teams working on a small experiments to test a specific hypotheses. Whatever lessons they learn will have consequences that will impact not only the decisions they will make about the business models they are testing. Their lessons learned will also inform investment decision making by management boards, which will in turn inform the company's overall innovation strategy.

118

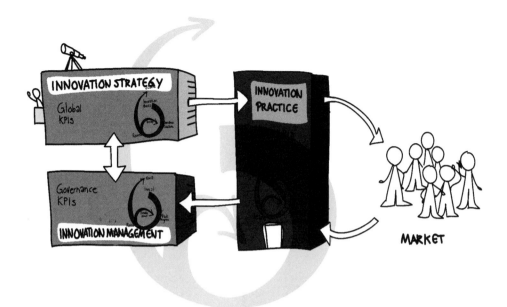

The relationship also works when it is considered in the opposite direction. Innovation strategy informs the types of products that management boards will invest in, which ultimately impacts the business models that product teams will be testing when they run their granular experiments. This cycle could be viewed as an innovation engine that is based on a simple *create-test-learn* loop. This loop is part of every cog in the engine, showing up in different forms as shown in Chapter 5. A single experiment is a *create-test-learn* loop, so is every business model iteration.

The innovation framework stages that guide product development, are a *create-test-learn* loop in which only validated business models are taken to scale. An investment decision in a specific product is a *create-test-learn* loop via which decisions to double-down investment and move a product to the next stage are based on learning. Innovation strategy is a *create-test-learn* loop via which our innovation thesis is revised on the basis of learnings from our investment decisions. In fact, the entire ecosystem is a *create-test-learn* loop in which innovation strategy is tested via innovation practice, and the lessons learned are tracked via innovation management, which in turn inform the revision of strategy. We will now move to Part II of our book, which is a deeper dive into the last part of our ecosystem: *innovation practice*.

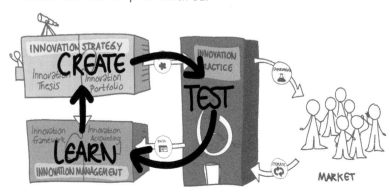

PART 2

PRAC

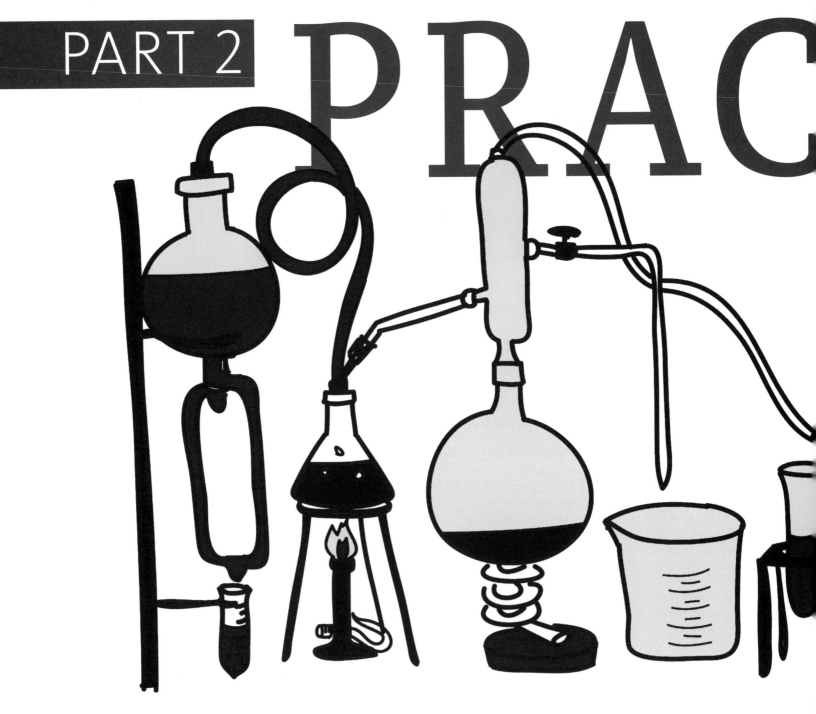

Practice
[praktIs]

The actual application or use
of an idea, belief, or method,
as opposed to theories
relating to it.
The customary, habitual,
or expected procedure or
way of doing of something.[1]

Innovation practice is the cutting-edge face of an innovation ecosystem. This is where the rubber meets the road. It is where ideas are generated, tested and taken to scale. The other elements of the ecosystem cannot thrive without a great innovation practice in place. For example, a company cannot evolve its innovation thesis or balance its port-folio, if product teams are not testing new product ideas with customers.

At the core of innovation practice is one fundamental principle: *no product idea should be launched and taken to scale before the business model has been tested and validated.* The specific practices outlined in this part of the book are in service of that one core principle. Indeed, the entire innovation ecosystem should be designed to evolve on the basis of market learnings.

Innovation practice is also firmly rooted in our innovation framework (i.e. *create ideas, test ideas, scale ideas, renew ideas*). The point of the framework is to ensure that product teams are engaged in the appropriate activities for their innovation stage. The goal is to prevent *premature scaling*. To illustrate practice, each stage in our innovation frame-work will be presented as a chapter in this second part of the book.

'Invention is, by its very nature, a disorderly process. You can't put a Six Sigma process into that area and say, "Well, I'm getting behind on invention so I'm going to schedule myself for three good ideas on Wednesday and two on Friday". That's not how creativity works.'

George Buckley, Former CEO of 3M

CHAPTER SIX

Creating Ideas

At the heart of innovation is the lightbulb moment. Creative ideas can come up in *spontaneous* eureka moments, or when teams are *deliberately* trying to solve specific problems. Sure, there is hard work and discipline involved in getting a new product successfully to market. But without that magical 'aha' moment of creativity, companies would have no new product ideas to work on. These creative 'aha' moments always seem sudden and unexpected. Ideas 'pop-up out of nowhere' without a clear logical cause. This can make creativity seem mysterious or mystical.

Despite this, researchers have been able to identify the social and psychological factors that influence creativity. These include individual factors such as *tolerance of ambiguity*, *openness to experience*, *risk-taking* and *self-confidence*.[2] One interesting finding from the research is that multicultural experiences seem to enhance creativity.[3] In fact, there are quite a few examples of creative individuals who did their best work while they were living abroad. Picasso, Händel, Hemingway and Stravinsky all created their most well-regarded work while living abroad.

William Maddux, a Professor in Organizational Behavior at IN-SEAD, has been working with colleagues to understand more about why and how living abroad enhances creativity. They have found that it is not merely travelling to foreign countries (e.g. going on holiday) that enhances creativity. Instead, creativity is enhanced when individuals spend time living abroad, learning and immersing themselves in foreign cultures.[4] More recently, Maddux and colleagues found that bicultural individuals, who were able to identify with both their home and host cultures, showed enhanced creativity.[5] What they found was that these biculturals had greater levels of *integrative complexity*, which is the ability to consider and combine multiple perspectives and points of view.

This ability to combine multiple points of view lies at the heart of creativity. 'Aha' moments arise when unique insights are combined to create something novel. What the research shows goes beyond the idea that companies should send their employees to live abroad, although this is probably a good idea. The research reveals an underlying process that results in enhanced creativity; i.e. *exposing individuals to experiences with multiple perspectives and worldviews*. It is the combination of these various perspectives in novel ways that results in new ideas.

125

Tim Berners-Lee, the inventor of the World Wide Web, was right when he described *innovation as serendipity*. Serendipity is the occurrence of events by chance in a 'happy or beneficial way'.[6] Serendipity facilitates creativity when teams make accidental but novel and useful discoveries. This can occur while innovators are looking for something different to what they end up discovering, or when they find what they are looking for but do it in a totally unexpected way. A lot of great products, such as the Post-It Note, were discovered while the inventors were working on something else.[7]

The idea that innovation is serendipity does not mean that the most innovative companies are just lucky. It is possible to create our own luck.[8] For starters, every employee in our company must be able to articulate our innovation thesis. Once this is well understood, the company is ready to unleash its people's creative genius. To encourage creativity, companies should create environments that are rich with multiple experiences, insights and perspectives; they should provide the tools and context for employees to use those insights for creative ideation. The practices we outline below can help a company design its ecosystem to create and benefit from serendipity.

Innovation Is A Team Sport

Creativity is a characteristic that is often used to describe individuals. But the idea of the lone genius is a myth. Even famous inventors such as Thomas Edison where in reality representing the 'work of many men'.[9] We have defined innovation as the combination of great new ideas and sustainably profitable business models. Our innovation framework involves multiple steps from idea generation, testing business models and scaling growth. In taking products from idea to scale, innovation will inevitably involve interactions among people with different expertise from multiple departments within the organization. In writing about innovation at Bell Labs, James Gertner notes that:

"Almost by definition, a single person, or even a single group, could not alone create an innovation. The task [is] too variegated and involved." [10]

Bell Labs was created on Jan. 1st, 1925, by the consolidation of Western Electric's Research Laboratory. The lab was co-owned by Western Electric and AT&T. Over the years, the lab has had several owners; but it is now owned by Nokia. Bell Labs is one of the most productive R&D labs in history; inventing a large number of the technologies we use today. Bell Labs scientists invented the facsimile machine, the first long-distance television transmission, the first binary digital computer, the transistor, the laser, cellular technology, the UNIX operating system and the first fiber-optic technologies.[11] Fourteen scientists from Bell Labs have won Nobel Prizes, and the lab has even won Grammy and Emmy Awards.

The most famous scientist to emerge from Bell Labs was probably Bill Shockley, who won a Nobel Prize for his work on the transistor. Shockley later moved to California and his attempts to commercialize a new transistor design based on silicon, are considered to be responsible for the creation of California's Silicon Valley. Indeed, the famous 'Traitorous Eight' scientists and engineers who left Shockley's Semiconductor Labs are responsible for dozens of historically important Silicon Valley corporations including AMD and Intel.[12] Such is the historical impact of the work that began at Bell Labs those many years ago.

But how did Bell Labs manage such feats of innovation? The answer lies in how the lab organized work among its scientists and inventors. The lab was designed to ensure that people of diverse knowledge and expertise worked together in close proximity, where they could have plenty of meetings and serendipitous connections.[13] After World War II, Bell Labs moved into a new campus in Murray Hill, New Jersey. At this new campus, interdisciplinary teams were created that combined theorists and engineers. According to Jon Gertner, the Murray Hill campus was deliberately designed so that "...everyone would be in one another's way".[14] At Bell Labs, theoretical science was combined with applied engineering to produce wonderful inventions such as the first communications satellite (i.e. Telstar 1).[15]

Interdisciplinary collaboration creates insights by exposing people to ideas from other disciplines besides their own area of specialization. This in turn creates tremendous opportunities for serendipity. The challenge in most companies is that people are organized into specialist departments such as marketing, sales, finance, technology and HR. This means that people spend most of their time interacting with people who share their expertise and worldview. In order to encourage creativity, companies have to break down these silos and there are several ways to do so.

Breaking Down Silos

At the most basic level, companies should create multidisciplinary teams in which colleagues from different departments work together. These teams should be focused on solving specific problems, working on specific products or delivering specific aspects of a product. When innovation projects are commissioned, or work is being done within innovation labs, multi-disciplinary teams *must* be used. This should not be viewed as an optional choice. Where possible, these teams should sit together so as to minimize gated handoffs and increase real-time collaboration.

127

To be effective, the teams must be small and relatively independent. It is recommended best practice to have small teams with not more than eight to ten people in them. At IDEO, they pioneered 'hot teams', which are small multi-disciplinary teams that are empowered to take specific innovation projects to completion.[16] Amazon's Jeff Bezos has a rule that innovation teams should be small enough to be well fed by two pizzas.[17] The reason for having small teams is that the more people you have in a team, the more lines of communication you have to keep open. This increased complexity can make effective collaboration difficult. Innovation requires teams that can quickly go through the *create-test-learn* loop and make decisions.

At Spotify they have developed an engineering ecosystem that is based on multi-disciplinary *squads* that are responsible end-to-end for the stuff they build. Each squad sits together, will have long-term goals and may use agile practices to achieve these goals. The squads are autonomous but they work within the boundaries of company strategy. Also within the ecosystem are *chapters*, which are competency based teams such as quality assurance, user experience or engineering; and *guilds* which are broader communities of shared interests, where people gather to share ideas on specific topics such as leadership, design thinking or web development.[18]

128

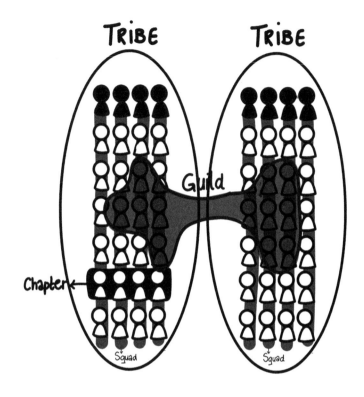

Source: Kniberg, K. & Ivarsson, A. (2012). *Scaling Agile @ Spotify with Tribes, Squads, Chapters & Guilds.*

Beyond interdisciplinary representation, it is also important to ensure that the teams are cross-functional in terms of personalities. Tom Kelley describes some characters for hot teams at IDEO that include the visionary, the troubleshooter, the craftsman, the entrepreneur and the technologist. A cross-functional team must have introverts and extraverts, analytical thinkers and creatives, serious intellectuals and fun-loving disruptors. These individuals, working together with mutual respect, will be more creative than a group of individuals who are highly similar and cohesive. Below is our list of eight personality types that innovation teams should have:

- *Miss Happy-Go-Lucky*: This is the life the party. This person makes sure the team is having fun while they work. Innovation requires elements of playfulness, especially during ideation. Miss Happy-Go-Lucky serves the role of resident fire-starter and mess-maker.
- *Mr Visionary Creative*: Great ideas are also driven by creative vision. These are people who can see the world, not as it is, but as they would want it to be. Every team needs its dreamers and visionaries to fight for the creative ideals that underpin a product idea.
- *Miss Pragmatic*: But all dreams have to be checked against reality. The pragmatist makes sure we review our product ideas and identify any risky assumptions. They also make sure we test these assumptions before we take our product to market.
- *Mr Analytical*: Innovation is also about figuring out a sustainably profitable business model. Both in financial and operational terms, innovation teams need someone with an analytical mind. We are not only creating cool new things, we are building a business.
- *Miss Get Stuff Done*: This is the action person. No analysis paralysis and endless experiments. Innovation is also about getting stuff done. A hard-driving team member pushes us to complete a minimum viable version of the product and ship

it to the market early. We can figure out the rest as we go!

- *Mr Perfectionist*: But let's not be too hasty. Good quality products also ensure that we deliver value to customers in a manner that sustains their loyalty to our brand. This is particularly important for established companies. As learnings from the market inform our iterations, Mr Perfectionist serves as the quality assurance check for our product.
- *Miss Consensus*: With this cast of characters working together, team meetings can often become contentious. A team member that helps the team collaborate well is highly useful. As much as we want diverse opinions at the table, in the end we need to make decisions and move forward positively as a team.
- *Mr Supportive*: Finally, teams consist of people with different needs. There is an element of innovation teamwork that is about supporting and encouraging each other. Failing fast can only work in teams where individuals feel safe to make mistakes. As such, supportive colleagues are a key element of the team.

129

These are the various personalities that are important to have in innovation teams. These roles are not gendered and each can be done by any person, male or female. We also don't mean to imply that every team should have exactly eight people in it. It is possible for people to have strengths in more than one of these areas. The point is to make sure we go beyond creating teams based on professional discipline alone and also consider the mix of personalities among the team members.

But it is also not enough to just have the right mix of people in a team. How the people work, collaborate and interact with each other will determine their creative success. In an interesting research project on how 'a collection of creatives can become a creative collective',[19] Andrew Hargadon and Beth Bechky found that it all starts with *help seeking*. Individuals working on innovation challenges have to be willing to seek help from their colleagues. However, this help seeking behavior only facilitates innovation if it is met with reciprocal *help giving* from those colleagues who are receiving requests. An authentic and engaged interest in helping others is important. Working collaboratively also requires individuals that can absorb and use feedback. *Reflective reframing* happens when

people take a fresh look at what they know, using the perspectives they are getting as feedback from colleagues. There is no point in seeking help if you do not use what you are learning to rethink your original ideas. If help seeking and help giving are the two sides of the innovation coin, then reflective reframing is the process via which these two sides combine to create value.

The role for leadership within the company is to *reinforce* the shared values and beliefs that reward and promote collaborative problem solving. For example, *help seeking* needs an environment in which it is not viewed as weakness or incompetence. *Help giving* must also be recognized and celebrated. Teams must be given the time and space for collaborative engagement. Heroically trying to solve problems as an individual must not be rewarded. Our goal is to create an environment in which a collection of different types of people work together to become a creative force.

Communities of Practice

The Spotify model we described earlier is great because it is not only designed to create cross-functional teams, it is also deliberately designed and managed for interaction, sharing and collaboration. The chapters and guilds within Spotify allow individuals who may not be part of the same squad to meet and learn from each other regularly. Such networking among people who share interests is a great way to encourage the interactions that may result in serendipity.

Communities of practice are a key element of any innovation ecosystem. In Silicon Valley, it is not just the density of startups and entrepreneurs that creates serendipity; it is also the community and the levels of interaction among people working at different startups. The Homebrew Computer Club was a community of computer enthusiasts that met regularly between 1975 and 1986. It was within those interactions that Steve Wozniak and Steve Jobs were able to create the first Apple computer.

reflective framing

help giving

help seeking

addition to this, companies can also host regular events for face-to-face interaction. At these events employees can demo and share their work, have conversations about the challenges they are facing and share best practice. Such regular events put into practice the ideas of help seeking, help giving and reflective reframing. Companies can also create open communities that include external speakers such as startup founders, scientists, policy makers and academics. A regular unconference, such as a Leancamp, can be organized with attendees choosing their own topics for discussion on the day.[20]

The community and networking events should be promoted as opportunities for interaction and sharing. There should be no pressure on employees to come up with creative new products at an unconference. With the right tools and practices in place creative ideation will happen naturally. Communities of practice also need to have consistent investment and active management. They should not be viewed as an unnecessary expenditure or a nice-to-have. They should be seen as critical to the company's ongoing success. Peer-to-peer collaboration ensures that innovation best practices are more widely adopted and used within the company.

131

The lesson to learn here is that companies should not only create cross-functional teams; collaboration can also be encouraged by creating communities in which colleagues regularly interact with each other. These communities can be created using both virtual and physical tools. Companies can create virtual platforms via which people write articles, host webinars, share knowledge, best practice and innovation tools. Such interactions are especially helpful for those companies that find it difficult to have their cross-functional teams co-located.

In

Go And See

In addition to internal cross-functional collaboration with colleagues, customers can also be a rich source of insights. Since innovation is ultimately about delivering customer value, a company must stay connected to its customers in order to develop a deep empathy and understanding of their needs. This means that employees have to be allowed to regularly get out of the office and go see how customers live their lives. *Getting out of the building* has become a mantra for entrepreneurs to test their product ideas with customers before they start building. However, getting out of the building can also be a great source of inspiration for coming up with new ideas.

Design thinking encourages innovators to spend time developing empathy for customers, before coming up with ideas. Such empathy can *not* be found by running focus groups or handing out surveys and questionnaires. It is important to go out into the world and see people living their lives. This *customer safari* allows you to see what people do, what comes naturally to them and what they find challenging. By speaking to customers in their context, you can also learn what they are trying to accomplish in their lives when they do certain things or choose particular products.

132

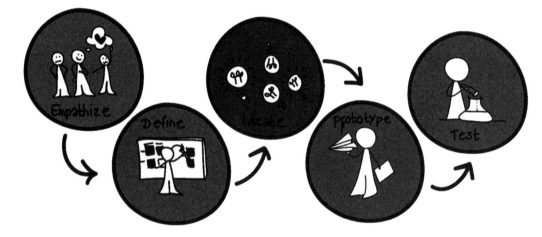

Adapted from Brown, T. (2009). *Change by Design.* New York City: Harper Collins.

Observing customers can help teams identify potential early adopters. These are the individuals who are so desperate for a solution that they would be willing pay for a minimum viable version. Extreme users and edge cases can also be 'found in the wild'. These people can help you define the boundaries of how far you may have to go to make your product useful. There will also be customers who have come up with clever hacks to solve their problems or are using your products in a unique way. All these insights will help you develop empathy for customers before beginning ideation.

What is important when making observations is to keep an open mind. If we bias our observations with ready-made solutions, then we may fail to see better options that are available to us. An enquiring mind that is curious about people's lives is an absolute necessity. Not only should you observe from a distance, you can also participate in tasks that help customers accomplish their goals. This will give you an authentic feel for what your customers go through day-to-day. Remember, our goal is to get as many unique perspectives on the problem space as we can.

1

OBSERVE

2

OBSERVE & TALK

3

OBSERVE, TALK & PARTICIPATE

The World Keeps Turning

Analyzing trends and changes in our business environment is another great source of product ideas. With the world changing at such a fast pace, companies cannot afford to keep their heads in the ground. They must pay attention to changes in their business environment. Several companies have specialist market research departments that study the competition and important business trends. PESTLE analysis is often their main tool of choice. We have also been part of organizations that have teams focused on researching future technologies and how they may impact the business.

But paying attention to the world should not be viewed as the work of specialist researchers only. Companies must encourage employees to take note of trends and changes in the world. What is more important is that these insights are shared widely within the business. Companies should not allow research on trends to stay hidden in the files and desk drawers of the market research department. This is where communities of practices, networking events and platforms for sharing become really useful. Sharing business environment learnings is a great way to keep innovation teams abreast with what is going on around them.

133

Beyond researching future trends, companies can also invent the future via investments in R&D. For some companies, such as pharmaceuticals, R&D is not optional; it is the only way to do business. It is beyond the scope of this book to delve into how companies can create a great R&D strategy.[21] From our perspective, R&D labs should not function as silos. To be part of a company's creative culture, people working in R&D labs should share their projects and progress with colleagues on an ongoing basis. This helps inform colleagues about technologies that may be available; which helps to inform new product ideas. In return, the feedback the scientists receive from colleagues can also inform the R&D process.

Idea Generation

With all this interaction and interdisciplinary collaboration going on, your company will be buzzing with activity. There is a method to all the madness. We are trying to create an environment that is filled with opportunities for serendipity and creative insights. We are looking for people to be exposed to multiple perspectives because we know this is how creative 'aha' moments happen. If we succeed, ideas will start to come from everywhere. We want to take advantage of this energy by creating tools and activities that encourage people to generate lots of ideas.

"The best way to have a good idea is to have a lot of ideas."

Linus Pauling

In his book *Originals*,[22] Adam Grant illustrates that the best way for people to come up with great ideas is to have them generate a lot of ideas. As the number of ideas people generate increases, there is a greater chance of something really groundbreaking coming through. This was the case for Shakespeare, who in his lifetime wrote 37 plays and 154 sonnets. Some of these were not very good (e.g. *Timon of Athens*), but some of them are classics (e.g. *Macbeth, Othello, King Lear*). The same is true of Mozart, Beethoven and Bach, who created a handful of pieces that are considered classics, but wrote over five hundred pieces each during their lifetimes. So rather than have teams sit around racking their brains to come up with that one great idea that will save the company, we need to have our teams working to generate as many ideas as possible.

This is where tools such as *visual thinking* come into their own. A lot of our business activities use the 'left side' of the brain; communicating using words and numbers. Business language has a tendency to be stiff, formal and rigid. To generate loads of ideas, a certain playfulness is needed. Visual thinking provides a unique perspective to business problems by allowing people to use the artistic 'right side' of our brains to solve business problems. The use of pens, papers, sticky notes and drawing opens up the creative side of the human mind.

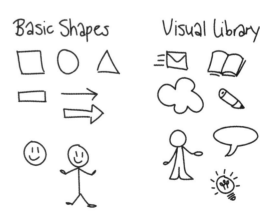

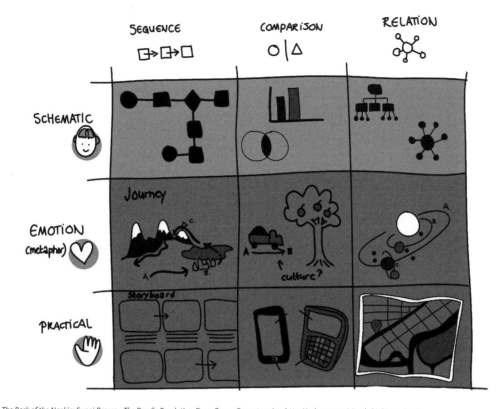

Adapted from: Dan Roam - *The Back of the Napkin*; Sunni Brown - *The Doodle Revolution*; Dave Gray - *Gamestorming*. http://xplaner.com/visual-thinking-school/

Most people will complain that they cannot draw to save their lives. But it is also very difficult to describe complex ideas verbally. A quick sketch or doodle really helps to get your ideas across to others. This makes visual thinking a great collaboration tool. Visually communicating and sharing ideas can also spark ideas in others. As such, this is a method we will be referencing a lot throughout the rest of the book. Below are some general tips for visual thinking:

- If you can draw the simple shapes in the visual alphabet, then you can use visual thinking. The point is not to become Picasso, but to use pictures to communicate ideas.
- An ideation workshop should include different types of people, who should all have an opportunity to draw their ideas. Drawing is not for designers only; accountants, managers and programmers should all get a chance to draw.
- Visual thinking tools include paper, pens, sticky notes, whiteboards, pictures and Sharpies. Even physical objects such as Play-Doh and LEGO can be useful for illustrating and prototyping ideas.
- The use of visual frameworks such as the one below can also help teams organize and communicate their ideas. For example, Dave Gray and Sunni Brown differentiate three types of drawing frameworks; time (or *sequence*), difference (or *comparison*), and systems (or *relationships*).

Using visual thinking and other tools, there are several ways to generate ideas within companies. We will describe three main methods that we have observed being used most often: *Brainstorming, Open Calls* and *Idea Competitions*. In addition to generating a lot of ideas, *idea selection* is also an important part of our innovation framework. Innovation is ultimately about choosing the right ideas to work on. With loads of ideas being generated, the number of available options can create paralysis. This is the paradox of choice. So, for each idea generation method we describe, we will also provide guidance on how teams can make choices about specific ideas to work on.

The Brainstormer[23]

Brainstorming is a great method for generating ideas. However, most companies do not use this method as often as they should. And when they have a brainstorming session, it's an all day event at some off-site venue. Brainstorming sessions should be an integral part of the culture in a company. They should be considered as one of the main tools that a company uses whenever it is trying to come up with ideas to solve any challenges it is facing. Brainstorming should also be used for coming up with product ideas, especially after teams have been out of the building observing customers and gathering insights.

The other challenge is that those companies that do have brainstorming sessions do not use the right methods for success. The sessions are often too long (e.g. all day off-site), whereas IDEO recommends sixty minutes as the optimal time for a brainstorming session. Other counterproductive practices include having every person take their turn to speak in a predetermined sequence or having the boss speak first. Such practices do not get people's creative juices flowing. Remember, our goal is to generate as many ideas as possible. Below are some tips for running a great brainstorming session:

1. *Get Focused:* A good brainstorming session has to be focused on a clear problem statement. Part of the reason for getting out of the building is to develop a point of view about customers and their needs. Our *innovation thesis* and *portfolio goals* can also serve as a good reference point for sharpening the focus of our brainstorming sessions. It is not good to simply ask people to come up with cool ideas without any guidance. Serendipitous interactions should be harnessed to tackle a specific problem that is the focus of the brainstorming session.

2. *Apply Ideation Rules:* To get people comfortable with ideation you can set some simple rules. These can be clearly shown on posters or a whiteboard during the session. What we are really trying stop is people criticizing ideas too soon, which causes other people to start editing their thoughts. So we can put in place simple rules such as '*quantity not quality*', '*visual thinking*', '*generate then review*', and '*having fun is allowed*'.

3. *Build Then Jump:* Brainstorming sessions tend to have a curve on which ideation builds up slowly and then reaches a point of intensity before tapering down. The role of a facilitator is to spark conversations during the slow build up phase and then allow the conversation to flow afterwards. When the conversation seems to be tapering off, another cycle can be sparked by 'jumping' to a different topic.

4. *Make Use of Space:* Use the space in the room to capture ideas. Papers, sticky notes and Sharpies are a good way to do this. Encourage the team to use visual thinking. Cover the wall with their drawings and ideas, before having them step back to review and organize.

5. *Use Warm Up Exercises:* Before getting into the specific ideation session itself, the facilitator can help the team stretch their mental muscles by doing some warm up exercises. For example, teams can use creative exercises such as coming up with as many uses for a pen as they can think off. Alex Osterwalder recommends the 'silly cow' exercise where teams sketch ideas for three business models based on a cow.

6. *Use Physical Objects:* In practice, a good brainstorming session is highly visual. Sketches and sticky notes will be

everywhere. However, teams can go a step further by bringing physical objects into the room. These can be competitor products, alternative products and inspiring technologies. The objects need not be directly related to the topic under discussion. We are just looking for inspiration. Teams can also bring in materials for prototyping ideas such as foam, duct tape, LEGO bricks, Play-Doh, string and stickers.

Adapted from: Kelley, T. (2007). *The Art of Innovation*. London: Crown Business.

A well-run brainstorming session will produce a lot of ideas. However, since teams cannot work on every idea, choices have to be made. A key brainstorming discipline is making sure that no criticism of ideas happens during the idea generation stage. First, we ideate, then we critique. Making use of space, combined with visual thinking, means that all the ideas we have generated will be posted on the walls ready for review.

1. Allow team members to present each of their ideas quickly. Use a timer and allow people to only speak for five minutes. That is five minutes for all their ideas, not five minutes per idea!
2. Spend another five minutes during which team members ask questions about any ideas they didn't fully understand.
3. After presentation and review are completed, the team can then spend time integrating similar themes or ideas.
4. Now it's time to vote. Each team member can get three to five stickers which they can use to vote for their favorite ideas. They can vote for as many ideas as they have stickers or place all their votes on one idea.

After voting, there will be three to five top ideas that will have been identified. This is a good time to bring in people with super votes. In the book *Sprint*, Jake Knapp and colleagues argue that every design sprint should have a *decider* (or two).[24] This person is usually someone with a leadership role within the organization who has the power to approve innovation projects. If budget for the innovation project has already been approved, then decider status can be allocated to a product manager, product owner or any other team leader.

A good decider will make final decisions based on the innovation thesis and the company's portfolio goals. When there are several ideas that are aligned to the thesis and portfolio goals then other criteria can be used as well (e.g. ease and cost of implementation). Having a decider with final approval in the room during voting is useful for getting executive buy-in. It helps to ensure ideas do not become orphans that go no further after the brainstorming session is over.

Having a decider in the room is also useful at limiting decision paralysis and endless team discussions. Once we have our top three ideas, the decider chooses one and we are ready to go. It is important to note here that the decider's choice should not

137

be taken as the ultimate validation for the idea. We still have to get out of the building and test our ideas. More on that in Chapter 7.

Open Calls

One of the many barriers to innovation in large companies is the requirement that any proposals for new ideas have to move through various layers of management decision making before they get investment. Such processes ensure that only those individuals with an appetite for corporate politics, writing business plans or a deep passion for their idea will work to push their ideas through. If companies need to generate a lot of ideas before they find a few good ones, such convoluted decision making will undoubtedly stifle innovation.

Companies need a process that allows anyone in the company to come up with an idea and get a chance to test it. This what Adobe created with their Kickbox program.[25] The Kickbox is a red box that is sealed with a fire alarm graphic that says "pull in case of idea". Inside the box you will find a set of cards, tools, notebooks, sticky notes, a chocolate bar and a $10 Starbucks gift card.

The cards and tools inside the box provide a step-by-step guide of what you need to do to generate, prototype and test an idea. Employees are not only given instructions and tools; as a way to unleash innovation, the Kickbox also contains a prepaid credit card with $1000 on it. An employee can use the card on any resources they need to test and develop their idea, without having to justify or explain the expenses to a manager.

To ensure that the company generates a lot of ideas, Adobe allows any employee across the organization to get a Kickbox. There is a two-day workshop available at which employees learn how to use the Kickbox. This is not mandatory, but strongly recommended. There are also no absolute limits to the number of Kickboxes an employee can have access to. If they work on an idea and it fails, this does not stop them getting access to another box. Indeed, some of the more successful ideas have come from employees on their second Kickbox.[26]

What Adobe has created is a great process for serendipity. Having an open call for ideas that allows every employee to participate gives Adobe a chance to find great ideas from people that would normally be excluded from innovation. Providing employees with resources and tools to test their ideas, shows that Adobe is committed to supporting innovation. The Adobe Kickbox program illustrates the following principles that companies should follow when making open calls for ideas:

1. Every employee, regardless of role and status, should be allowed to participate.
2. Provide employees with clear objectives or an innovation thesis for the call.
3. Provide a small investment or limited resources for testing ideas.
4. Provide clear guidelines for testing ideas, including tools and resources.
5. Training and support from innovation coaches should be available to employees.
6. There should be a clear process of what happens to an idea after it has been successfully tested.

When running an open call for ideas, the criteria for obtaining future investment should be clear. Within Abode's system, idea selection for future investment is based on merit. Anyone can get access to the red box and the $1000 credit card. But that is all they get. To move further, they have to 'beat the box'. The only way to 'beat the box' is to use the resources that Adobe have given you to demonstrate the viability of your idea. If you are successful at showing viability, you can get access to a blue box and further investment to develop the idea.

Other companies use time as a resources to generate ideas via open calls. At 3M, employees are allowed to spend 15% of their time working on ideas of their choice.[27] 3M employees can use the open technology platforms to prototype and test ideas. At Intuit, they have 10% unstructured time for employees to work on projects they are passionate about. Intuit also has an innovation lab (*Intuit Labs*), where people can get support to develop and test their ideas.[28] For a long time, Google allowed its engineers 20% time to work on personal projects. Products such as Google News, Google Talk and Gmail, were developed using this allotted time.[29]

But even when time is used as a resource, there must be a clear process for what happens with ideas once they are successful. For example, an internal review at 3M found that despite liberal policies in terms of resources to develop ideas, some promising ideas did not receive further investment for development. This led 3M to set up *Genesis Grants* to fund nascent ideas, and the *Pacing Plus Program* to accelerate ideas that have the potential to be successful.[30]

Another challenge with open calls for ideas, is that it can create a scattergun approach to innovation. This can generate a lot of noise and very little value. In 2013, Google axed its 20% time policy. Google's rationale for axing the policy was that it was developing a more focused innovation strategy.[31] For a large company such as Google, this decision makes sense. Even with open calls for ideas and unstructured time for employees, some strategic guidance is critical. The innovation thesis and balanced portfolio targets should be used to set the objectives of any open call for ideas.

Idea Competitions

In addition to open calls, a lot of companies run idea competitions. This process typically involves a company setting up an online platform on which employees can submit ideas. There is then an awareness campaign to make employees aware of the competition via various channels (e.g. email, internal blogs and posters in key public spaces). Employees submit their ideas to the platform and some sort of voting process takes place. This

typically involves other employees commenting and voting on the platform. The top ideas are then taken to a management decision making committee, who makes the final decision on the winners.

Idea competitions can be a fun way to get engagement from employees. There is quite a buzz that can be created by the excitement of competing and winning. However, the ultimate goal in running idea competitions is to use serendipity to discover breakthrough ideas that can make a contribution to company revenues and growth. Idea competitions should not be treated as a fun side show in which the winning ideas get no further focus or investment after the competition is over. Below are five principles of running successful idea competitions.

1. *Open to All*: As with open calls, every employee should be allowed to participate regardless of role and status.
2. *Strategic Objectives*: Every idea competition should have a clear objective. Employees should not be asked to just submit any idea they can think of. Strategic objectives that are aligned to an innovation thesis should be made clear to all employees who participate in the competition.
3. *Idea Shaping*: Beyond just voting and commenting, companies can deploy platforms that allow employees to collaboratively shape each other's ideas. As we have already noted, no one employee can generate a fully formed breakthrough idea by themselves. Allowing employees to shape each other's ideas creates serendipity by taking advantage of 'creative collective' innovation principles of help seeking, help giving and reflective reframing.
4. *Idea Selection*: There should be clear selection criteria. Allowing employees to vote is a very popular method, but this can turn the idea competition into a popularity contest, with well known and well-liked employees winning. Furthermore, most employees do not really understand how innovation works, so their voting choices may be constrained by this limited knowledge. A potential solution is to educate employees on innovation and provide clear voting guidelines. Another solution is to have an informed decision making body that selects ideas based on the company's innovation thesis and balanced portfolio goals.
5. *What Happens Next?*: There must be a clear process of what happens after an idea wins the competition. How will it be tested, developed and taken to scale? If nothing happens after an idea wins the competition, this can create a less than inspiring environment for idea generation in the future. It is also a limitation of idea competitions that only one, two or three ideas get the chance to be tested. We believe that top 10 or top 15 ideas should get a chance to be tested via a process similar to the Kickbox. Only after testing should the winners be announced. Those ideas can then get investment for further development.

Adapted from Glaveski, S. (2015). 'How to Run an Effective Idea Generation Campaign.' *Innovation Excellence*: http://innovationexcellence.com/blog/2015/04/20/how-to-run-an-effective-idea-generation-program/

Capturing Ideas

When a large number of ideas are being generated, not all ideas will get a chance to be worked on. Furthermore, not all ideas that are worked on will succeed. Some of them will fail. The challenge for companies is to ensure that these ideas do not fall through the cracks in terms of company-wide knowledge. In their study of 3M, Dr Raghu Garud and colleagues discovered that there is an asynchronous nature to innovation. Ideas that make no sense to invest in or even fail in the market at one time, can later be reused in other projects or redesigned into successful products. As such, companies need to create platforms where all these ideas are captured and tagged.

At 3M, they have a system of technology platforms that are open to all employees. The platforms capture all the research, knowledge and product development work happening on a particular technology (e.g. microreplication). These platforms allow other researchers and innovators to use the available knowledge and resources in whatever projects they are working on. Within 3M, this process is referred to as 'bootlegging'. The technology platforms are treated as a company-wide resource for innovation during the 15% unstructured time.

Companies should ensure that the ideas generated by employees are captured and kept on an open platform. The decisions about whether or not to invest in any idea must also be recorded and tagged for future innovators to look at. Even ideas that are tried and end up failing in the market must be logged and kept on this platform. This will help companies take advantage of the asynchronous nature of creativity and innovation. Indeed, part of the research and idea generation process should involve encouraging employees to look at the open platforms to find inspiration in ideas that have been developed by their colleagues.

141

Idea Review

The goal of *idea generation* is to end up selecting one idea that the team can focus on. Once a specific idea has been selected, the next step is not to build your 'wonderful' product and launch it to the market. To repeat our fundamental principle; teams should not be taking their ideas to scale prematurely. We are also not going to be writing twenty-five page business plans. Instead, the selected ideas should be reviewed for key assumptions and gaps in knowledge (i.e. *idea review*). These assumptions and gaps are what we will then test in the next stage of our innovation journey.

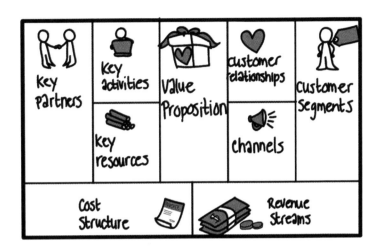

Source: Osterwalder, A. & Pigneur, Y. (2010). *Business Model Generation*. New York City: John Wiley & Sons

Source: Maurya, A. (2012). *Running Lean*. Sebastopol:O'Reilly.

The best way to review an idea, is to make the assumptions underlying the idea visible to teams. There are several tools that can be used to capture and review assumptions. In large company contexts, we have found it beneficial to use Oster- walder's Business Model Canvas. This canvas has nine sections; *key partners, key activities, key resources, value propositions, customer relationships, channels, customer segments, cost structure* and *revenue streams*. Other colleagues, especially those working with startups, prefer to use the Lean Canvas by Ash Maurya. Adapted from the Business Model Canvas, this canvas also has nine sections; *problem, solution, key metrics, unique value proposition, unfair advantage, channels, customer segments, cost structure* and *revenue streams*.

When using these canvases, the best way to extract assump- tions from people is to ask them to imagine their idea as a product in the world. What value would it be bringing to cus- tomers? What problems would it solve? How would customers hear about it, buy it and have it delivered? How much do we think it might cost to make? What would our revenue model be? How much would we charge customers? The team can discuss and capture these assumptions on the canvas. Imagin- ing our product already succeeding in the world and mapping it on a canvas is good way to make explicit what we, as a team, are assuming will happen if we succeed. Ash Maurya calls this capturing our 'Plan A'.

Identifying Risky Assumptions

After we have mapped out our assumptions on the canvas, the team should now spend time reviewing these. Within our canvas, there will be ideas we have mapped that are well rooted in knowledge. However, there will also be ideas we have mapped that are merely assumptions. These are ideas for which we have no knowledge or evidence of their correctness. For example, we may be assuming that customers have a need that they do not have. This distinction between assumption and knowledge should be identified, and all sticky notes with untested assumptions should be clearly marked with a red sticker or an "X".

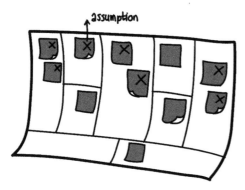

At the end of this idea review process, we can then step back from our canvas and see how many ideas we placed on it are knowledge versus assumptions. Our work going forward, is to reduce the assumption-to-knowledge ratio, such that our canvas has a lot of knowledge and very few or zero assumptions.

This is the definition of a validated business model:

VALIDATED BUSINESS MODEL = KNOWLEDGE > ASSUMPTIONS

Within our identified assumptions will be ideas that are critical for the success of the business model. For example, the success of our product may hinge on the willingness of customers to switch from a competitor. In contrast, other assumptions on the canvas may not be as critical to success. The assumptions that are critical to success should be clearly identified on the canvas (e.g. using green stickers or a 'Y').

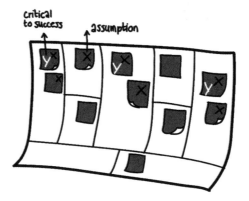

Assumptions that have also been identified as critical for success (i.e. sticky notes with both red and green stickers), can be described as our 'riskiest assumptions'. These ideas are critical to the success of the business model, but we do not yet have evidence that they are correct. If it turns out we are wrong, then there is a high likelihood that our product or innovation project will fail. As such, in the testing phase of our innovation journey, we have to prioritize testing these risky assumptions first.

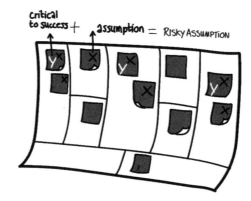

143

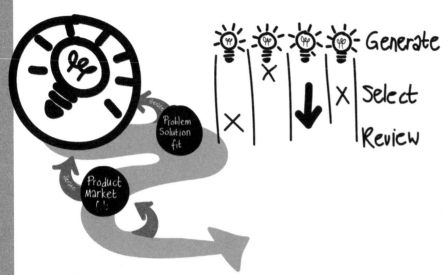

1. The first criteria is alignment to strategy and the innovation thesis. Decision makers must try as much as they can to ensure that the vast majority of ideas that get worked on are aligned to strategy.
2. The second criterion is balanced portfolio goals. This criterion ensures that companies do not keep working on the same types of ideas. Ideas that help a company to balance its portfolio across the three innovation types must be prioritized (i.e. *core*, *adjacent* and *transformational*).
3. The final governance question for decision makers is how well the team has identified their assumptions and made plans for testing. Once the team has prioritized the risky assumptions they want to test, they are now ready to move on to the next stage of the innovation journey.

READY TO TEST IDEAS

With all the activity that is happening during the idea creation stage, disciplined innovation management is needed. The thousand flowers blooming should be corralled and pointed toward achieving our strategic goals. A combination of our innovation framework and innovation accounting can be applied to tracking and managing ideation. At the most basic level, teams that are working on generating ideas can track a few *reporting KPIs*. For example, they can track activity metrics such as the number of ideas generated and the number of ideas that have been chosen for further exploration. Once an idea is chosen and is getting prepared for testing, an impact metric for the team is whether or not risky assumptions have been identified.

From a *governance KPI* perspective, the key decision to be made is whether the idea is ready to move to the testing stage of its innovation journey. When we described *brainstorming*, *open calls* and *idea competitions* we provided some guidance as to how ideas can be selected for further work. Regardless of how ideas are generated and submitted to decision makers, there are three key criteria that must be considered:

A company can create submission forms for teams and scorecards for decision makers that can be used to evaluate ideas. The forms and scorecards must cover the key criteria identified above. In addition to these, other criteria can be used to make decisions (e.g. costs, market size, timing). However, these criteria should be considered after and weighed less than the key criteria above. If a company places more weight on costs or technological constraints, it will end up working on exactly the same types of products. As such, innovation thesis and portfolio balance must take precedence. If, upon analysis, there are several ideas that meet these key criteria, then the other criteria can be used to whittle them down further.

Global KPIs measure how well our investments in innovation are contributing to the overall health of the company. At this early stage, there are not many global KPIs to measure. The focus is mostly on activity metrics such as the number of ideas generated for each innovation type (*core, adjacent, transformational*) and innovation substage (*generate, select, review*). Over time as ideas are tested and validated, other global KPIs such as innovation contribution and cost savings come into play.

Innovation Accounting for Creating Ideas

CREATE IDEAS	GENERATE	Is the idea aligned to our company's strategic goals and innovation thesis?
	SELECT	Does this idea help us meet our goals for achieving a balanced portfolio?
	REVIEW	Has the team identified their risky assumptions and made clear plans to test them?
	OTHER CRITERIA	Costs, Timing, Resource Availability, Skills Availability, Technological Constraints, Potential Market Size?

KPIs	ACTIVITY METRICS	IMPACT METRICS
REPORTING	number of ideas generated number of ideas chosen assumptions identified	hypotheses developed minimum fail criteria set
GOVERNANCE	number of ideas submitted number of decisions made products moved to next stage average amount invested	alignment with thesis alignment with portfolio assumption-to-knowledge ratio
GLOBAL	number of products by innovation type (core, adjacent, transformational) number of products per substage (generate, select, review)	Not Applicable

Innovation Activity: Idea Selection

One of the things we have noticed in our work is the difficulty businesses have in choosing ideas to work on. After brainstorming sessions or idea competitions, when a variety of ideas are on the table, managers tend to revert back to previous decision making practices. Ideas are chosen on how much money they can make immediately or whether the ideas utilize current capabilities. Such criteria are a good way of ensuring that the company works on the same things it has always worked on. Our innovation accounting framework focuses on two main questions at this early stage:

1. Is this idea aligned with our company's strategic goals and innovation thesis?
2. Does this idea help us meet our goals for achieving a balanced portfolio?

To help decision makers with prioritizing ideas, we developed a five step method for mapping ideas along the dimensions of innovation thesis and innovation portfolio. We gather a small group of decision makers, usually a cross-functional team, in a room for about sixty minutes. They bring with them the ideas they are trying to choose from (e.g. from a brainstorm session, an open call or idea competition):

1. We ask the team to put all the ideas onto sticky notes, with one idea going on each sticky note.

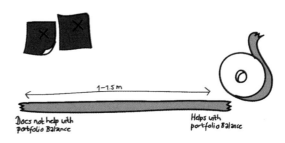

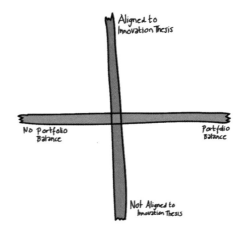

2. Next, we ask the team to draw two intersecting lines on about one to one and a half meters each on a whiteboard. Along the vertical line, we ask them to write at the top "Aligned To Innovation Thesis" and at the bottom "Not Aligned to Innovation Thesis". On the horizontal line, we ask the team to write on the right "Helps With Portfolio Balance" and on the left, "Does Not Help With Portfolio Balance".

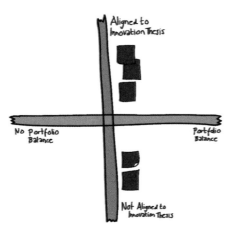

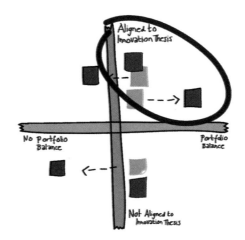

3. After this, we ask them to map each idea along the two dimensions, starting with innovation thesis. Each idea is ranked in terms of how well it aligns with the innovation thesis. At the top will be the ideas that align with the innovation thesis the most.

5. In the end, the ideas in the top right quadrant represent the ideas that should be chosen for further development. Management can then select more specific ideas from this set using other dimensions if they need to (e.g. budget, ease of implementation, market size and revenue potential).

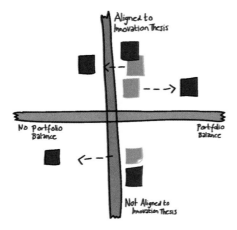

4. Then, without changing the vertical raking, each idea is ranked horizontally in terms of how much it helps balance the company's portfolio. On the right will be the ideas that help the most.

Innovation Activity: Business Model Prototyping

The business model canvas is a great tool to capture assumptions and document our Plan A. However, the canvas is also a great tool for ideation. Rather than focus on the first business model we come up with, teams can prototype several business models. Prototyping several business models is great for innovation because it deals with the 'local maxima' problem of optimizing and refining on our original ideas too soon, before we explore the problem space.

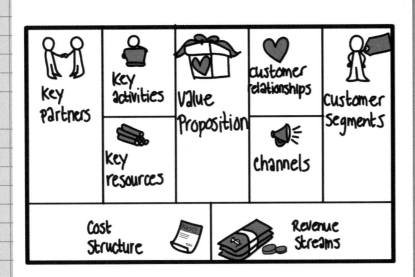

Source: Osterwalder, A. & Pigneur, Y. (2010). *Business Model Generation*. New York City: John Wiley & Sons.

For a business model prototyping session, we gather a cross-functional team in a room for a two to three hour workshop. We use Ao size business model canvases that are usually placed on the wall. We give the team basic business model design rules such as:

- Write on sticky notes and stick them on the canvas - do not write on the canvas.
- Visual thinking - use words and images to illustrate your ideas.
- Put one idea or assumption per sticky note - don't make lists of assumptions.
- Do it together as a team and allow every team member to contribute.
- Loads of ideas - quantity over quality, you can review the sticky notes later.

After a warm up exercise (e.g. the silly cow), the team is asked to collaboratively build their first business model canvas. This is their Plan A; i.e. how they imagine the product will be created and sold in the market. We give the team twenty to thirty minutes to do this. After they have mapped their first model, we ask them to take a picture of the model and store it in the 'fridge'.

Now the prototyping session begins in earnest. To develop various business models, we ask the team to imagine a series of 'what-ifs' and then map the appropriate business model. For example, we ask the team to imagine that they are not allowed to use the internet or mobile application to sell their product. How would this change their business model? Below are a few 'what if' scenarios we use:

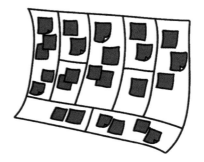

- Whatever your current revenue model, please charge ten times more. Now develop your value proposition to justify the extra charge.
- Give your core value proposition to customers for free. How are you now going to make money?
- Is your business model B2B or B2C? Whatever it is, keep the same value propositions and design the opposite model. If your model is B2B, make your business model B2C and vice versa.
- How would your business model change if you had to cut all your prices by 75%?
- How would your business model change if your costs went up by 50%?

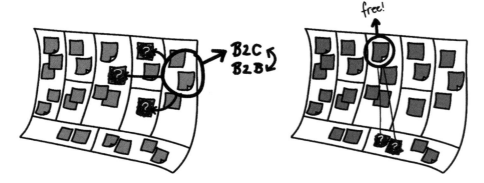

These are just a few examples. Teams and coaches can develop their own scenarios that are relevant to their business and context. The 'what-if' scenarios need not be realistic, they are just tools to spark ideation. We give teams fifteen to twenty minutes to work through each scenario and we use three to four scenarios depending on time constraints. At the end of each scenario, we ask teams to take pictures of their newly designed business model.

When they have mapped a few business models for different scenarios, we then ask them to review their first business model from the picture they took. Is there anything they would change now, given the outputs of the ideation session? We then give them fifteen to twenty minutes to come up with a final Plan A. It is this final business model that will be reviewed for risky assumptions.

Innovation Activity: Assumptions Prioritization

For this short workshop, all we need is a flat surface such as a table, a whiteboard or a wall. We also need a roll of masking tape, sticky notes and sharpies. The assumptions prioritization session utilizes the following six key steps:

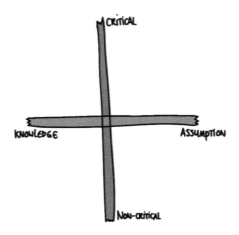

1. We ask the team to take from their business model canvas all sticky notes that have been identified as being assumptions rather than knowledge.

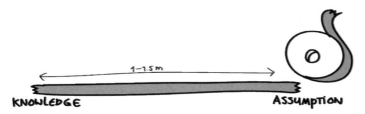

3. At the middle point of the horizontal line, we will use the masking tape to draw a perpendicular line that stretches across both sides of the horizontal line (i.e. 1m-1,5m). We are than going to mark the top end of the line with 'critical for business model' or simply 'critical' and the bottom end with 'not critical for business model' or simply 'non-critical'.

2. Using the masking tape, the team will then create a one to one and a half meters line on a flat surface (please note: marker pens also work for this). On the left end of the line, the team writes: 'we have a lot of knowledge' or simply 'knowledge'. Similarly, on the right end of the line, the teams writes: 'we have no knowledge' or simply 'assumption'.

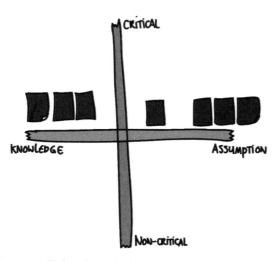

4. The teams will then be asked to rank the assumptions by placing them on the horizontal assumption-knowledge line. The assumptions for which we have some information will go towards the left, whereas the rest of the assumptions will be placed on the right.

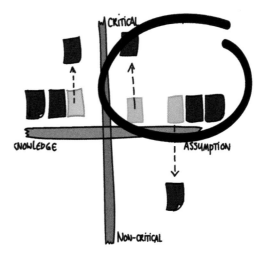

6. The assumptions that end up in the top right quadrant are the risky assumptions that have to be prioritized for testing in the next innovation stage.

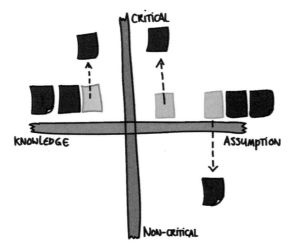

5. Without changing their relative position to the horizontal line, the team will then start moving the sticky notes up or down the vertical line based on the degree of the importance each assumption has in relation to the business model.

CONVERSATIONS ON INNOVATION
Timan Rebel

CO-FOUNDER AT NEXT AMSTERDAM

Timan Rebel has over fourteen years of experience as an entrepreneur and had an earlier successful exit in 2007 with SB/SD, the largest social network in the Netherlands for teenagers at that time. Timan was co-founder of Snowciety and Fast Moving Targets, CTO of Peermatch, Mobypicture and Sol United, as well as Entrepreneur in Residence at The Next Web. He started the StartupBus movement in Europe in 2011 and acted as lead mentor at Rockstart Accelerator, where he has mentored over 45 startups. He recently set up NEXT Amsterdam with Esther Gons, which is a startup studio that invests in founders to help them turn their ideas into successful revenue-driven startups. To help innovators, they have been creating tools that help with business model design and testing ideas.

CS: TELL US WHY YOU CREATED THE NEXT CANVAS? DOES THE WORLD NEED ANOTHER CANVAS?

TR: Well yes. At NEXT Amsterdam, innovation accounting - ways to keep track of what you have learned and validated over time - is a really BIG thing. Since this is hardest *before* any metrics are in place or revenue streams, we have experimented with several ways to visualize progress over time from ideation to scale. We based our revised canvas on Ash Maurya's Lean Canvas. We realized that certain segments are tackled together: you really need to understand the problem of a specific customer segment, to be able to produce a value proposition on which you can base the solution. With this knowledge, we reordered segments joining up related ones. The order is what simplifies a seemingly chaotic process for most startups. Moving from left to right over time and the order in which these become important, moving towards a scalable business model. This helps startups that often ask us, where do I start? How do I decide what to work on or experiment with first? Especially the search for a working business model can feel like going around in circles, and innovation accounting a tedious task. This canvas helps them with taking the right steps and keeps track of the progress the team is making.

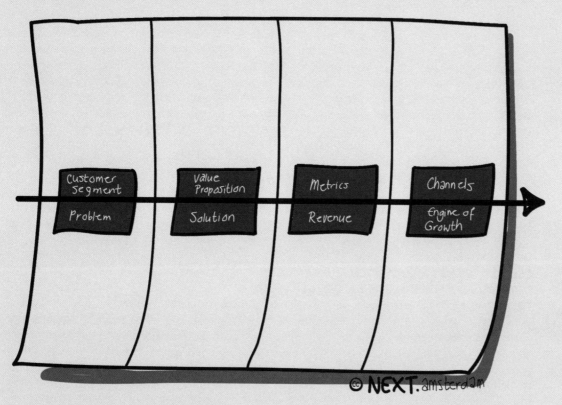

© NEXT.amsterdam

153

CS: CAN YOU EXPLAIN IN MORE DETAIL EACH SECTION OF THE CANVAS AND HOW THE PAIRS GO TOGETHER IN TERMS OF ASSUMPTIONS?

TR: We split our canvas vertically into a product and customer track. The segments in the customer track corresponds to the segments in the product track and vice versa. For example, you first want to identify the customer segment and the problem that segment is facing. The customer segment and problem segment together form the first step of our canvas. There are four steps in total. Each of the four steps of our canvas links to an innovation lifecycle stage and going from one step to the other results in a promotion.

Prove there is a problem. When you first start your startup or project, you need to identify the customer segment and the problem that segment faces. Once you have identified and verified those assumptions you can move to the unique value proposition and the actual solution. That step also brings you past the ideation phase.

Prove your solution. The next step is the unique value proposition and solution phase, proving that your solution is the one your customer is looking for and thereby reaching 'Problem/Solution' fit.

Prove people will pay. Now you want to prove that your customers want to pay for your solution. To do that you need to start experimenting with possible revenue models and identify the right metrics to measure the usage of your solution. When you have proven your customers want to pay and your metrics all look good, you reach the magical 'Product/market-fit' and are ready to scale.

Prove you can scale. This is the last step of our canvas, and most often the hardest step. Only here do you start proving the channels and growth engine.

The good thing about the direction of the NEXT canvas is that startups recognize if they are working on premature scaling. Working on validating channels when the solution hasn't even been proven yet, is visibly skipping steps.

CS: HOW IS THE CANVAS USED IN PRACTICE? IS IT STRICTLY FOR BUSINESS MODEL DESIGN?

TR: Where the Lean Canvas and Business Model Canvas are great for brainstorming, the NEXT Canvas is designed with tracking of progress in mind. When you fill in the canvas for the first time you start at the beginning with the customer/problem step. You write down your assumptions and define those that are most risky. After the brainstorming however, the NEXT Canvas and experiment cards can also be used as a progress tracking tool. We usually use two types of stickies to identify validated/invalidated assumptions. When done right, you see the validated color grow from left to right, indicating more and more validated assumptions and promotions to the next steps.

CS: WHAT CHALLENGES DO YOU FIND INNOVATORS FACE WHEN TESTING THEIR IDEAS AND HOW DO YOU HELP THEM MANAGE THE PROCESS AT NEXT?

TR: The biggest challenge is to keep testing ideas. It is easy to start with Lean Startup and Innovation Accounting. Filling in a canvas, writing down some assumptions, even running an experiment or two. It gets really hard when you want to incorporate Lean Startup and Innovation Accounting in the day to day activities of your company. At NEXT we developed an Innovation Sprint and Experiment Cards to make it easier to run multiple experiments over time. We learned that a process or framework helps people to get grips with Lean Startup.

The Innovation Sprint is a simplified Kanban board with a list of experiments to run, running experiments and finished experiments. Every experiment is represented by an experiment card, holding all important information of an experiment. From the hypotheses and context to the success criteria. By using experiment cards, starting an experiment is as simple as filling out a form.

Besides the Innovation Sprint and Experiment Cards, our NEXT Canvas is ideal to use as a progress tracking tool. Because the canvas is laid out over time you can see how far you are proving the riskiest assumptions and if you are skipping steps. In our online tool (https://nextinnovation. tools) it is even easier to create experiments, just by clicking on a sticky note and writing down the specifics of the experiment and adding them to the innovation sprint board.

CS: HOW DO YOU THINK A LARGE ESTABLISHED COMPANY CAN USE THE NEXT CANVAS?
TR: A startup usually has only one business model they need to prove. Doing that without a framework is possible. If you don't find a repeatable business model you simply fail and run out of time and money.

It gets much harder when you are running multiple innovation projects at the same time in a larger established company. Not only do you want to have an overview of progress, challenges and insights from every single project, you also want to see which metric is effective to measure the state the project is in and what it needs to reach at least to continue.

The NEXT canvas gives a visual overview of the status of every innovation project. In what phase is the project, what is already validated and what key insights have been found during the experiments.

155

'Enlightened trial and error succeeds over the planning of the lone genius.'

Peter Skillman, GM Core UX at Microsoft

CHAPTER SEVEN

Testing Ideas

There are very few product ideas that ever succeed in their original form. PayPal started out working on cryptography software, then money transfer via PDA, before they landed on their successful web-based payment system model.[32] Flickr started out as an online game,[33] YouTube began as an online dating site[34] and Instagram was an iPhone location app called Burbn.[35] There are many more examples of successful companies that had to change and adapt their original ideas before they found success. Success with an idea in its original form is extremely rare. This is why innovators have to test their product ideas before launching them at scale.

Saras Sarasvathy is Professor at the Darden School of Business at the University of Virginia. She and her colleagues have studied experienced entrepreneurs and how they go about setting up their businesses. Her research findings challenge the *causal approach* to innovation in which entrepreneurs are viewed as setting their goals and then assembling the necessary resources to execute. Instead, she found that entrepreneurs *effectuate* their way to success; they begin with whatever resources they have at their disposal at the time and then figure out the rest as they go.[36]

The five principles of effectuation provide a method for innovators to start working on their ideas without knowing all the facts. Starting where we are and taking incremental steps allows us to learn and adjust as we go. The effectuation method is well aligned with our principles of incremental investing, testing ideas before scaling and alignment with internal stakeholders. The discipline to assume that we might be wrong, focuses innovators on taking small steps when developing their ideas. These steps allow effectuation to take place. As some of our assumptions are shown to be wrong, we can then change and iterate our business model.

Effectuation and Corporate Startup Similarities

PRINCIPLE	EFFECTUATION	CORPORATE STARTUP
BIRD IN HAND	Start with the possibilities within your means. Begin by asking who you are, what you know and who you know.	Start where you are. Review your idea. Map your first plan. Identify risky assumptions. Make plans to test.
AFFORDABLE LOSS	Don't go all out with high risk investments. Understand what you can afford to lose. Choose goals that have limited and affordable downside.	Use incremental investing. Start with a small investment to test risky assumptions. Increase investment as assumptions turn into knowledge.
LEMONADE	Invite and use unexpected surprises. Leverage 'bad news' as clues to what will really work in the market.	Expect to learn about customer needs and viable business models. Use lessons learned to refine your ideas.
PATCHWORK QUILT	Build partnerships with stakeholders who are committed to your project. Partners reduce uncertainty and provide more resources (i.e. birds in hand).	Work with internal stakeholders and key partners to ensure your product does not become an orphan. Align your idea with company strategy, innovation thesis and portfolio goals.
PILOT-IN-THE-PLANE	Focus on activities within your control. Take action to create rather than predict the future.	Start working on your idea in incremental steps. Use market feedback to create better products and business models.

Adapted from Sarasvathy, S.D. (2009) *Effectuation: Elements of Entrepreneurial Expertise.* Cheltenham: Edward Elgar.

Innovation as Science

One aspect of testing ideas that spooks corporate management is the notion of embracing failure. Among Lean Start-up's greatest hits is the idea of *'failing fast'*. This has become a popular part of the lexicon around entrepreneurship and innovation. It is often misrepresented as meaning the *'celebration of failure'*. It is true that companies should not be spending money on doomed projects. Such projects should fail fast and be stopped. But this is neither the point nor the aspiration!

Others have tweaked the mantra to *'learn fast'*. This is more in line with the intended spirit of the original mantra. The badge of honor is not failing. The badge of honor is *validated learning*. To build a cultural tolerance for failure, management has to understand that innovators are not being blasé about failing. Before we take products to scale, we are testing our assumptions. The quicker we learn that we are wrong, the quicker we can change and refine our business model. In effectuation terms, we are trying to make lemonade!

In addition to this, testing ideas is *not* about throwing things on the wall and seeing what sticks. It is a systematic process in which we apply the scientific method to innovation. When most people hear the word *scientist*, they imagine people wearing white lab coats and carefully handling test tubes. However, science is a set of principles that can be applied in any context to test the validity of our assumptions and theories. We do not need to wear lab coats, we just need to understand and apply the core principles of science described below:

- *Skepticism:* Do not believe your own hype. Trust us. Your product is NOT as cool as you think it is. Faith and intuition may be valid bases for making decisions sometimes. But for innovation, an exclusive use of intuition in decision making can be dangerous. Launching products on the basis of faith can lead to failure more often than success.
- *Empiricism:* Rather than rely on faith, innovators should base their decisions on data and evidence. By getting out of the building and talking to customers, we are able to make more informed decisions about what goes into our products. This can help the company to make products that people want.
- *Hypothesis Driven:* The data we collect as evidence is not useful without a framework for interpretation. So before getting out of the building, we need to transform our assumptions into hypotheses: "if activity X *is performed*, then result Y *is expected*". After developing such hypotheses, any evidence we collect can be benchmarked against our expectations. This makes learning easier and faster; and also allows us to make systematic progress.
- *Falsifiability:* It is important that the hypotheses we develop are falsifiable. Karl Popper viewed falsifiability as more important than verification because even with a number of signals supporting the correctness of our assumptions, a single experiment showing we are wrong can be more logically and financially decisive.[37] As such, we need to ensure that we develop hypotheses that are *testable* and have *minimum fail criteria,* so that it is possible to quickly see when our assumptions are wrong.

159

Applied Science

But what does science actually look like when it is being practiced in corporate environments? At the heart of everything is the *create-test-learn* loop that we presented in Part I of this book. Testing ideas follows a set of simple steps that any innovation team can apply to their work.

"In general, we look for a new [scientific] law by the following process. First, we guess it... then we compute the consequences of the guess.... then we compare the computation results to nature or... experiment or... experience, to see if it works. If it disagrees with [the] experiment, it's wrong. In that simple statement is the key to science."

Richard Feynman, Physicist

The first steps in the process of testing ideas were described in Chapter 6. An innovation team should capture their Plan A using a business model canvas. This plan should then be reviewed for assumptions. All identified assumptions are then ranked in terms of how important they are to the business model (i.e. risky assumptions). The plan is to test the riskiest assumptions first. As such, once the riskiest assumptions have been identified, the team should then select a specific assumption to work on. The key goal of working on an assumption is to transform it into a falsifiable hypothesis by setting minimum fail criteria.

The process of setting minimum fail criteria is where we have seen a lot innovation teams struggle. The key mistake teams make is that they try to set their minimum fail criteria before designing the experiments to test their assumptions. Fail criteria cannot be stated in general terms in a vacuum; they have to be connected to a specific experiment. So before setting minimum fail criteria, teams should first brainstorm ideas for how they are going to test their chosen risky assumption.

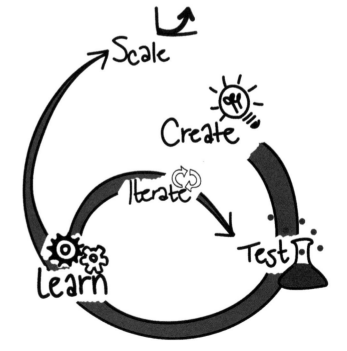

 *Disclaimer: We use the term 'experiment' in this book to refer to its general colloquial meaning of testing and trying out stuff. We do not use it in the scientific sense where independent variables are manipulated to check their effects on dependent variables, while controlling for confounding factors.*

After coming up with a few ideas for how to test the assumption, the team can then choose one or two experiments to focus on. The team should be clear about what they are going to do (e.g. create a landing page), who they are going to run the experiment on and what they are going to measure. Only at this stage can the team then set their minimum fail criteria. These criteria should state clearly the outcome that would make the team accept that the experiment failed to support their assumption. When they have completed this process, the team is now ready to run their experiment.

At the end of the experiment, the data should be analyzed and key lessons captured. The key question at the end of each experiment is whether our assumption has been supported by the evidence and what the implications of our findings are for the business model. On the basis of the outcome, the team can decide what to do next. If our assumption is supported by the evidence, we may decide to persevere with our idea and move on to test the next set of assumptions. If our assumption is not supported by the experiment, we have the choice to change the assumption and adapt our business model (i.e. pivot), or stop the project altogether.

161

STEPS	ACTIVITY
CAPTURE IDEA	Map our Plan A to a business model canvas.
IDENTIFY ASSUMPTIONS	Go through the canvas identifying all untested assumptions.
PRIORITIZE ASSUMPTIONS	Identify those untested assumptions that are critical for success.
BRAINSTORM TESTS	Choose one assumption and brainstorm how to test it.
FALSIFIABLE HYPOTHESES	Choose one experiment to focus on and set minimum fail criteria.
GET OUT OF THE BUILDING	Run the experiment with customers in context.
CAPTURE LEARNINGS	Review whether your assumptions are supported by data.
MAKE DECISION	Persevere, Pivot or Stop.

Exploratory Testing

There is one exception to the testing ideas process we have described above. Sometimes innovators are not exactly sure what they are looking for. They would like to go out into the world and see what is happening before they get clarity on their own ideas. This is referred to as *exploratory* or *generative research*. In developing exploratory tests, the team should follow the first few steps we outlined above (i.e. capturing and identifying their assumptions). However, instead of setting minimum fail criteria, the team should set learning goals. These goals clearly outline what we are trying to learn or find out by getting out of the building.

It is up to every team to decide how they are going to test their ideas. Our process just encourages teams to make their choices explicit. Generative research is useful for learning about customers, products and markets. However, it is limited in terms of the confidence with which we can reach firm conclusions. Without setting minimum fail criteria in advance, some cognitive bias can creep into our decision making and take us down the wrong path. As such, after conducting generative research, we encourage teams to develop testable hypotheses with minimum fail criteria and run experiments.

The Innovator's Toolbox

At the most basic level, the innovator's toolbox contains two broad methods; *listening to what customers say* and *observing what they do*. Using these broad approaches, we can test our assumptions about customers, markets, products and business models. Our tests can be exploratory (i.e. *generative research*) or based on clear testable hypotheses (i.e. *evaluative research*). We have put together a brief list of the research tools that innovators can use to test their ideas. This is a simple guide of some commonly used methods and tactics. For a more exhaustive guide on innovation research tools we recommend Tristan Kromer's *The Real Startup Book*.[38]

163

DESK RESEARCH
This can be a great method to test our assumptions without having to get out of the building. Innovators can review market research reports (e.g. trends in technology or the economy). Social media comments, online conversations and Google Trends are also great tools for learning about what customers are searching for, their opinions on topics and issues they find frustrating and what they do to solve their problems.

CUSTOMER OBSERVATION
Observation is great way to get out of the building and see customers in context. For example, with B2B clients, an innovation team can get permission to spend time at the client's offices watching how they work. This can give us insights into what people struggle with or find difficult. As noted in Chapter 6, it is also possible for us to be *participant observers* who both observe customers and help them with their tasks.

"Observation is a passive science, experimentation an active science."

Claude Bernard

CUSTOMER INTERVIEWS

Talking to customers is the most popular method innovation teams use when they get out of the building. It is a quick and cheap way to gain access to customers; and when used correctly it can provide great insights into what customers say, feel and do. Talking to customers can be used to explore customer needs or test solution ideas.

THE LANDING PAGE

Before building your product, you can test whether your value proposition resonates with customers by creating a simple landing page. On this landing page, you can present your value proposition and then see if it resonates with customers. The best way to measure resonance is to have a call to action on the landing page. You can ask customers to sign up for a free trial, pre-order and leave their email address. In fact, asking people to pre-order is a great way to measure their willingness to pay. Physical paper flyers or digital flyers sent via email can also mimic the same effect.

TEST ADVERTISING CAMPAIGN

Another way to test your value proposition is to run a test advertising campaign. Similar to the landing page, you can present different value propositions and measure which ones get the best click-through rates. Test ads can be even used to test the names of products and also whether a certain advertising channel (e.g. Google or Facebook) is a good way to reach potential customers.

THE EXPLAINER VIDEO

When your proposed value proposition, product or service is complex, explainer videos may be a good way to ensure customers understand your offering. The video can be added to a landing page or an email campaign as part of value proposition testing. As usual, there has to be some call to action connected to the video (e.g. a 'Pre-Order' button). We want to measure customer behavior, not just their opinions.

THE COMPREHENSION TEST

Landing pages, flyers and ad campaign tests only work to the extent that customers understand the value proposition. If customers don't understand the offering then the experiment may fail. This can make it hard for innovators to make decisions. Did the experiment fail because customers don't like the offering or because they don't get it? As such, before running your main experiment you might want to run comprehension tests to ensure that customers understand the offering. Typically, customers are presented with the value proposition on a flyer or landing page for five to ten seconds; after which they are asked to describe the offering in their own words. If customer descriptions of the offering align with your intended value proposition, then you are good to go. If not, then make improvements to your messaging and test again.

CROWDFUNDING

Will customers pay for the product? That is the perennial question. With landing pages and test ads you can test this by having customers pre-order the product. Crowdfunding is also a good way to test the willingness to pay. It can be used to fund an innovation project via contributions from a large number of customers. However, because most large companies are not starved of resources, crowdfunding can instead be used as an initial measure of customer interest. There will still be further work to do to create a more viable business model.

PRE-SALES - LETTER OF INTENT

This method is particularly useful for companies that sell products and services to other businesses. To learn whether your customers will pay for your product before you build it, you can have them sign a letter of intent. Indeed, you could ask them to pay a fully guaranteed 50% deposit for the product, which you promise to deliver within a certain time period. You can also promise that if the customers are not satisfied with the product, they can get the 50% deposit back in full. If you find customers will not sign up for your product even with such guarantees, then you have to pause and explore why that is the case.

DIGITAL PROTOTYPE

Prototypes are a great method for building a product with help from customers. In order to learn which features of your product resonate the most, you can create low fidelity digital wireframes or high fidelity software mockups. You can then present these to customers for feedback. Indeed, digital prototypes are a great way to learn about how customers might use your product. If your features, buttons or workflows are confusing to customers, you can quickly learn how to make them better.

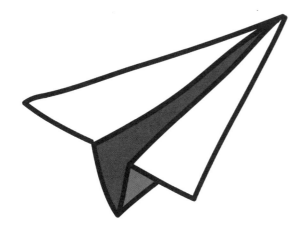

169

PHYSICAL PROTOTYPE

If your company makes and sells physical products, then prototyping can be a great way to test your ideas. Physical prototyping is not only great for testing what resonates with customers, it is also useful for testing whether the company has the capabilities to create the product. Will the technology work? Can this be done? The R&D labs in companies like 3M focus on testing the viability of different product ideas.

CONCIERGE

Even when the intention is to build a digital platform, teams can begin by delivering their value proposition physically. For example, an education company building a platform to connect tutors with homeschooled students can begin by connecting them to each other manually. As they learn more about their customers' needs, they can begin automating elements of the process, testing their revenue model and other parts of the business model.

WIZARD OF OZ

This method can again be used when the intention is to create an automated process. Similar to the concierge approach, the product or service is delivered manually, but the customer is presented with a digital experience. For example, an assessment company may want to automate the creation of test items. They can create a platform where examiners enter topics of choice, and while the customers are having a 'digital' experience, the test items are being generated manually in the background.

A/B TESTING

A/B testing is sometimes referred to as split testing. This approach allows you to compare variants of your products or value propositions to see which one performs better with customers. As an experimentation tool, this method is normally connected to a call to action such as downloads or purchases. For example, you can compare two versions of a web page to see which one has better purchasing conversion rates.

171

CO-CREATION

Companies can also work with customers to co-create products and services. This approach is particularly powerful when conducted with early adopters who have a deep understanding of the customer jobs to be done. Several large organizations, including BMW and Pearson, have set up co-creation labs where they work with customers to help design and improve products.

USABILITY TESTING

As your product or service begins to take shape, usability testing is a great way to find out how easy your product is to use by testing it with real users. Typically, users are asked to complete tasks connected to the value proposition, while the product team watches. This method is a great way to refine products and ensure that we are delivering value to customers. It is also possible to run user tests on competitor products. This is a great way to discover what works or doesn't work for customers and create better experiences.

The above list of tools is not complete. It is just a flavor of the options that innovators have at their disposal to test their ideas. The tools can be used on their own or combined to create even better methods. Furthermore, as we will discuss later, some of these methods have to be adjusted and tweaked to suit the context of large established organizations. In our work, we have found that there is no limit to the creativity of innovators when it comes to designing experiments. The value of their work truly shines when they are able to validate their business models, even while working in environments with legacy constraints.

Tracking Progress

The main goal of running experiments is to make decisions about what to do next with our business model. As such, we need a tool to track the experiments we are running and the decisions we are making. It is also possible to run more than one experiment at a time. So if we are not tracking progress and decision making, we can easily lose track of what we are doing. To help with both designing and tracking experiments, we have developed an experiment canvas.[39]

The experiment canvas is our innovation accounting tool for *reporting KPIs*. It is the tool that teams can use to track the assumptions they are testing, the experiments they are running, the lessons they are learning and the decisions they are making. At the macro level, a product team needs to learn whether their business model as a system, works in a sustainable way. At the micro level, the team needs to track whether a single experiment they ran to test a specific assumption, produced positive results. The experiment canvas helps teams to do both types of innovation accounting.

An innovation team needs a large copy of the canvas hanging on a wall, sticky notes, Sharpies and sticky dots. The canvas is most useful after the team has already thought about the tests they want to run. It is not an ideation tool, but rather a tool to capture and track the experiments we are running and the decisions we are making. Below we describe each block of the canvas.

- *Tested Assumption:* The team needs to select one of their riskiest assumptions from the business model canvas and place it on this block of the experiment canvas. This assumption will be the focus of our experiment design.
- *Impact Business Model Block:* Use sticky dots to mark the area on the business model canvas template that is relevant to the chosen assumption (e.g. customer segment or key partners).
- *Cohort:* Write down the group of people you have selected to test your assumptions on. It is important to be as specific as possible (e.g. marketing managers from leading telecommunication companies or young mothers shopping at the nearby mall).
- *Experiment:* Describe the type of experiment you are going to perform. What exactly are you going to do (e.g. interview customers, set-up a landing page, create a paper prototype).
- *Fail Criteria:* Outline the minimum outcome for which we would conclude that our assumption has not been supported by our experiment.
- *Timebox:* Experiments should not be allowed to run without limits. Instead, they should be timeboxed. In this section, we indicate how long we expect the experiment to run for.

At this stage we are ready to get out of the building and run our experiment. At the end of the experiment, we can then analyze our data and complete the remaining parts of the canvas.

- *Result:* In this section we capture the outcome from the experiment. For example, we can indicate the number of downloads we got from our landing page. We should compare this with our minimum fail criteria.
- *Learning:* Here we describe the key lessons we learned. Did the experiment support our assumption? What other things did we learn from customers? We should capture this on sticky notes and place them on the canvas (i.e. put one insight per sticky note).
- *Decision:* Now it's time to make a decision. Do we persevere, pivot or stop? Please note that if we consider the results of the experiment to be inconclusive, we can also make the decision to run another experiment.

TESTED ASSUMPTION												

IMPACTED BUSINESS MODEL BLOCK

Grey out the Business model block impacted by hypothesis

	1	2	3	1	2	3	1	2	3	1	2	3

COHORT

Define the user group that the experiment is designed for

EXPERIMENT

Design the experiment using the minimum set of requirement that is needed to test the hypothesis

FAIL CRITERIA

Specify lowest limit for not proceeding or persevering

TIMEBOX

Set the time the experiment is going to run for

Launch Experiment   Launch Experiment   Launch Experiment   Launch Experiment

RESULTS

Record all the findings of the experiment focusing on the fail criteria

LEARNINGS

Document the key lessons learned from the experiment

DECISION

Write down the decision taken based on the results and learnings

173

Each lane on the canvas represents one experiment. The canvas is designed so that teams can run multiple experiments to test one assumption or aspect of their business model. A team can also run parallel experiments to test different parts of their business model. The ultimate goal is to transform our assumptions to knowledge so that we end up with a validated business model.

Validated Business Model = Knowledge > Assumptions

How To Avoid False Signals
A major challenge with getting out of the building and running experiments is false signals. These can be false negatives (e.g. concluding that people don't want the product, when they do) or false positives (e.g. concluding that people want the product, when they don't). To avoid false signals there are a few things to consider and account for before, during and after running an experiment:

FAIL CRITERIA VS. SUCCESS CRITERIA
Innovation experiments are different from scientific research in one major way; we are not trying to achieve *statistical significance*, we are trying to achieve *financial significance*. Scientists are normally searching for universal truths that can explain the phenomenon in the world. Innovators are simply looking for a sustainable business model. However, because innovators are usually quite passionate about their ideas, there is a risk that they can take any signal they get as a sign that their idea is good.

This is why we recommend setting fail criteria, rather than success criteria. Success criteria focus innovators on 'proving' their idea is right. This can become a slippery slope. For example, if a team sets their success criteria at a 30% conversion rate, and the data comes back at 28%, do they consider the experiment as a failure? We have never met innovators that would do that.[40] Most of the teams we have coached would quickly make the decision that this is close enough to push ahead.

If the team makes three or more successive decisions like this, it increases the possibility that they are slowly steering their project away from success. They are doing it by small degrees and it doesn't appear to be a problem until it is. So rather than set success criteria, we recommend that teams think hard about the lowest level at which they would consider that the experiment has failed. It is essentially the point at which a team would say, if things are this bad, then we should not keep going (i.e. if only two out of ten people want the product, then our business model is dead).

This is a good way to limit the potential influence of false signals. Of course teams can always 'cheat themselves' by setting very low fail criteria. Dan once worked with an innovation team in a European government agency. After deciding to interview twenty customers, the team set their fail criterion as one out of twenty. This would be enough for them to make the decision to build a software solution. Dan had to remind them of the potential for false signals if they set their fail criterion that low. If teams follow our tips for setting minimum fail criteria, they can quickly figure out the lowest level at which their idea would fail. This is where they should set the benchmark. The criteria must be set and agreed before teams run their experiments, not after. If teams try to set their criteria after the experiment has been run, then cognitive biases in favor of their ideas will influence them to make bad choices.

Tips for Setting Minimum Fail Criteria

EARLY ADOPTERS	Early adopters are individuals who have a problem that is serious enough for them to be actively looking for a solution. If the team chooses to run their experiment with a group of early adopters, then the fail criteria should be set at a high level and strictly adhered to (e.g. 70%-90% conversion rates). This is because if a group that is regarded as early adopters will not support our assumptions, then our idea has little chance of success.
FIND ANALOGS	Before setting our fail criteria, we can analyze our industry for products, companies or business models that are similar to ours and use their success rates as the basis for our fail criteria. For example, a conversion rate of 5% is considered good for a software-as-a-service or SaaS model.
BACK OF THE NAPKIN	The team can use back of the napkin calculations about what would constitute a profitable business model for them (e.g. target revenue). These numbers need not be accurate but ballpark figures to help us get started. For example, if a team calculates that they need customers to be willing to pay $100 for the product to break even, this can inform how they set their fail criteria. As we research and test our ideas, our ballpark figures will become more accurate and help us set more informed criteria.

TALKING TO HUMANS

We encourage innovators to get out of the building and talk to customers. But customers can also be the greatest source of false signals. When talking to customers, innovators need to be very careful. There are usually a few dynamics at play that can take you in the wrong direction. The first one is *social desirability*. In most social interactions, humans are thinking about the impression they are making on others with their words and actions. Social pressure also means that people may not want to hurt your feelings with negative opinions. So if you present your idea and ask people what they think, they will tell you what they think you want to hear.

The second problem is that people may not have the *ability to introspect* and gain access to what they really think about stuff. However, because we live in a society where people have to give reasons for their choices and behaviors, people will confabulate these reasons. In other words, because you asked, they will come up with something. But even in those rare situations where people have access to their real thoughts and feelings on a subject, they may lack the *language or willingness* to share their thoughts with you. They know what they think, but they do not want to tell you.

Finally, people are terrible at predicting what they will do in the future.[41] During an interview, people can state confidently that they intend to buy your product, sign up for your platform or download your application. However, when the time comes they can behave totally differently. It is not that people are lying. At the time of the interview they may authentically believe they will buy something in the future. But when the prospect of pulling out real money arises, they may not want to do it.

These dynamics are the reasons we do not recommend focus groups as a research tool for innovators. Focus groups exacerbate the dynamics of human interaction in counterproductive ways. They have in them people who are really not sure what they think, trying not to hurt the moderator's feelings, while trying to make a good impression on the other participants. The social pressure for conformity in these situations can be high. This is a recipe for disastrous false signals![42]

Rob Fitzpatrick has written a clever little book about talking to customers entitled *The Mom Test*.[43] In the book, Rob argues that innovators should *not* ask customers questions that if they asked their own mum, she could lie to them. Instead, innovators should only ask customers questions that if they asked their own mum, she would have to tell them the truth. The mom-test should be applied to every question innovators plan to ask customers. Below is a brief guide that teams can use to decide whether their questions are *mom-test-compliant:*

STOP fishing for compliments

Bad Questions:
- Do you think our idea for Product X is a good idea?
- We have this awesome idea for an App... Do you like it?
- This is that secret project we have been working on... What do you think?

These questions are bad because:
- They expose the innovator's ego.
- They make it seem as though the innovator is fishing for compliments.
- This forces people to say something nice to you.

What to do instead:
- Try as much as possible not to talk about your idea.
- Instead, speak to customers about their lives and the problems they have.
- For example, you can ask:
  - *When you are trying to achieve your goals, what challenges do you face?*
  - *Talk me through the last time you tried to solve that problem.*

177

Don't pitch!
Listen and learn

nobody can predict
their future behaviour

Bad Questions:
- Let me tell you what other features our product offers.
- No no, I don't think you get it... our product also does this.

These questions are bad because:
- You are pitching! You have finally found a customer brave enough to tell you that your idea is rubbish and you are pitching!
- So now you are really exposing your ego.
- The customer will tell you whatever you want to hear, to get rid of you.

What to do instead:
- Whatever you do, don't pitch.
- Negative feedback is gold dust. Use it to make lemonade.
- For example, you can ask:
  - Okay, so which problems do you really care about solving?
  - What are you doing right now to solve those problems? Do you have any suggestions we can use to improve our offering?

Bad Questions:
- Would you buy a product that solved this problem?
- How much would you pay for this?

These questions are bad because:
- They are future facing.
- People don't know what they are going to do in the future.
- People will confabulate an answer.

What to do instead:
- Try not to ask about future behavior.
- Instead, run experiments that test whether the customers will really do what they say they will do (e.g. a landing page with a 'Buy Now' button).
- If you have to talk to customers, you can ask:
  - How do you currently deal with this problem?
  - Have you purchased any solutions for your problem?
  - How much is this problem currently costing you to solve?

Adapted from Fitzpatrick, R. (2014). *The Mom Test*: Amazon CreateSpace.

LEARN THEN CONFIRM

Some innovation teams have a methodology bias. For example, some teams only do interviews or focus groups. Other teams hate talking to customers so they are happier running email campaigns or doing online A/B testing. Using just one research method can bias the results you get or the conclusions you reach. For example, talking to customers is often a poor indicator of actual behavior, and running A/B tests may not give you insights into why a particular option is preferred. We recommend that teams triangulate their tests by using more than one method from the innovator's toolbox.

Rob Fitzpatrick and Salim Virani suggest that innovators should *learn* then *confirm*. In other words, talk to customers then get them to do something. For example, if customers give you a strong indication that they have a particular problem they would pay to be solved, then run a second experiment where you ask them to sign a letter of intent, pay a deposit or sign up for a free trial. This will provide clearer evidence of whether you are on the right track. If the customer will not even sign up for a free trial, then the problem to be solved may not be that serious.

As an example, Dan once worked on a news app that was designed to increase the number of articles that get shared. His team went out and talked to customers. The majority of customer said that they don't usually share news but when they do, they share it directly with friends and relatives who they know are interested in that specific topic. After this, Dan and the team then looked at usage data to triangulate their results. They found that the percentage of people sharing news in their app was less than 10%. However, the majority of those people (80%), were sharing using email. This confirmed the interview data and allowed the teams to make more informed product decisions.

Additionally, when we run experiments some of our assumptions will not be supported by the data. In that situation, teams may need to change or adapt their assumptions (i.e. they will need to pivot). Pivots can be dangerous moments for false signals. It is true that we would have made a change on the basis of what we have learned. But just to be sure we are on the right track, we need to *learn* then *confirm*. So a pivot represents a new set of assumptions that need to be tested. Once we have iterated our business model, we need to get out of the building to confirm that our iteration is valid.

179

INNOVATORS + EARLY ADOPTERS = EARLYVANGELISTS

Established companies have a major cultural challenge when it comes to innovation. They are too used to operating at scale. So when new ideas are being developed, the constant questions to innovators are about scaling. How many customers will this serve? How much revenue? How fast will it grow? Clayton Christensen admonishes executives to be *impatient for profit, but patient for growth*. What this means is that executives should push innovators to find a profitable business model before they push for the product to be taken to scale.

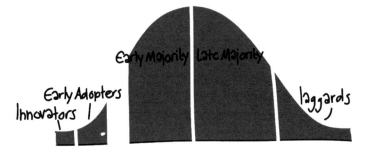

Source: Moore, G. A. (1999). *Crossing the Chasm*. New York: HarperBusiness.

This means that at early on, innovators should not try to engage with the early majority or late majority markets. The quickest way to gain traction is to focus on innovators and early adopters. Steve Blank calls this group the *earlyvangelists*. The criteria for determining whether someone is an earlyvangelist is actually great way to manage false signals. According to Blank, an earlyvangelist:

HAS A PROBLEM
IS AWARE OF HAVING A PROBLEM
HAS BEEN ACTIVELY LOOKING FOR A SOLUTION
HAS PUT TOGETHER A SOLUTION OUT OF PIECE PARTS
HAS OR CAN ACQUIRE A BUDGET

If a customer does not fit this profile, then they are not an earlyvangelist. These criteria can be used as exclusion criteria when selecting customers to test ideas with. They are also useful for helping innovators sharpen their focus, define clear customer jobs-to-be-done, identify target segments and set good fail criteria. As already noted, if an innovation team is testing problem hypotheses with early adopters, they should set very high fail criteria (e.g. 70%-90%). This is so that when the experiment fails, it forces the team to think about who the early adopters really are and how to find them.

Only after validating the business model with early adopters, can innovators start thinking about entering the mass market. Targeting the mass market with untested ideas is a recipe for failure, in public! The aspiration is for ideas to reach profitability or at least break even while still serving the early adopter market. This success provides the momentum that can then propel the product towards sustainable growth.

EXPERIMENTS WITH 'REAL' PRODUCTS

'That will never work here!' This what we often hear from management teams in established companies whenever we present our innovator's toolbox. Among the top reasons given is the assumption that lean innovation only applies to software. When companies make 'real' physical products, they have strong questions about how to run experiments or build minimum viable products.

It is easy to forget that *The Lean Startup* movement was based on the lean manufacturing method developed by Toyota, a car manufacturing company. The idea of getting out of the building is based on Toyota's practice of Genchi Genbutsu, meaning "go and see".[44] The concepts of learning about what customers want, building prototypes and testing them with customers was also pioneered by product design firms such as IDEO, who work mostly on physical products. IDEO shot to fame as a company when it was featured on ABC's *Nightline* using design thinking methods to redesign the shopping cart.

The rise of the maker movement also provides some indication of how lean principles can be applied to physical products. The combination of open-source learning and the proliferation of design thinking principles, has helped spawn a growing movement of inventors, designers, hackers and tinkerers.[45] Powerful technologies such as 3D printing have provided tools for innovators to design and test product ideas without going through the expense of setting up manufacturing capabilities. Open 3D printing platforms like Ponoko provide access to anyone who wants to design and build prototypes affordably. The use of crowdfunding also helps makers test their value propositions before building their products at scale. Indeed, the money raised via such a campaign can be used to fund the development of the product.

practical

safety

flexible

Clearly these startup practices cannot be ported to established companies like for like. However, companies can apply similar principles even as they adapt the tactics. For example, the global fashion retailer Zara has applied lean principles to the way it runs its business.[46] Zara applies 'just-in-time' methods by holding low stocks and updating its collections continuously. New designs can arrive at their stores within fifteen days. Zara releases about a thousand designs to its stores every month. They release just a few items of each design and learn what customers are buying before increasing inventory on any particular item. This approach reduces waste and unsold inventory.[47]

General Electric (GE), is a well known global powerhouse that works in several industries including power, water, oil, gas, aviation, healthcare and transportation. Even in such a large company making complex hardware products, lean innovation methods have been shown to work. GE has been working with Eric Ries to set up FastWorks, which is a lean startup framework for developing new products. Their most famous example of applying this method is a refrigerator which went through several iterations and customer tests before it was manufactured at scale.[48]

The FastWorks process is the antithesis of typical manufacturing where product designs and business plans are made before several thousand products are manufactured and launched. To deliver the fridge using lean startup methods, GE had to redesign their process so that they can make just a few refrigerators to begin with. The process had to allow the GE team to iterate on the fridge several times before it was ready for manufacturing at scale.[49] This involved working with suppliers, manufacturers and even their internal finance teams.

There are unique challenges that face companies making 'real' products when it comes to applying lean innovation. However, there are also some similarities with how the principles are applied to software products. Regardless of the types of product you are making, a company can still apply the core principles of *create-test-learn* and validating business models before taking products to scale. Below are some things companies should consider when applying our innovator's toolbox to 'real' products:

- *Customer Development*: Even when creating physical products, it still important to understand the customer jobs to be done. There is no guarantee that a physical product will succeed by simply having great technology. The Segway was a great piece of technology. The inventors were so convinced of its greatness that they worked on the product in secret without testing it with customers. Their fear was that the idea might get stolen. Investors, including Steve Jobs, were convinced that the product was going to be a great success.[50] The product was indeed a cool idea. But commercial success was not at the levels expected. As such, working on a physical product does not negate the need to get out of the building and do some problem exploration.

- *Can It Be Done*: To a greater extent than software, new physical products often have technical risks. The question of whether the product can be made as expected looms large. As we are writing this, Samsung have just announced that they are scrapping their new Galaxy Note 7 because of issues with exploding batteries.[51] As such, in addition to validating customer needs, there is a need to test and develop capabilities for manufacturing the product.

- *Prototyping*: Before developing manufacturing capabilities, prototyping can be used to test product ideas. Minimum viable products created via prototyping can be used for two purposes. First, we can test our assumptions about whether we are creating a solution that will meet our customers' needs. Second, as our solution specifications emerge, we can start to test our capabilities to deliver the product to the market.

- *Manufacturing & Suppliers*: Once we know what we are going to build, we should start testing early whether our manufacturing capabilities can create the product. It is important to have early conversations with suppliers. The product we have in mind may have to be changed and adapted to suit the available capabilities. If new capabilities have to be created, this should be known early and tested in terms of timing and costs.

- *Distribution*: The storage and distribution of physical products is different to that of software, which needs no real physical space. As part of our business model validation, we have to test our channels for delivering value to customers. We need to know early the potential challenges and costs involved so we can include this in our pricing models.

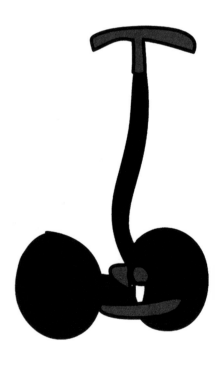

- *Pre-Orders*: While crowdfunding may not always be an option for an established company, getting pre-orders is certainly an option. There are two routes to this. We can get pre-orders early while we are still testing customer interest. This can be done with a full money back guarantee. If brand equity is a key challenge, then pre-orders can begin once we have validated our ability to create and deliver the value; but before we actually start manufacturing at scale. This will serve as a final test of the market potential of our product.

- *High Customer Expectations*: When we start to make and distribute our product it is important to realize that customer expectations in terms of quality are much higher for physical products than for software. We anticipate that Samsung's problems with the Note 7 will be more harmful to its brand than the famous Fail Whale was to Twitter's brand. As such, as we start to ramp up production, quality assurance should become a key focus.

Prototyping can be done using rapid *create-test-learn* loops. Jake Knapp's five-day sprint methodology can be used for this purpose.[52] However, some of the challenges with physical products mean that there will be times when our *create-test-learn* loops require much longer lead times. This is fine, as long as we are going as fast as we can. It may be difficult to iterate at the same speed as a software team, but we have found that most teams can go much faster than they think. Furthermore, several experiments can be run in parallel. This means that while we wait for results from an experiment with a long lead time (e.g. a prototype from a supplier), we can be testing our other business model assumptions.

183

Testing Ideas Without Hurting the Brand

Unlike startups who are usually just starting out in business, large companies have trading histories and reputations. Part of this reputation is captured in the company's brand. A lot of work goes into developing and protecting this brand, and rightly so. Customer relationships are also an important part of this mix. Sales Directors are wary of any activity that might compromise their relationships with customers. So when they hear an innovation team talking about 'moving fast and breaking things', their reaction is "...over my dead body!"

This is not an unreasonable response. Goodwill and reputation are hard for a company to regain once they are lost. As such, it is important to ensure that whatever we do with innovation does not damage our company's reputation. This tension between having to test ideas before we scale, and protecting the brand is another expression of the innovation paradox. How well this tension is resolved will determine a company's ability to innovate successfully. Below are some guidelines on how innovators can test ideas without hurting their company's brand and reputation.

- *Informed Consent*: Deception can hurt a brand. If customers find out that they were unknowingly part of an experiment, they may not be pleased. One way to deal with this is to tell customers that you are running a test upfront and ask them directly whether they are willing to help. Customers who participate in interviews, usability tests or concierge experiments often do so knowing what they are getting into. Of course once people know they are part of an experiment, they tend to modify their behavior slightly. In such situations, it is key to ensure that our questions, tools and methods are '*mom-test compliant*'.

- *Consent In Advance*: Another solution is have a pool of customers who consent in advance to take part in future experiments. These customers can also be asked to consent that when we run experiments we do not have to divulge to them details that are critical to the validity of our experiments (e.g. whether or not they are part of a control condition). In exchange, we can guarantee customers that we will not harm or embarrass them. This is similar to medical research. Participants consent to be part of a medical trial with the understanding that they may be part of the group that unknowingly receives the placebo.

- *Alpha Beta*: Another way of gaining informed consent from customers is by making it clear that the product is still in 'beta'; and that you are actively looking for customer feedback. This is easiest for online products that can simply be labelled as 'beta' on the logo or landing page. For example, Google's Gmail was in beta for over five years, becoming the subject of geeky internet jokes. However, in that time, Google were able to comfortably test various features such as integrated chat, anti-spam technology, group chat and video chat.[53]

- *Early Adopters*: Connected to consent is the issue of who we run our experiments with. In the early stages of the innovation journey we do not recommend targeting the mass market. If we make mistakes in the wider market, then our brand is in trouble. We recommend running experiments with early adopters. These individuals have the problem we are trying to solve, are aware of having that problem and have been actively looking for a solution. These customers are more likely to be willing to help us by trying out our solutions and giving us feedback. If we succeed in developing a solution that solves their problem, these early adopters are more likely to actively refer others to our product (i.e. they may become earlyvangelists). Such positive recommendations will benefit the brand.

- *Innovation Sandbox*: If we have an online product that is already getting used by customers, then we need to ensure that our experiments do not harm our customers' experience. Creating an innovation sandbox can help with this challenge. We can create an area of our website where we test new features by releasing them to only a few customers to begin with. If we see that the features are well received, we can then roll them out to all our customers; and if there is a problem, we can roll the features back, adapt or kill them.

- *White Label*: Another way to test ideas without harming the brand is not to use the brand at all. Going off-brand can save the company from the media fanfare that is often involved in new product launches. When we go off-brand we can test our ideas and fail fast quietly. Going off-brand also allows an idea to be tested on its own merits. When Toyota were thinking about launching a gas payments platform, a key question for them was whether anyone would care about the product if it wasn't a Toyota product. So they quickly set up an off-brand website and drove traffic to it via Facebook ads.[54]

- *An Innovation Brand*: Being associated with innovation can also add equity to a brand. As such, one way to test ideas is to create an innovation brand that is associated with the main company brand. Examples of this include Google X, Telefonica Labs and Intuit Labs. This makes clear to customers that any product with the innovation brand associated with it is still being tested. This lowers expectations, while improving a company's reputation for being innovative.

- *Debrief and Reward*: After running experiments, another way to improve your brand reputation is to debrief and reward customers. After each test, explain to customers why you are running the experiment, why you value their contribution and why you could not tell them everything at the beginning. After that, ask if it is still okay for you to include their data in your analysis. In addition to this, give customers great rewards for being part of your experiment. These can include access to some of your products or services for free.

185

The above are some of the things you can do to mitigate the effects of experiments on your brand. If your company operates in highly regulated environments such as banking and health, then testing ideas can be more challenging. The best way to resolve this challenge is to do some upfront work with the legal, finance, brand management, sales and marketing to develop guidelines for what innovators can and cannot do when running experiments. These guidelines should be simple enough for all to understand, but cover the most important potential challenges for the company. The rule can then be that, if innovators want to run experiments outside the guidelines, they should then get clearance from the relevant departments.

READY TO SCALE

The key to running innovation experiments is speed. We want to run as many experiments as we can before we run out of budget. But we are not just running these experiments for the sake of it. Our ultimate goal is to consolidate the knowledge into a repeatable and scalable business model. We are codifying what works and doesn't work before we launch our business at scale. As such, tracking progress towards that end goal is key for innovation success. Teams that do not focus on their overarching business goals are more likely to spend their time running experiments, proud to be using lean innovation but making no real progress.

At the most granular level of tracking progress are the *reporting KPIs*. The experiment canvas we presented earlier serves this purpose. First, a team can track the experiments they are running and the outcomes from those experiments. Activity metrics in this case include the number of experiments run, number of customer interviews and number of prototypes built. Impact metrics include assumptions validated/not validated and decisions made (i.e. pivot or persevere). We can also measure the speed and cost of the experiments we are running (e.g. cost-per-learning, learning velocity and validation velocity).

In addition to reporting KPIs, we can track progress along business model milestones using *governance KPIs*. We have defined innovation as the combination of new ideas with sustainable business models. A business model is sustainable when we have made something people want and we can deliver this value profitably. As such, innovators should use their experiments to:

- Understand customer needs and their jobs to be done.
- Develop a solution that meets customer needs and helps them complete their jobs to be done.
- Confirm that customers will pay more for the solution than it costs to create it.
- Find the right channels and partners to deliver value to our customers.
- Make sure that we have found a market large enough to grow customer numbers, revenues and profits in the future.

When innovation teams review their risky assumptions and make decisions about what to test first, this innovation journey should be taken into account. There is no point in developing, testing or scaling a solution before the customer jobs to be done are well understood. There is also no point in testing our channels or revenue models before we know what product we are going to be selling. Innovation is a non-linear process with many false starts and do-overs. However, there is a hierarchy of knowledge that every team must systematically acquire before taking a product to scale.

To manage investments in innovation teams, a company can create submission forms and scorecards. At Pearson, they have pioneered the concept of a *product council*. This is an investment decision making board that incrementally invests in innovation projects using product lifecycle stage-gates. To unlock investment, teams have to demonstrate success and progress in answering key questions along the innovation journey. For example, a team will not receive investment to build and test a solution until they show evidence that they have validated customer needs. In line with our innovation framework, these forms and scorecards can be based on the following key criteria.

187

TEST IDEAS	Problem	Has the team validated customer needs and identified the customer job to be done?
	Solution	Has the team tested their solution with customers, found that the solution meets their needs and that they are willing to pay for it?
	Business	Has the team found a sustainable way to create their product, the right channels to deliver it to customers and the right price point for profitability?
	Other Criteria	Market size, competition, trends (social, technological, legal and economical).

We use *Global KPIs* to measure how well our investments in innovation are contributing to the health of the company. Testing ideas provides some early indication of potential benefits. This is most clear during the later sub-stages at which we are testing the business model. Activity metrics for global KPIs include number of products per innovation stage (i.e. *problem, solution, business*) and percentage of products aligned to the innovation thesis. In terms of impact metrics, we can start to get some early indication of process improvements, new market segments and innovation conversion (i.e. through the number of old customers switching to our new offerings).

The number of validated new business models that are ready for scale is also a great global KPI indicating the health of a company's innovation pipeline. Our experience is that very few companies can point to a pipeline of new business models that they are getting ready to scale. This does not bode well for future revenue growth. A balanced portfolio with products at various stages of their innovation journey is essential. However, even with validated business models, the transition from testing to scaling has to be managed well. It is easy to mismanage this process and ruin potentially great products. How to scale ideas is the focus of the next chapter.

Innovation Accounting for Testing Ideas

KPIs	ACTIVITY METRICS	IMPACT METRICS
REPORTING	number of experiments run	experiment results
	number of customer conversations	decisions made (*pivot or persevere*)
	number of customer interviews	cost-per-learning
	number of customer observations	time-cost-per-learning
	number of prototypes/MVPs built	learning velocity
	number of hackathons/design sprints	validation velocity
GOVERNANCE	number of products in pipeline	stage-gate criteria
	number of applications submitted	assumption-to-knowledge ratio
	number of decisions made	% of products at problem-solution fit
	number of products moving stages	% of products at product-market fit
	average amount spent per stage	% of products ready for scale
GLOBAL	number of products by innovation type (*core, adjacent, transformational*)	process improvement metrics
		number of patents granted
	number of products per substage (*problem, solution, business*)	new business models ready to scale
	% of products aligned to thesis	cost savings
	number of patent filings	innovation conversion
	partnerships and collaborations	new market segment entered

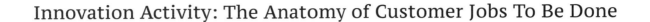

Innovation Activity: The Anatomy of Customer Jobs To Be Done

Customer observations and interviews are a great way to understand customer jobs to be done. When we get out of the building we have to explore customer jobs as processes, not single events. This understanding can help innovators add value to the customer at each stage of the job process. To that end, we have developed a method for magnifying and dissecting customer jobs to be done.

After getting out of the building to explore customer needs, a cross-functional team can then spend two to three hours in a workshop using our magnifier canvas with sticky notes and Sharpies. At the beginning of the session, we have the team identify the job to be done they want to focus on and place a sticky note in the designated box on the canvas. Then we ask the team to gather around the canvas and start brainstorming each element of the chosen job to be done.

TRIGGER

 DEFINE JOB

 PLAN JOB

 EXECUTE JOB

What triggered the job?
Was it an intrinsic or extrinsic trigger?
Was it a result of a previous Job?
Is this Job addressing a need or pain?

How does the customer define the job?
What is the temporal component of the customer's expectation?
What is the object of the customer's expectation?
What is the context of the customer's expectation?

How is the customer planning the job?
Are there any inputs that need to be prepared before executing the job?

How is the job being executed?

JOB TO BE DONE

ALTER

 ASSESS OUTCOME

 CONCLUDE JOB

Is an expectation's component going to be altered?
Which one?
Is the solution altered?
Is the job altered?
When is the customer most likely to alter something?

How is the customer assessing the outcome?
Is the customer assessing all outcomes?
When is the customer assessing the outcomes?

How is the customer disposing of the job?
Is there a new complementary job that the customer is trying to get done?
How is the customer feeling?

- *Trigger:* First, we ask the team to list the possible causes that might trigger a person to initiate that particular job. For example, the triggering source can be extrinsic (e.g. advertising, word of mouth, peer pressure). The source can also be intrinsic with regards to a specific need that the individual wants to fulfill. This need can be the result of a previous job or an ongoing pain point.

- *Define Job*: Next, the team thinks of how the customer might define the job and lists possibilities in the relevant block. The team needs to take a customer perspective on this task and understand that how customers define their jobs forms the foundation for purchasing decisions. In fact, a major part of the definition step is the setting of expectations about outcomes.

- *Plan Job*: Following the definition, the team needs to think about how the customer plans the job. This includes how the customer prepares the inputs or the environment in which the job will be executed. From mapping out this step, the team can later think about the ways in which planning can be simplified.

- *Execute Job*: Although this might seem like the most trivial step, the team still needs to map out how the job is currently executed by the customer. This is because there may be opportunities to improve or add value to this.

- *Assess Outcome*: Following the 'execution' step, the team then captures how the customer assesses the quality of the job against the expectations they set earlier. Customers often compare the results obtained to the results they expected. This can reveal how satisfied customers are with the outcome.

- *Alter*: Innovation teams need to be aware that mid-course corrections happen with a lot of jobs. This is because customers continually assess outcomes while the job is still being executed. If the results match their expectations, the customer can move onto concluding the job. But if the results are not satisfactory, they may have to go for alternatives, or accept the lower standard. As such, the team needs to think about what happens if the outcome of the job differs from expectations. This can be an opportunity to create value.

- *Conclude Job*: Finally, the team then needs to capture the actions that the customer does to conclude the job. With trivial jobs the conclusion step can be very simple. However, with more complex jobs the conclusion step may very well be a long process. Even though the majority of customers may not notice the conclusion step of a job, a team can add value by developing solutions that provide a simplified conclusion process.

Magnifying the customer job to be done is a great way to improve solution ideation. This is because reviewing every step of the job reveals several opportunities to add value. As such, before teams start thinking about solutions, we recommend that they spend time analyzing the anatomy to the job to be done.

Alessandro Vigilante

VICE PRESIDENT AND HEAD OF US WEST COAST INNOVATION ECOSYSTEM AT FIDELITY INVESTMENTS

Alessandro Vigilante is a VP at Fidelity Investments where he is responsible for identifying the most relevant technology companies in the Silicon Valley, assessing them and bringing them to the attention of the relevant Fidelity executives. Before moving to California, Alessandro worked in London, in the same role for Europe. Prior to Fidelity, Alessandro held a number of important executive positions where he has helped to develop, design and launch a number of enterprise level flagship products for telecommunication companies. He is a judge and mentor for a number of Startups Accelerators and an MBA guest lecturer on Corporate Entrepreneurship at SDA Bocconi (Milan, Italy) and IE Business School (Madrid, Spain). In this conversation, Alessandro speaks to us about how to manage the challenges of running experiments in large enterprises with B2B business models.

CS: SO YOU HAVE SOME EXPERIENCE WITH TESTING IDEAS IN LARGE ENTERPRISES?
AV: Yes. Basically, back in 2011 I set up the innovation team at a large B2B telecommunication infrastructure company. We set it up from scratch and ran it for three years.

CS: WHAT TYPES OF EXPERIMENTS WERE YOU DOING IN A B2B TELECOMS COMPANY?
AV: The experiments were typically looking for disruptive technologies that could help us go to market much quicker. Basically, we were experimenting with those technologies. The reality was that once the prototype was built and once the business case was made, we still had to go through the approval of the business unit to bring things to market. From sales, marketing, product manage-

ment, and so on. Again, what we were basically doing was finding technology partners that were capable of working with us on stuff that wasn't available commercially, and then to help us basically build the business case and allow us to bring this technology to market earlier. That's what we did.

CS: WERE YOU EXPERIMENTING JUST ON THE PRODUCT SIDE, OR WERE YOU EXPERIMENTING ALSO ON MARKET SIDE?

AV: We were experimenting also on the market side. There were two types of experiments we were doing on the market side, we called them hard prototypes and soft prototypes. Hard prototypes were things that really existed and that we were actually bringing to customers; however, customers could not buy them. Customers could look at them, could join a test for a specific time. It was sort of a beta where customers were asked to do a survey at the end or we were actually interviewing them. It was B2B so don't imagine mass market approach. It was two or three customers, having a conversation with them. Soft prototypes were used in the case of an underdeveloped technology or when the technology wasn't available at all, and we could not technically build something to show our customers. In this case we were relying mainly on wireframes.

CS: HOW WERE LEGAL, COMPLIANCE AND MARKETING INVOLVED IN SUPPORTING THE EXPERIMENTS?

AV: In general, legal was okay with us doing experiments. Some people didn't like the approach, the regulatory folks in particular. In some cases, the regulatory team actually wanted to stop us from doing things. The reality is that, at first, I just ignored them. I had a massive advantage of having the sponsorship of the CEO. Any problem I was getting, was basically just a matter of escalating. Just a matter of saying, "Dear Regulatory Director, if you have a problem with this, just speak to the CEO, or to my boss," who was the CTO at the time. Let me say, was it a constructive relationship with them? No. Was I playing dirty? Yes. But it worked.

The reason why I could play dirty was because we would stop building after the prototype stage. Once the prototype was proven, we were basically bringing this into the business simulator, and the business simulator was then responsible for bringing these to market. We were sort of handing over the problem of legal and regulatory for bringing this to market. For the experiment it wasn't important. Later when I changed roles - I was leading the strategy and business development department and we were also tasked with bringing the ideas to market - I actually had to work with legal and regulatory at a very different level.

Two things made a tremendous difference. The first was my boss, who was really supportive of the experimental approach. The second thing was finding people in legal and regulatory that were on-board with our method or at least wanted to know more about our method, and try working with them. To sum it up, if you talk about legal and regulatory, yes, in general they are a problem when it comes to experimenting, but if you go down one level and look for specific individuals in those teams that can help you, and that are highly regarded within your organization, if you're lucky enough, you can find those individuals and bypass the official process. The official process of saying go to the gate of the legal team and get someone assigned, or the gate of the regulatory team, and so on and so forth. Well, actually if you build one-to-one relationship with the people in those organizations that you know can make it happen, things are extremely easier. From the moment I found an idea to the moment we launched, it was less than three months, all with the support of legal and regulatory.

CS: HOW WERE YOU IDENTIFYING THESE PEOPLE?
AV: On one hand we were trying to understand the degree of impact on the organization an individual had and on the other, how cooperative they were when presented with our method. Let me give you an example: once I did some revenue share agreements with companies that legal would have labelled as completely unstable - basically a startup. We had to protect against data bankruptcy. We had to protect, actually we had to gain base, so we had to add some equity back in case they are being sold or their value increases. We had to hand over regulatory responsibilities for the businesses that we were delivering. We had to look into the data privacy for our customers that we were sharing with them.

It was some pretty complex stuff. Nonetheless, the guys that we identified within the legal department were amazing from this point of view, because they were very oriented towards innovation, and they had the authority to do things within the organization. What this means is that at some point, when I had to go to the head of the department, to get a signature, because he was the only one authorized to sign on behalf of the group, he signed immediately because he knew that the document that I was bringing to his attention was something that I didn't write myself and it was actually written by someone in his team.

CS: HOW DID YOU SET UP YOUR SUCCESS CRITERIA FOR THE EXPERIMENTS?
AV: We started from the business case - we knew how much financial return was expected from an idea from the business case and we just worked backwards from there.

CS: WHAT HAPPENED AFTER AN EXPERIMENT IF THE SUCCESS CRITERIA WASN'T MET?
AV: We were updating the business case and letting the idea owners and managers know that they will not meet their business case estimate with the current idea - it was up to them to decide whether or not 'kill' the idea or they would pivot it and we would start a new experiment.

'Sustainable growth is characterized by one simple rule:
New customers come from the actions of past customers.'

Eric Ries, Author of *The Lean Startup*

CHAPTER EIGHT

Scaling Ideas

In November and December 2015, Tendayi worked with an innovation team from a large global bank. The team had developed a number of minimum viable products that were receiving positive responses from customers. The product ideas were great and some had the potential to positively move the needle within the bank. However, the team's progress had stalled, with only a couple of ideas gaining traction with management. The team had been busy developing prototypes and testing ideas. But when they tried to scale their ideas, there were only a few executives there waiting to embrace and celebrate their progress.

Innovators working in large companies often think that they have an advantage when it comes to scaling ideas. The company they work for is already operating at scale, with a reliable business model that is generating revenues and profits. So these intrapreneurs don't worry about growth until they have finished testing their idea. They think that once they have created a new product with promise, it can simply be plugged into the mother ship's scaling machine… and voila! They have built a rocket and now all they need is the rocket fuel.

199

Large companies have more financial and human capital resources than startups. However, it is not inevitable that these resources will result in the successful scaling of any product. When a new product is highly similar to the current crop of successful products, an established company can easily use its current resources to take it to scale. However, those same resources may not be as useful at scaling transformational innovations. Successful growth is not inevitable just because a team is part of a large company. There are several challenges that innovators need to manage and overcome before they can achieve success.

The Functional Matrix

The first challenge to address is whether the core business itself is structured appropriately for innovation management. As we discussed earlier, quite a number of large companies are set up as functional organizations. In such companies, functions such as marketing, engineering and finance are siloed from each other. Products are then managed across these functions in a matrix structure.[55] What this often means is that there are no product level or division level P&Ls.

In a functional organization, financial numbers tend to accrue to the company's main P&L. This increases the role of the CEO and executive team in making decisions on products. However, the lack of product level P&Ls can hide a lot of non-performing products. Since everything accrues upwards, the main goal becomes to improve the overall profitability of the company. There is no specific person that is responsible for the performance of any single product. As such, very few people know with sufficient precision, which products are losing or making the most money.

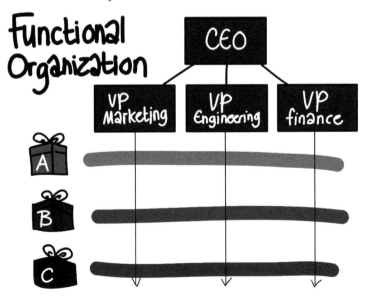

It is challenging for a cross-functional team that has been working on an innovation project, to find a comfortable entry point back into a functional organization. They will be immediately faced with siloes and handover issues. Functional organizations are also problematic from an innovation lifecycle perspective. Without product level P&Ls, it is difficult to measure how much traction a specific product is getting in the market, and whether a company should continue to pour resources into the product. To be fair, it is not totally impossible for a functional organization to get to product level P&Ls or to innovate. Rather, it is a challenge because the company is not structurally organized to manage products individually along their innovation lifecycle.

Our framework works best in organizations that have the capability to track specific products along their innovation journeys. We have found that an innovation ecosystem is much easier to set up and manage in large companies that are structured as divisional organizations.[56] In such a structure, products are organized as mini-companies with their own marketing, engineering and finance. There are some centralized functions such as HR, infrastructure and legal. However, each product or division has its own P&L and specific individuals that are accountable for success.[57]

A great example of the divisional approach is the retail giant Whole Foods Market. Each Whole Foods store is an autonomous profit center with its own P&L.[58] Within the store, teams that work in various departments such as produce or deli, are also autonomous and responsible for the success of their department. There is transparency within the company, such that different stores can see how other stores or departments are performing; and which products are selling well. This model has been getting adjusted over time to cope with scale and competition;[59] but it has helped Whole Foods succeed by serving local needs and sourcing local products.

Divisional Organization

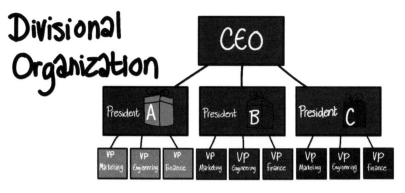

In divisional organizations, managers can see which products are at which stage of their innovation lifecycle. This creates both the autonomy and transparency that is critical for innovation success. With product level P&Ls, it is also easier for innovation teams to manage the growth of their product. Scaling does not happen in one big bang. There is constant work to be done fine tuning the engine of growth and making sure that it is working well. This means that innovators need to have access to growth metrics, so that they can track whether their business model improvements are having the desired impact.

Transition Management

For teams that work in innovation labs that are set up separately from the core business, the attempt to scale new products can be a moment of truth. As they look to their company to provide resources and support to scale, they can find themselves in choppy political waters. A lot of innovation teams tend to find out late in the game that nobody in the company is interested in their products. They are often disappointed to watch their great ideas with a validated business model become orphans.

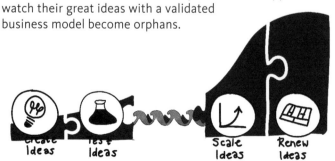

Create Ideas   Test Ideas   Scale Ideas   Renew Ideas

We are strong advocates for building an innovation ecosystem within a company, even if the innovation work happens in a separate lab. Innovation labs that run invisible guerilla movements have no choice but to become visible if they want their ideas to get sufficient resources to support scaling. Our approach ensures that the work being done in the labs is aligned to the company's strategic goals (i.e. innovation thesis and balanced portfolio). This increases the chances that management will make the decision to transition products from the lab to the main organization.

But even with strategic alignment, we have learned that it is critical to have the involvement of key stakeholders, early in the life of an innovation project. The involvement of key stakeholders helps the innovation team to learn quickly whether the company has divisions or managers that will be willing to invest in taking the product to scale. The innovation team that Tendayi worked with at the large global bank, eventually put in place a rule that they would no longer take on any innovation projects that did not have a business sponsor from the main company involved. Over time they have been learning that having a sponsor makes it easier to later find support and resources for scaling ideas.

Spin-Out/Spin-In

Transitioning products into the main company is not the only option available to innovation labs. There is also the option to *spin-out*, rather than *spin-in* successful innovations. New products that are ready to scale can be set up as separate companies or autonomous divisions within the company. Well managed spin-outs provide innovation teams with the independence to manage the growth of their product. However, even this decision making will involve senior executives.

Managing spin-outs is a complex process with many factors to consider. However, from a scaling perspective, we believe there are two overarching criteria that can be used to make decisions. The first criterion concerns whether the product idea is aligned with our strategic goals (i.e. thesis and portfolio). If the product is not aligned with strategy then the company must explore options to divest from the project or sell the technology to other companies. If the product is aligned with strategy, then a second criterion comes into play; i.e. does the company already possesses the capacity and capabilities to scale the product?

If the company has the capabilities to scale, then it makes sense to spin the new product back into the company. However, if the company does not have the capabilities to scale the product, and there is no real commitment to develop the capabilities within the current business, then it makes sense

to spin-out the new product as a separate entity. Regardless whether a product is spun-in or spun-out, a disciplined innovation management process must be followed. Spun-in products must not have their growth stifled by traditional management practices; and spin-outs must not be left to wander in the wilderness without proper strategic guidance.

COMPANY SCALING CAPABILITY		ALIGNED TO STRATEGY	
		LOW	HIGH
HIGH		DIVEST/SELL	Spin-in
LOW		DIVEST/SELL	Spin-Out

A Different Language

Effective innovation management requires people in a company to speak the same language around products, business models and innovation stages. The challenge we have found is that innovation teams sometimes speak a different language than their colleagues in the main business. We teach innovation teams to be able to understand and describe their engines of growth (i.e. sticky, viral, paid). What we have learned, with some surprise, is that a lot of established companies do not have a lexicon to describe their growth engines; despite the fact that they are running an already successful business at scale!

Not having a shared lexicon around growth engines can create problems for innovation teams. Managers from the core business can fail to understand the growth needs of new products.

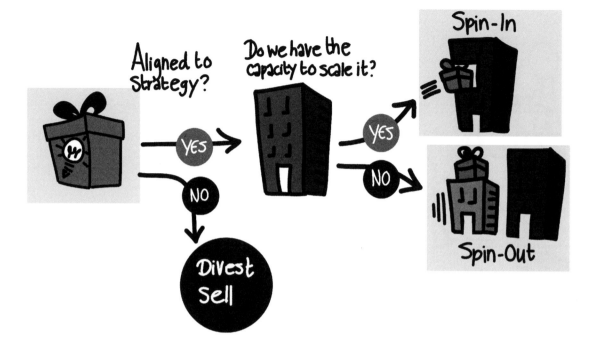

Instead, they will try to force new products to scale via the same distribution channels and sales methods they have always used. This can be a challenge when large companies acquire startups, then try to 'achieve synergies' by making the newly acquired team use the company's core capabilities to scale. If the startup has been using a different engine of growth, 'achieving synergies' can actually mean lower growth rates or even failure.

The point of testing our ideas is for the market to tell us the right channels and engines of growth to use. These should not be predetermined by the existing structures of the main company. If we learn that the best way to scale a product is different for what our company has traditionally done, it is then critical that the company develops the capacity and knowledge to manage this new growth engine; or spin-out the innovation

team as a standalone company or autonomous division. To align language, we believe that it is important for managers to understand the different engines of growth.

Engines of Growth

An innovation team can perform one-time actions that increase customer numbers and drive revenues (e.g. a Super Bowl advert). However, these one-time actions may not lead to sustainable growth. To scale their products in a sustainable way, innovation teams need *traction*. A product can be defined as having traction when the actions of current customers consistently drive new customer acquisition and revenue growth. In other words, the team has to develop a repeatable system that is not reliant on one-time stunts to drive customers to their product. In *The Lean Startup*, Eric Ries describes three main engines of growth that can be applied to most products.

Retention Rate = ((CE-CN)/CS)) X 100:

- CE = number of customers at end of a certain period
- CN = number of new customers acquired during that period
- CS = number of customers at start of that period

Let's imagine a subscription product that tracks its retention on a monthly basis. They start a particular month with 1220 subscribers. During that month they lose 96 customers, but also get 240 new subscriptions. At the end of that month, they will have 1364 customer in total. According to the formula above:

- 1364 - 240 = 1124
- 1124/1220 = .92
- .92 X 100 = 92%

THE STICKY ENGINE

With the sticky engine, the key behavior that drives growth is whether customers keep coming back to use our product. Delivering amazing value is the most reliable way to maintain customer loyalty. With loyal customers, our product will have good retention rates, which increases the likelihood of sustainable growth. If the rate at which the product acquires and keeps new customers is greater than the rate at which customers abandon the product, then scale will be achieved.

The ability to retain customers is particularly important for membership or subscription based products. It is also important for products that require repeat purchasing, such as dogfood or shaving razors. Jeff Haden in *Inc. Magazine* describes a simple formula that can be used to calculate a product's retention rate:[60]

This product has a 92% retention rate (or an 8% churn rate). Such a product can grow customer numbers by slowly adding a few customers every month. For every hundred customers it acquires, at least 92 will stick around for a period. Whether 92% is a good retention rate depends on the product and the costs of acquiring or keeping customers. The goal for an innovation team is to achieve their optimal retention rate by fine tuning their engine of growth over time.

- *Purchase Frequency*: This represents the average amount of purchases that are made by a single customer during our defined time period. It is calculated by adding together the total amount of purchases we received; then dividing that number by the total number of unique customers we served.
- *Customer Value*: This is the average monetary value that a single customer brings to the product over a certain period of time. This is calculated by multiplying the purchase value with the purchase frequency.
- *Customer Lifespan*: This is the average length of time that a customer stays with the product before they stop making purchases.

Customer Lifetime Value (CLV) is then calculated by multiplying our customer value with the customer lifespan:

205

THE PAID ENGINE

With the paid engine, the key customer behavior that drives growth is the amount of money they spend on our product during a certain period. This growth engine relies on paid marketing, advertising or a sales force. As such, there are costs associated with acquiring new customers. To achieve sustainable growth, the cost of customer acquisition must be less than the financial value that those customers bring over their lifetime using the product. According to Kevin Donnelly on the Shopify Blogs, you need the following elements in order to calculate your *customer lifetime value* (CLV):[61]

- *Purchase Value*: This is the average amount a customer spends when they order the product. It is calculated by adding together the total amount of money we receive over a certain period (e.g. a month), and dividing that amount by the total number of orders that were placed.

Once we know the lifetime value of our customers, we can now make decisions about the sustainability of our growth engine. We just need to answer one key question: what is the average cost of acquiring a customer? These costs can be calculated by dividing the amount we spend on marketing with the total number of customers we acquire.[62] If the cost of acquiring a customer is less than their lifetime value, then our engine of growth is working well. The actions of customers - in this case the amount of money they are spending with us - can pay for our engine to acquire new customers.

- *Conversion Rate*: This is the average number of new customers that respond to the outreach by purchasing or subscribing to our product. This is calculated by dividing the total number of new customers that respond, with the total number of new customers reached within a certain period. For example, if each current customer reaches six people on average and only three of those people respond, then the conversion rate is 50% or .50.

The viral coefficient is then calculated by multiplying the average reach metric with the conversion rate. So in the example above, the average reach is six people and the conversion rate is .50; meaning that the viral coefficient is 6 x .50 = 3. If a product has a viral coefficient greater than 1, then it has a great engine of growth and it will grow customer numbers exponentially.

THE VIRAL ENGINE

With the viral engine, the key behavior that drives growth is the extent to which customers are willing to market our product for us. This marketing can be done via word of mouth; i.e. customers actively referring new customers to our product. Customers can also market our product inadvertently as a side-effect of using it; i.e. current customer usage activity exposes new customers to our product. To measure how well our viral engine is working, we need to calculate the *viral coefficient*. To make that calculation, innovation teams need the following metrics:

- *Average Reach*: This is the average number of new customers that a single current customer reaches (e.g. by inviting them to use our product). Reach is calculated by dividing the total number of customers you currently have using the product, with the total number of new customers that have been reached within a certain period.

Viral Coefficient = Average Reach X Conversion Rate

The speed at which a product will scale depends on the length of its *viral loop*; i.e. the time it takes for current customers to reach new customers and get conversions. Using the example above, if the product started with a thousand customers, has a viral coefficient of 3, and the viral loop is one month; this means that after the first month the product will have four thousand customers, the second month 13 000 customers, the third month 40 000 customers and so on. If the viral loop holds, then after ten months, the product will have over 22 million customers! These amazing rates of growth explain the rapid rise of social networks such as Facebook and Twitter.

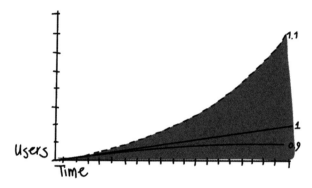

Sustainable Traction

Growth engines are powerful tools for understanding how products can be taken to scale. Product teams can use more than one growth engine to scale their idea, and they often do. However, we feel that it's important to at least identify one main driver of growth. This is because innovators tend to drown in growth metrics. Focusing on one main engine, especially during the early stages of growth, helps to ensure that the team does not suffer from data analysis paralysis. Instead, the team can focus on the few key metrics that matter.

In that regard, it is important to recognize that all metrics are not created equal. Innovators always need to be reminded why they do their work. Beyond vanity metrics, such as the number of customers using our product, the ultimate measure of success

is whether we are able to create value and deliver it profitably. A great viral coefficient with a low churn rate means that we are able to increase our customer numbers and levels of engagement. This may indicate that we have a great product, but on its own this is not an indicator that we have a great business model.

We have seen products that are growing customer numbers; but each customer they are getting is not providing sufficient revenues to cover their costs. While they can boast about their popularity with customers, such a product will still fail because the business model does not work. The ultimate measure of whether our growth engine has been successfully optimized is reaching break even or profitability.

Created Value > Captured Value > = Cost of Value Delivery[63]

In *Scaling Lean*, Ash Maurya presents a great *value equation* for measuring sustainable traction. First, our product needs to create more value for customers than the value we capture back from them. This value-for-money perception is key to gaining loyal customers. Second, we need to ensure that our costs for delivering value to customers are less than the value we capture back from them. This means that over time we can reach break even and profitability. A great *growth engine* coupled with a working *value equation* means that our product has sustainable traction.

Premature Optimization

During the early stages of innovation, *premature scaling* is the challenge that innovators have to guard against. However, once they have found something that works, innovators have to deal with a new challenge; i.e. *premature optimization*. When product teams first enter the growth phase, they immediately come under the pressure of expectations from management. The team have found a business model that works. So now management expects growth rates and profit returns that are similar to other products in the core portfolio.

207

This pressure to grow fast forces teams to focus on optimizing rather than tuning their growth engine. The problem with premature optimization is that during the early stages of innovation, the team has been working mostly with early adopters. The transition to the main market needs to be managed well. Mainstream customers are more demanding in terms of product quality and reliable service. The channels and marketing messages to reach them may also be a little different. Furthermore, the goal is not just to scale as fast as possible with the product as it is; we want to scale and get better as we grow.[64] As such, the same innovation disciplines of *create-test-learn* apply even as we take our ideas to scale. Premature optimization happens when teams abandon this iterative approach and focus on just executing their growth plans.

Within our innovation framework, scaling ideas is broken into three sub-stages. The first sub-stage focuses on *tuning the engine*. The goal here is to make sure that the business model is still working as expected when the product transitions to the mass market and the team is growing. The team focuses their attention on refining their value equation and growth engine.

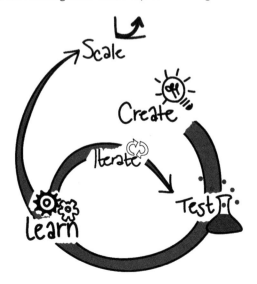

The questions they are tackling mostly concern their margins (i.e. cost structures and revenues) and channels into the main market. They are looking to create a repeatable process before accelerating their growth.

Once the team is satisfied that their business model can work at scale, they can move on to *accelerating growth*. Now the company can pour resources and energy into grabbing as much market share as possible. It is important that the team executes their growth strategy to reach the market, create awareness and generate sales. However, even as we accelerate growth, the *create-test-learn* loop allows us to sense and respond to any changes happening in the market and improve our product. The team must also monitor its environment for competitors and changes in customer preferences.

Every product inevitably reaches its peak where growth slows down. The market is saturated and the product has become a cash cow. *Exploitation* is this final sub-stage of scaling ideas. The goal here is to generate as much value from our cash cows as possible, before moving on to new opportunities. At this stage, it is okay for the company to focus most of their energy on optimizing costs and other elements of their business model. We call this activity *mature optimization* because this is the right time to place the majority of our focus on execution. What is clear from our approach is that scaling ideas is not simply a matter of increasing investments in an innovation project. Taking new products to scale must be managed systematically using an iterative approach. In the early stages of growth, teams may have to slow down in order to grow faster during the later stages. In *Scaling Up Excellence*,[65] Robert Sutton and Huggy Rao describe scaling as not just an 'air war' but a 'ground war'. Innovation teams need to have the grit to take systematic steps to ensure that customer value keeps improving as the product scales. Sutton and Rao note that:

"Scaling is akin to running a long race where you don't know the right path, often what seems to be the right path turns out to be the wrong one, and you don't know how long the race will last, where or how it will end, or where the finish line is located."

209

Given this reality, the innovation principles from earlier stages remain the same across the innovation lifecycle - benchmark growth hypotheses (i.e. *create*), implement growth tactics (i.e. *test*) and monitor growth outcomes (i.e. *learn*). If growth rates are as expected, scale up what is working. If growth rates are not as expected, change elements of your business model or growth tactics and try again.

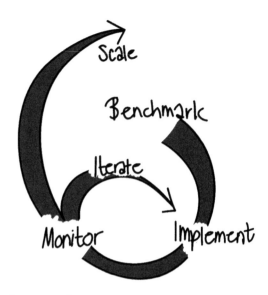

Scale

Benchmark

Iterate

Monitor

Implement

Growth Hypotheses

Our growth strategy should not be implemented in a vacuum. If we are going to be constantly tuning our engines of growth, we need to set the goals that we are navigating towards (i.e. by setting our minimum success criteria). This is the point in the innovation journey when it's finally right for the team to set their three to five year financial growth targets. But unlike traditional business planning, these growth targets are not wishful thinking. They are based on the learnings that the team gathered while validating their business model.

In addition to this, innovation teams are not making *growth projections*. Instead, they are benchmarking their *growth hypotheses*. This minor difference in labeling is not an artificial play on words. It represents a fundamental difference in orientation. Traditional business planning and financial projections have an air of inevitability that orients teams towards execution (i.e. premature optimization). In contrast, growth hypotheses are tentative and orient teams towards consistently tuning and monitoring their growth engines.

Growth hypotheses are most useful when they are specific and actionable. As such, every innovation team should decide on a specific revenue target to aim for. They can apply what they have learned so far about their business model and size of the market. They can also make reference to their company's strategic goals around gaining share in certain markets or future revenue targets. Using these inputs, the teams can decide on the right revenue or profit target within three years.

Once this long term target is set, it can then be broken down into the business relevant units of value (e.g. customer numbers or number of new subscriptions). Imagine a team whose goal is to reach $10 million in annual revenue after three years. There are some simple 'back of the napkin' steps that they can follow to set some milestones. We acknowledge that there are more rigorous accounting methods that can be used. Our steps simply illustrate the principle of setting specific business model benchmarks before teams implement their growth tactics:

Step 1 - On the basis of their business model, the team must decide the relevant units of value that amount to $10 million in annual revenues. What number of purchases is needed, what number of customers and at what lifetime value? What are the retention rates or viral co-efficient that will help the team achieve this revenue goal? For example, the team can calculate that it needs 100 000 customers with a lifetime value of $100 to reach their target.

Step 2 - Using these units of value, the team can then measure where they are today in relation to their target. In our example, the team may learn that they currently have only 9000 customers with a lifetime value of $80.

Step 3 - The difference between where the team is now and where they need to be in the future, can then be used to set annual growth hypotheses. In our example, the team needs 91 000 new customers to reach their target and they also need to increase the customer lifetime value. These goals can be broken into annual targets (e.g. Year 1 = 15 000 new customers at $85 CLV; Year 2 = 26 000 new customers at $95 CLV; Years 3 = 50 000 new customers at $100 CLV). These targets can be adjusted on the basis of retention rates and other key metrics (e.g. decreasing costs of customer acquisition).

Step 4 - To be actionable, these annual growth hypotheses can be broken down further into quarterly or monthly targets. This granular breakdown allows the team to monitor progress and learn early whether they are on track to reach their goal.[66]

Once the growth hypotheses have been set, they should be captured in a visible and transparent place for both the team and management to see. As the team does their work, progress can then be measured against these minimum success criteria.

Jack Sparrow Is Back

Another way to benchmark and track progress is to use the growth funnel. Regardless of the business model, innovation teams have created awareness for the product via their customer *acquisition* channels. Once they have their customers' attention they must somehow drive them to have an initial experience with the product (i.e. *activation*). The goal is to give customers the best experience possible so that they become loyal customers who provide us with repeat business (*retention*); and tell others about the product (*referral*). If the team successfully achieves these steps, they will have sustainable *revenues* and profits.

211

In *The Definitive Guide to Growth Hacking*, Neil Patel and Bronson Taylor simplified the pirate metrics growth funnel into three steps; *getting customers*, *activating customers* and *retaining customers*. These three steps do not explicitly reference referrals and revenue. Patel and Taylor argue that referrals can be viewed as a different method of getting customers; and revenues can be viewed as another form of customer activation. This three step model simplifies the funnel without losing the fidelity that teams need to manage growth.

Growth funnels are powerful tools for benchmarking and tracking progress. For example, a team can learn that they are activating only three out of every hundred customers they acquire (i.e. 3% conversion). However, their growth hypotheses require them to activate at least forty-five customers out of every hundred (i.e. 45% conversion). This information helps the team know what to focus on. At this moment, there is no point in increasing their customer acquisition efforts. They have to first fix their customer activation rates. Growth funnels reveal bottlenecks restricting the path towards growth. The team's job is to develop tactics to remove these bottlenecks.

Growth Tactics

With their targets and benchmarks in place, the team can now begin doing the hard work of optimizing and accelerating their growth engine. This is the grinding part of the work. There are several tactics and tools that they can use to spur growth. Not all tactics will have a positive impact on growth and the team has to slowly figure out what works. Patel and Taylor differentiate among growth tactics aimed at getting customers, activating customers and retaining customers.[67] Below we provide an incomplete guide of some of these tactics. Teams can also use their creativity to come up with even better growth hacks.

To *get customers*, innovation teams can use:
* *Pull Tactics*: This involves giving customers a reason to come to your product through enticements and incentives. Pull tactics include subtle marketing techniques such as blogging, writing magazine articles, conference talks, social media campaigns and features in marketplaces such as app stores.
* *Push Tactics*: This approach is more aggressive and involves getting customer attention in more direct ways such as paid advertising, marketing campaigns and direct sales teams. Both pull and push tactics apply to the paid engine of growth. There are costs involved in such customer acquisition activities that have to be recouped via revenues.
* *The Product*: This involves using the product as its own marketing and promotion tool. Tactics include network invitations (e.g. customers inviting friends on their email contact lists to your product), social sharing (e.g. allowing customers to talk about your product on social networks) and incentives (for example, Dropbox grew by giving customers more storage space if they got their friends to sign-up). Such tactics mostly apply to the viral engine of growth and progress can be measured via the viral coefficient.

To *activate customers*, innovations teams can use:
* *Copywriting*: This applies to all types of products, but is most important for web based sales. The key is to ensure that customers clearly understand our value proposition. Sometimes teams fail to activate customers because their value proposition is not being communicated clearly. Teams must test different forms of copywriting until they get to the language that has the best activation rates.
* *Calls To Action*: We have seen teams who are great at acquiring customers, but once the customers are engaged it is not clear what is expected from them. How do they buy the product, sign-up or subscribe? Whether we are selling physical or digital products, we must have clear calls to action for our customers.
* *Onboarding*: For complex products, especially in B2B settings, the way teams onboard customers can increase or decrease their activation rates. It is important to provide support and clear guides that help customers use our product for the first time. Our goal is to help customers to experience our value proposition as quickly as possible.
* *Pricing*: Teams must also test their pricing strategy to ensure that it is helping with activation. Pricing techniques include flat pricing, tier pricing, free trials, freemium, bundling and discount pricing. It is beyond the scope of this book to discuss pricing techniques in great detail, but this is an important part of every product's growth strategy.[68] Our pricing has to both provide us with good margins and lead to sufficient customer activation rates.

213

To *retain customers*, innovation teams can use:

- *Value Improvement*: The best way to retain customers is to make them happy. Teams must consistently focus on improving the value that their product delivers. Operating at scale does not mean that we stop working to make our products better. There should be ongoing work to improve our product's ability to help customers with their jobs to be done.
- *Customer Experience*: Products that are easy and fun to use inspire customer loyalty. Product teams must constantly learn about their customers' experiences with their products or service. Usability testing is one method teams can employ and the lessons learned should be applied to improving the product.
- *Rewards and Incentives*: A lot of companies tend to focus on giving good deals to new customers only. This neglect of current customers can lead to lower retention rates. Instead, companies should rollout the red-carpet for current customers by giving them rewards and incentives for their ongoing support.
- *Community Building*: We can treat our customers as simply consumers of our product. An alternative approach is to build a community around the product. This can be an exclusive club that customers join after purchasing our product. Memberships can come with extra benefits such as free accessories or community support. Customers that are part of a community are less likely to leave our product.

These are some example of tactics that teams can use to tune and improve their growth engines. The discipline is to ensure that we do not apply the tactics all at once. Teams must remember that they are always trying to learn what works or doesn't work. As such, when they get a marketing budget, they must incrementally spend it on one or two tactics at a time. The plan is to employ a growth tactic and measure the impact on the growth engine before we ramp-up our efforts.

It is also important to recognize that behind every growth metric are real people. Sometimes the best way to learn why a particular growth tactic is not having the desired impact is to just talk to customers. For example, if a team finds that they are having trouble with customer activation on their website, they can simply walk into a restaurant and ask a few customers to use the site while they watch. They can then have conversations to learn what customers are finding difficult about using the website. Such simple activities can provide insights into what is stopping customers from engaging more fully with our product.

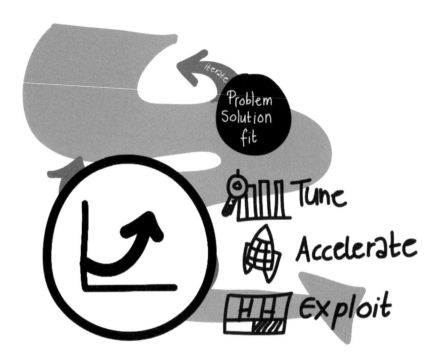

Problem Solution fit

iterate

Tune

Accelerate

Exploit

MONITORING PROGRESS - INNOVATION ACCOUNTING

At this stage of the innovation journey, there is not as much focus on activity metrics. Teams can still track the number of experiments they are running to test their growth tactics, the number of customers they are reaching and the validation velocity for their experiments. However, growth tactics have no intrinsic value within themselves. Teams can come up with really creative growth hacks, but the proof is in the pudding. What matters is whether the tactics we are employing are helping us achieve our hypothesized growth targets.

At the most granular level of monitoring progress are *reporting KPIs*. These metrics measure the impact of our growth tactics on the growth engines. We have already described some key metrics that teams should measure when we presented the growth engines, the value equation and the growth funnel. Key reporting KPIs include acquisition rates, costs of acquisition, activation rates, retention rates, viral coefficients, customer satisfaction, revenues and profit margins.

The challenge most innovation teams face is that they tend to track their reporting KPIs using aggregated data (e.g. the number of customers to date). If a team is trying out different growth tactics and product improvements, then aggregated metrics do not allow them to measure the impact of each unique activity they undertake. Instead of using aggregated metrics, teams should break their data into cohorts. A cohort is a group of customers that have received the same treatment. Depending on the frequency of their experiments, a team can track weekly or monthly cohorts.

The power of cohort analysis is that it shows more clearly whether our growth tactics are having the desired impact. For example, last week's cohort can show a team that they have a 10% retention rate within their growth funnel. If the team does some work to improve the stickiness of their product, then the impact of this work will be most clearly visible in the following week's cohort of new customers (e.g. retention improves to 20%). However, if this new cohort data is mixed together with the previous week's data, the teams will now be measuring retention using a mix of data from two groups that have had different product experiences. Cohort analysis separates these two groups and gives teams cleaner data to track progress with.

In addition to reporting KPIs, an investment board can track a team's progress along their growth milestones using *governance KPIs*. It is important to note here that the measures of growth we have described so far remain the same across all the substages of scaling ideas (i.e. retention rates, revenues, profits etc.). There are no unique growth metrics for each sub-stage. What differs from a governance perspective are the types of questions that these metrics are applied to answering. A product's progress can be monitored using monthly or quarterly reviews. The growth hypotheses that the teams set can form the basis for these reviews. These benchmarks, along with the governance questions, can be used to make decisions about ongoing investment in the product.

217

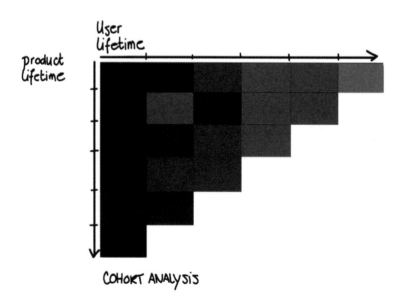

COHORT ANALYSIS

SCALING IDEAS	TUNE	Has the team identified and optimized their engine to grow customer numbers, revenues and profits?
	ACCELERATE	How fast is the team growing customers' numbers, revenues and profits and are the growth rates improving?
	EXPLOIT	As growth rates have slowed down, how well is the team optimizing costs and operational efficiencies?

The scaling ideas stage is also the right time for investment boards to start measuring returns on investment. Unlike *global KPIs* that focus on the overall performance of our investments in innovation at the company or portfolio level, an investment board is mostly interested in measuring returns from specific product investments. During the acceleration and exploitation sub-stages, the board can use traditional accounting metrics such as return on investment (ROI), net present value (NPV), accounting rate of return (ARR) and payback period.[69]

When products are being taken to scale, their impact on the company's bottom line becomes much more clear. This makes it easier to measure *Global KPIs*. The ultimate measure of impact is *innovation contribution*. This is the percentage of revenue and profits coming from products launched within a certain period (e.g. three years). Other metrics include *customer satisfaction*, *cost savings* and *innovation conversion* (i.e. percentage of old customers switching to new products). The company can also measure how well new products are doing at *gaining market share* in areas that are viewed as strategically important for the business.

Also of interest from a strategic lense is how well the company is doing in terms of its innovation thesis and balanced portfolio goals. It is important to track metrics such as the number of new products under each type of innovation (i.e. core, adjacent and transformational) and the percentage of new products succeeding at scale that are aligned with our innovation thesis. If we find that only a small percentage of our most successful products are aligned to our innovation thesis, it may be time to review and refine the thesis.

218

Scaling Excellence

Scaling a product is an exciting time for any team. Most ideas fail or run out of money before they get to this stage. So getting here is a major marker of success. But we don't want teams to celebrate too soon because scaling is also fraught with major challenges. The process we have described in this chapter helps teams to grow systematically. While speed is critical, growing systematically is much more important. When a product grows well, the team is able to maintain their focus on delivering value to customers.

In order to scale excellence, innovation teams must maintain a clear focus on their purpose, values and standards. Most teams realize late in the process that it is possible to grow a product while simultaneously destroying value. Starbucks made such a mistake early, when it scaled in a manner that hurt their customer experience. In 2007, founder and chairman Howard Schultz intervened in a now famous memo that was leaked to the press.[70] The key lesson here is that teams must never lose sight of the customer job to be done. The values and philosophy that led to early success need to be sustained as the product scales.

This is of course harder to do as the team grows in numbers. Adding new team members can create the complexity and bureaucracy that impairs communication and creativity. In most organizations we have worked with, teams grow by simply adding warm bodies. We believe that teams should try as much as they can to add new people that are aligned to their values and principles. For example, Facebook puts all new engineers through a six week bootcamp program where they work on projects that help them learn the company's code base, but also the company's product development culture.[71] At Zappos, after four week of training, new hires are offered $2000 to leave if the company is not a fit for them.[72]

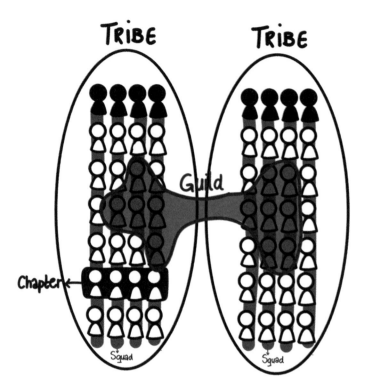

Source: Kniberg, K. & Ivarsson, A. (2012). *Scaling Agile @ Spotify with Tribes, Squads, Chapters @ Guilds.*

219

As teams grow, it is also a challenge to maintain small sized cross-functional teams. There is a tendency to add more people to the same teams and keep everyone together. However, it is possible to scale the small team structure by creating autonomous sub-teams that collaboratively work to deliver value. The Spotify model we described in Chapter 6 is a good example of this. Although they are working on the same product, the Spotify squads are cross-functional teams with autonomy to deliver value on specific elements of that product. This model might not work for all companies. However, innovation teams have to figure out how they maintain their scrappy innovative culture, even as they scale their idea.

KPIs	ACTIVITY METRICS	IMPACT METRICS
REPORTING	number of growth tactics tested	cohort analysis
	number of experiments run	pirate metrics *(acquisition, activation, retention, revenue, referral)*
	number of customers engaged	
	number of channels tested	Growth Engines *(lifetime value, retention rates, viral coefficients)*
	number of usability tests run	revenues and profits
	validation velocity	
GOVERNANCE	number of products in pipeline	stage-gate criteria
	number of reviews submitted	average growth rates
	number of decisions made	growth hypotheses validated
	number of products moving sub-stages	return on investment *(ARR, IRR, NPV)*
	average amount spent per sub-stage	process improvement metrics
GLOBAL	new products by type of innovation *(core, adjacent, transformational)*	innovation contribution
		cost savings
	% of products aligned to thesis	innovation conversion
	number of patent filings	market share *(new segments, shelf space, share of wallet, distribution footprint)*
	number of products built using lean	patents granted
	partnerships and collaborations	customer satisfaction

Innovation Activity: Stakeholder Radar

Our work has shown us that innovation will not succeed unless key stakeholders within the main business are well managed. As such, it is advisable for an innovation team to scout, understand and map their company's internal environment. To support this work, we have developed a Stakeholder Radar.

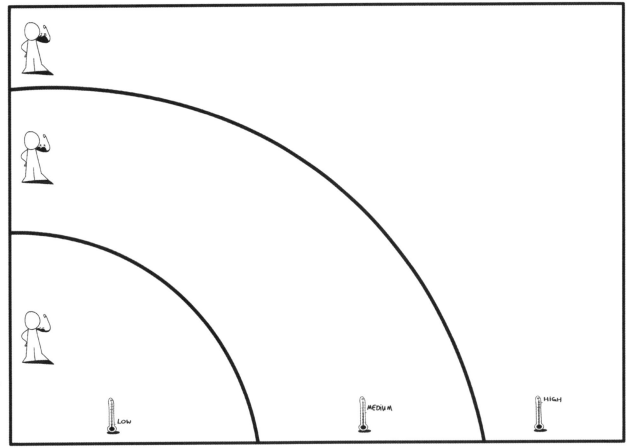

Power in the organization

Degree of interest

The workshop to map stakeholders lasts about sixty to ninety minutes, depending on the complexity of the company. For the workshop, teams need the Stakeholder Radar, sticky notes in three different colors (e.g. yellow, blue and red) and Sharpies.

Step 1: Before the workshop, the team should spend at least a week researching their company. They can look at organizational charts and also speak to key informants.

Step 2: After the research period, the workshop can then take place. We often start by asking the team to list on individual sticky notes the names of all the key stakeholders for their project. We ask them to put these names on the neutral colored sticky notes (i.e. yellow).

Step 3: Once this activity is completed, the team is then asked to place each sticky note on the Radar based on each individual's level of power in the organizations and their degree of interest in the project.

Step 4: We then inform the team that they will need to closely manage the stakeholders that have high power in the company and high interest in their project. For the stakeholders that have medium power and medium interest, we advise the team to keep them in the loop on what's happening in the project. For the stakeholders that have low power and low interest, we advise the team to continue monitoring them.

Step 5: To add another degree of fidelity to the picture - and ultimately make the entire exercise more actionable - we ask the team to color code the Radar using the blue and red sticky notes. We ask the team to review all stakeholders and identify those that are *supporters* versus *critics*. The names of the stakeholders that are supporters of the project are rewritten on the blue sticky notes and the names of the ones that are critics of the project are rewritten on the red sticky notes. This exercise should be done without changing the stakeholders' position on the radar.

Step 6: We then have the team review the Radar and make active plans of how to manage the stakeholders who have high power in the company and high interest in their project, but are also strong critics. This is the group where the highest risk for the future success of the project sits.

We complete the workshop by encouraging teams to revisit the Radar every now and again since their internal environment can change (e.g. supporters become critics) and new stakeholders might appear.

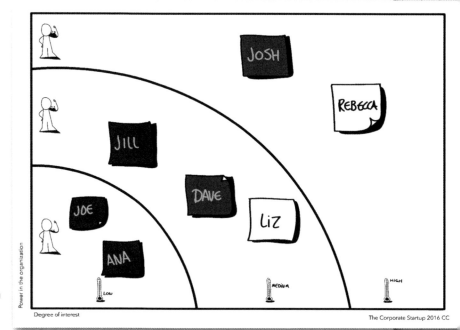

The Corporate Startup 2016 CC

CONVERSATIONS ON INNOVATION
Stephan Hoose

BUSINESS DEVELOPMENT AT JOSERA

Founded in 1941, Josera is a mid-sized family owned animal nutrition company. Over the last two years, Tendayi has been working with the company to help them adopt lean innovation principles and methods. This is an interesting challenge as Josera makes physical products (i.e. pet food) rather than digital products. The challenge is further exacerbated by the fact that Josera is a well established successful company in the highly traditional pet-food business. However, despite this success the owners and management are keen to stay ahead of the innovation curve and avoid disruption.

CS: WHAT ARE THE CHALLENGES THAT YOU HAVE FACED WITH INNOVATION?

SH: As a company, we have always been very focused on execution. This has helped us grow steadily and sustain the profitable success of our company. So we have had problems with generating ideas and recognizing good ideas. Because we have always used traditional management methods (e.g. business planning), we have also had challenges bringing new innovations to the market in a timely manner. Many of our employees did not realize that their input and ideas were wanted by management. They did not know where to place their new ideas. Some ideas were not brought to the attention of upper management, because somebody did not realize the idea's potential in the future. This is why we decided to put in place our lean innovation process.

CS: WHAT HAS MADE THE LEAN INNOVATION METHOD ATTRACTIVE TO YOUR COMPANY? HOW DO YOU THINK IT CAN HELP?

SH: Even though we are succeeding right now, we know we can not rest on that success. We need a way to generate and test ideas quickly. We have found that the business model design tools are much easier and faster to apply than other innovation tools. We are able to summarize an idea but at the same time get enough details to show the potential impact on the business. We are able to quickly identify assumptions and decide what to test first. The methods also help management to understand the proposed ideas, compare them to other ideas and make informed decisions on selecting the best ideas to move forward with.

CS: AS A COMPANY THAT MAKES PHYSICAL PRODUCTS, WHAT DIFFICULTIES HAVE YOU FACED APPLYING LEAN STARTUP METHODS?

SH: This has been the hardest part for us. We can certainly use common methods such as landing pages and concierge MVP's. However, given that we have a manufacturing process that is typical used for making big batches, we have had to learn that an effective way to test our assumptions is to build a small test product and to sell that product to the customers to learn from them that before we launch the 'real' product. This requires a bit of a change in our traditional product creation process.

225

CS: WHAT HAVE YOU DONE SO FAR TO IMPLEMENT LEAN INNOVATION IN YOUR BUSINESS?

SH: We are still at the beginning of using the methods in our company. Management and employees are highly motivated to focus on innovation. We have already selected promising ideas and are testing assumptions with our customers. Including our customers in our innovation process is so far our best learning.

'Success is a lousy teacher.
It seduces smart people into
thinking they can't lose.'

Bill Gates, Founder and former CEO of Microsoft

CHAPTER NINE

Renewing Ideas

We began this book with the story of Microsoft and Nokia. It was a cautionary tale of how stable and predictable profits can become a terrible drug. These two companies found massive success with innovative products, but that success became their Achilles' heel. The main effect of the 'drug of success' is hubris, with a small side effect of complacency. So even as we wrote about mature optimization at the end of the last chapter, successful scaling comes with a severe warning: Don't Over-Milk That Cash Cow! Companies must never allow themselves to be seduced into focusing solely on maintaining the financial success of current business models.

In July 2013, Benedict Evans published a provocative article entitled, "*The Irrelevance of Microsoft*". In the post, he powerfully illustrated how Microsoft's software, while still dominating the PC market, had only a small fraction of the mobile devices market.[1] With the PC market declining, while the mobile devices market was growing, Microsoft was strategically managing itself into irrelevance. Steve Blank tackles a similar topic in an article for *Harvard Business Review*. He argues that innovative companies are often founded by visionary CEOs.[2] However, when these CEOs depart, they tend to be replaced by world-class executors that are adept at optimizing operations and maximizing profits. These world-class executors succeed at improving the company's balance sheet and market valuation. What is often lacking from their tenures is a number of groundbreaking new product offerings.

According to Blank, this is the similarity between Steve Jobs' replacement at Apple (Tim Cook) and Bill Gates' replacement at Microsoft (Steve Ballmer). The jury is still out on Cook's tenure since he is only five years into the job at the time of writing this book. In contrast, when Steve Ballmer defends his tenure at Microsoft, he often makes reference to the revenues and profit numbers he achieved. Under his watch, Microsoft's annual profits grew threefold to over $21 billion.[3] If a company is making that kind of money, what is the point of worrying about relevance? Shareholders do not want their executives to miss out on clear revenue and profit opportunities. They want to get that money, while the getting is good!

227

While such a focus on profits is important, we feel that the long term sustainability of a company is connected to its ability to maintain its market relevance. At the time of Satya Nadella's appointment as Steve Ballmer's replacement at Microsoft, Bethany McLean wrote an interesting feature for *Vanity Fair*.[4] In that piece, she distinguished between a company's *strategic position* and its *financial position*. It is easy for companies to conflate the two positions and start to believe that strong financial numbers are a reflection of a strong strategic position. With money pouring in, these companies continue to believe their own hype until it's too late for them to respond to disruptive trends and startups. Since his appointment in February 2014, Satya Nadella has worked hard to bring Microsoft back to relevance. Under his stewardship, the company has found success with the launch of the Surface Book and the augmented reality headset Hololens. The company also successfully released the Windows 10 operating system and is using a new cloud-based business model with its Office products.[5]

228

As we have argued throughout this book, a company can stay relevant by creating transformational new products (e.g. Microsoft's Hololens). However, companies also have the option of staying relevant by renewing and refreshing their currently successful or declining business models (e.g. Microsoft Office Cloud). This chapter is about how companies can renew their business models after successful scaling and exploitation. We believe that product teams need to keep raising their heads and surveying the world around them. Are things still as they were yesterday? Is our business model still adaptive to its environment? Are we still delivering on the customer jobs to be done? What can we do to make our business model more adaptive?

The World Keeps On Turning
The success story of Nespresso has been well documented. They created an innovative business model whose pillars are coffee machines and pods that work together to make amazing coffee. What most people don't realize is that it took

nearly twenty years for Nespresso to find a business model that worked for the product.[6] Eric Favre, a Swiss engineer and Nestlé employee, invented and patented the Nespresso system in 1976. When Nestlé first launched Nespresso the focus was on selling the coffee machines to restaurants and businesses, but this approach was ultimately unsuccessful.

It was not until Jean-Paul Gaillard joined Nestlé that they were able to find a successful business model for Nespresso by focusing on high-end consumers. Nespresso finally achieved profitability in 1995 and by 2011 the product was generating annual sales in excess of 3 billion Swiss Francs (USD $2.9 billion).[7] Nespresso leveraged a great business model in which the manufacturing and sales of the machines were licensed to other companies. Nespresso then made the majority of its revenues from selling the coffee pods. A key part of this business model were Nespresso's patents that guaranteed a lock-in. Everyone with their machine had to come to them for the pods.[8]

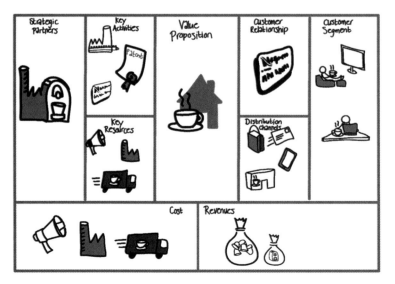

Source: Osterwalder, A. & Pigneur, Y. (2010). *Business Model Generation*. New York City: John Wiley & Sons.

However, Nespresso's success was soon under threat. In 2012, the patents protecting Nespresso's machine and pod system expired. This opened up the market for other companies to manufacture pods for the Nespresso machines. In May 2013, Euromonitor reported that Nespresso patents had been legally breached by a small British company called Dualit.[9] Other competitors also entered the market selling pods for Nespresso machines (including Douwe Egberts, Rosso Caffe and Artizan Coffee Company). Even the former CEO of Nespresso and father of its successful business model Jean-Paul Gaillard has founded the Ethical Coffee Company which makes biodegradable capsules for the Nespresso machine.[10]

In face of this competition, Nestlé has been launching and experimenting with various new products that leverage its existing capabilities. An example, is the Dolce Gusto machine which also uses a pod system, but targets the mass market with coffee based products like cappuccinos. Nestlé has also been experimenting with machines that can be used to make tea and baby formula.[11] Furthermore, Nespresso have renewed their main business model. Before the expiry of the patents, customers could only buy coffee pods on Nespresso's own website or its boutique stores. Now Nespresso coffee pods are available on Amazon and also in high street stores such as John Lewis.

The Nestlé story highlights that business models can expire. This can happen, not because of any mistakes that the company has made, but because the business environment has changed. In Nespresso's case, it was because its patents expired and this changed their competitive landscape. Technological, political and economic changes can also result in the business environment changing. At the time of writing this book, the UK is going through the challenges of having voted for Brexit. While the outcomes are still uncertain, companies whose business models rely heavily on Britain's EU membership have to start preparing for life in a different world. Their current business models may be expiring because they are no longer adaptive in a world that is changing rapidly.

229

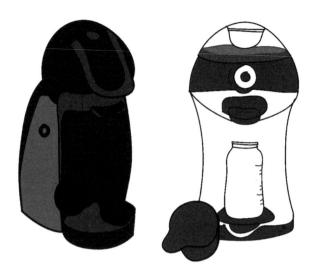

focuses on. In contrast, whether or not the product is helping customers achieve their jobs is more passive qualitative data that receives little attention.

This focus on financial data leads product teams to start optimizing their products or services for irrelevancy. Product 'improvements' become more about pushing customer numbers and revenues up, rather than providing value to those customers. For example, supermarkets often launch campaigns that are designed to bring in customers to do their shopping more often than they currently do. However, as Christensen and colleagues note, there are no customers on the planet that have a job called: "*I really need to spend a couple of hours going to the store today*".

Business environment changes are inevitable and can happen while people are not paying attention. Tendayi was once in New York in a Yellow Cab ride from JFK Airport to Manhattan. In a conversation with the taxi driver, he suddenly realized that it was 2016 but this man was unaware of what Uber was or how it worked! The taxi driver kept asking Tendayi how Uber drivers know where their passenger are, if the cars are hailed using an App. This taxi driver was sleepwalking through a technological change that may put him out of business. Innovation teams that scale their product successfully should never have that level of complacency.

Losing Sight of the Job

Most innovation teams succeed because they manage to create products that serve well defined customer jobs to be done. After achieving scale, it is quite easy for teams to lose sight of this core reason for their success. In their latest book, *Competing Against Luck*,[12] Clayton Christensen and his colleagues make the distinction between active data and passive data. They argue that when a product succeeds, customer numbers, revenues and profits become the active data that management

In the worst cases, neither financial goals nor customer jobs are considered when new features are added to a product. The hubris of success can make a product team feel that they know best what their customers need. If the team also knows that they have the market cornered with high switching costs, this lack of regard for customers can get even worse. The results are complex products that make it increasingly harder for customers to achieve their jobs. Microsoft's Word has many more features than the regular customer needs or uses. Such products are at risk of being disrupted by newcomers that have less complexity and simply focus on the customer job to be done (e.g. Google Docs). As such, regardless of scale, product teams and management must maintain a clear focus on customer jobs.

The Bonds That Bind

To deliver on a successful business model, companies often rely on key partners and suppliers. This value network can provide key resources such as raw materials and human talent; it can also help with marketing, sales and distribution. In a study on business model renewal, Christian Sandström and Ralf-Geert Osborne found that successful business models are hard to change because they are often based on an interdependent system of actors.[13] Most successful companies work with other companies that are beyond their control.

As such, when thinking about renewing their business models, companies that focus only on factors under their control are less likely to succeed. They will struggle with the constraints that are posed by their key partners. Sandström and Osborne suggest that companies should identify the critical actors in their network and align incentives before they can succeed at business model renewal. When Toyota renewed their business model using lean manufacturing methods, they ultimately had to work with their suppliers and distributors to ensure the alignment of systems and incentives.[14]

Analyze This!

Given the ever-present threat of business models becoming outdated, an important part of innovation is the continual renewal of successful ideas. The first step in idea renewal is for the team to analyze where they are in terms of their innovation journey (i.e. *business model analysis*). The key question that is addressed by this analysis is whether the current business model is still adaptive to changes that are happening in the business environment. To perform such analyses, the team must first map their current business model on a canvas. They then need to consider external factors that may impact sustainable success.

231

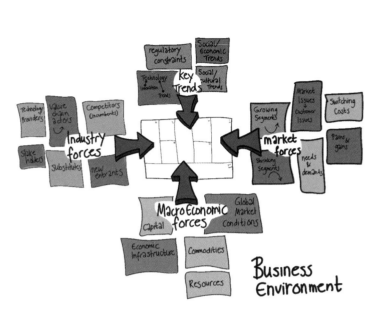

Source: Osterwalder, A. & Pigneur, Y. (2010). *Business Model Generation*. New York City: John Wiley & Sons.

BUSINESS ENVIRONMENT:

As we noted in Chapter 2, Alex Osterwalder and his colleagues at Strategyzer have developed the Business Environment Canvas. This canvas places the business model in the middle and allows teams to map four key environmental factors that may impact their business. These factors are *market forces* (e.g. growing or shrinking customer segments); *key trends* (e.g. changing technologies); *industry forces* (e.g. competitors); and *macroeconomic factors* (e.g. market conditions).[15] As we illustrate in the innovation activity at the end of this chapter, when the team maps the environment around their business model, they then have to decide whether there are any changes they need to make to their business model to make it more adaptive.

NETWORKS AND PARTNERS:

On most business model canvases will be a list of key partners that the team works with to deliver value. For each key partner, the team needs to first analyze how well the relationship is going. Is the partner delivering reliable value? In addition to this, the team can also review how dependent they are on that key partner to deliver on their business model. Finally, they can analyze how difficult it would be to replace that key partner should they need to. The best key partners are those that are highly reliable, but on whom the team are not highly dependent and can easily replace. The worst key partners are those that highly unreliable, but on whom the team are highly dependent and cannot easily replace. This analysis allows the team to note ongoing risks in their business model in terms of their network of partnerships.

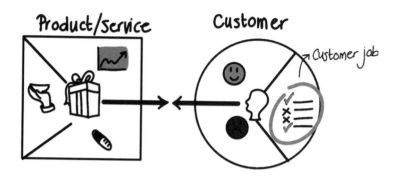

Source: Osterwalder, A., Pigneur, Y., Bernarda, G. & Smith, A. (2015). *Value Proposition Design.* New York City: John Wiley & Sons.

CUSTOMER JOBS:

This analysis zooms into the value proposition portion of the business model. What we have found is that a lot of companies cannot articulate the customer jobs that their products serve. This is particularly the case when the team has grown during the scaling phase. Companies usually invest little effort in socializing new members on the customer jobs to be done. As such, teams should revisit and discuss their customer jobs using the Value Proposition Canvas. Teams should also discuss whether there are any shifts in how customers are now doing the job. Are there new competitors that are better at serving the customer jobs? Are there cases of unusual and unexpected uses of our product? Is each feature of our product delivering value for customers? Which features are getting in the way of the customer job?

QUESTIONING OUR STORY:

Most teams we work with share an explicit or implicit narrative about the future of their product and business model. We work with such teams to challenge this narrative. Using the *premortem* method developed by Gary Kline,[16] we ask a team to imagine a future where their business model has totally failed. We then ask them to identify the factors on their business model canvas and in their business environment that are most likely to have caused that failure. When they finish their analysis, we then have a conversation about what changes they feel they need to make to the business model to avoid such potential failure.

These are the various methods that teams can use to analyze their current business models. This list is of course not exhaustive. Teams can come up with more creative ways to analyze their business models for risks and threats. Any aspect of the business model is up for review during the analysis step. Teams can analyze current channels, customer relationships, revenue models, cost structures, growth engines, key activities and key resources. The point is to put the business model under a holistic microscope with a view to finding ways to renew and refresh it.

Refresh And So Clean

After the analysis is complete, the team can look at their findings and start redesigning the business model (i.e. *business model redesign*). The team should brainstorm various ways to make their business model better and more adaptive. For example, after completing a business environment analysis, the team can break into two or three sub-teams that are each tasked with coming up with a redesigned business model. After 45 minutes, the sub-teams can come together and review what they have come up with. They can then pick the best elements of each other's business models and design a final version.

Another method we have found quite useful is the '*What Ifs*' approach to business model design (see also Chapter 6). Using this method, teams can turn their learnings for the analysis sub-stage into '*what if*' scenarios. For example, after a business environment analysis, a product team that is currently charging customers for its services can create the following 'what if' scenario:

What if a competitor starts offering a similar product to ours as a free service and we have to do the same; how would we adapt our business model to remain profitable.

This scenario can then form the basis of the business model redesign; which can be tackled in a number of ways (e.g. new revenue models, new channels, new customer segments, new technologies). Teams can use the business model prototyping method to create several different business models to tackle the same scenario, before settling on one model to take forward into testing and validation. As you may have noticed, business model redesign is not very different to what we described in the creating ideas chapter. It is ultimate still a method for developing and capturing assumptions. The only difference here is that the focus is on redesigning a current business model.

Hidden Assumptions

One challenge teams that are trying to renew their business model always face, is in managing the itch to execute. They are already operating at scale, so after a great redesigning session, the team feels inspired and wants to implement the new changes straight away. This is dangerous because redesigned business models are just as likely to have hidden assumptions as brand new business models that have been designed from scratch. As such, once a team has finished their redesign, there is a final step to go through that involves reviewing the revised model for any emerging assumptions that need to be tested (i.e. *business model review*).

Business model reviews are important because innovators tend to think that once they have succeeded with one business model, the lessons they have learned there will help them succeed with their next business model. However, in a review of large scale data from 6671 firms, Julian Frankish and colleagues discovered that having previously owned a business was unrelated to future success in a new venture.[17] Their research challenges the idea that entrepreneurial learning can be easily transferred from one business model to another. No two business situations are exactly alike. This is especially true for business model renewal, which is often triggered by some change in the external environment. Therefore, innovators must always be wary of ignoring their risky assumptions as this could lead to failure.

On their revised business model, the team should clearly identify all untested assumptions with a red sticker or an "X". At the end of this review process, the team can then step back from the canvas and assess their assumption-to-knowledge ratio. Redesigned business models tend to have fewer untested assumptions than brand new business models. Despite this fact, the team's work going forward is to reduce their assumption-to-knowledge ratio by testing their business model in context. This brings the innovation journey back full circle to the *testing ideas* stage, before the business model is again taken to scale.

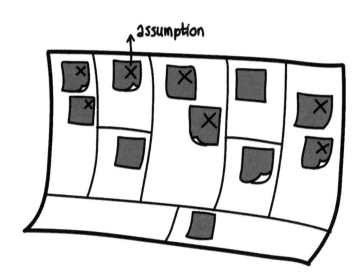

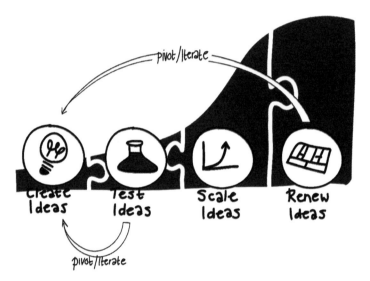

235

RECREATE-RETEST-RESCALE

The renewing ideas stage is slightly more complex than the earlier innovation stages in terms of accounting. In one sense, the stage is really a compression of all the previous three stages. It involves creative ideation as teams come up with new ways to deliver value and sustain profits. These renewed ideas will contain assumptions that have to be tested and validated. As such, in terms of *reporting KPIs* the team can track the same sorts of metrics as before (e.g. number of renewed models generated, number of renewed models chosen for testing and number of risky assumptions identified).

From a *governance KPI* perspective, the first step is deciding whether the redesigned business model is ready to move on to the testing stage. As shown in the table, key criteria include whether the team has successfully analyzed its business environment for potential threats and how well they have identified their risky assumptions and made plans for testing. When the team begins testing their assumptions, *governance KPIs* can then focus on whether the evidence is supportive of their assumptions. This assessment is done with a view to deciding whether to further invest in scaling the renewed business model.

RENEW IDEAS	ANALYZE	Has the team successfully analyzed their business environment for key trends and threats relevant to their business model?
	REDESIGN	Has the team redesigned their business model in manner that makes it adaptive to the changes in the business environment?
	REVIEW	Has the team identified the risky assumptions in their revised model and made clear plans to test them?

Renewing ideas is further complicated by the fact that we are dealing with a business model that is already at scale. As such, while the team is working on renewing their business model, all the KPIs for tracking and measuring growth still apply. The current business model needs to be continually monitored using monthly or quarterly reviews based on growth hypotheses. Returns on investments should also be continually monitored using accounting metrics such as ROI, NPV and ARR. In fact, these metrics can inform the decisions of whether a specific business model is ready for renewal. Three or four quarters of failing to hit growth targets through stagnation or decline can be used as a trigger for a business model analysis session.

It is important to note that innovators do not just renew business models for the fun of it. The work is always connected to important goals such as improving how the product delivers on the customer job to be done, revenue growth or increasing market share. As such, key metrics such as customer satisfaction, retention, referral and revenues can be used to the track if the renewed business model is having the desired incremental impact. There are also *global KPIs* that have to be considered in terms of the overall impact of the renewed business model on the company's portfolio and overall profitability (i.e. contribution and conversion). The key takeaway here is that the discipline of innovation accounting is sustained across the innovation journey.

237

Killing Our Babies

As much as innovators hate to admit it, there comes a time in every product's life when it has to be shut down. Not all ideas can be renewed and not all renewal efforts are successful. Renewing ideas can fail because technology has moved on and our product is no longer a fit (for example, cassette tapes becoming obsolete in the MP3 era). Customer tastes can also change, resulting in shrinking markets with very little growth potential. Smart companies with forward looking management disrupt themselves by successfully moving their new transformational products into the core of the business. In such cases, older products are retired for strategic reasons.

Rita McGrath describes two dimensions that companies can use to decide how to disengage from aging business models.[18] The first dimension concerns the potential future of the assets or capabilities driving the product (i.e. *asset is core to the business*, *asset has value but not to the company* or *asset is in decline*). The second dimension concerns how much time pressure the business is under (i.e. *little time pressure* versus *intense time pressure*). As shown in the table, there are six disengagement options based on the combination of these two factors. The least ideal options occur when the company is under time pressure. This is why it is important for companies to innovate before they absolutely need to.

	ASSET VALUABLE TO CORE BUSINESS	ASSET VALUABLE BUT NOT TO COMPANY	ASSET IN DECLINE
LITTLE TIME PRESSURE	**Orderly Migration** Customers can be systematically moved from current products to next generation products.	**Garage Sale** Systematically sell all assets that are no longer valuable to the company. Get best price possible.	**Run-Off** Figure out a way to support remaining customers while decreasing investment.
INTENSE TIME PRESSURE	**Hail Mary** Core business under threat. Divest quickly and try to find new products to develop quickly.	**Fire Sale** Sell all assets that are no longer valuable. Do it fast. No guarantee of getting best price possible.	**Last Man Standing** An option here is consolidation. But if this fails, exit quickly and take your losses.

Adapted from McGrath, R.G. (2013). *The End of Competitive Advantage.* Boston: Harvard Business School Publishing.

This takes us to the end of the innovation journey; which is also the beginning of the innovation journey. In a balanced portfolio, companies will have these endings and beginnings happening simultaneously across a wide range of products. Our hope is that over time companies are able to avoid complacency, booms, busts, bankruptcies and near death experiences. By using The Corporate Startup framework and our strategic innovation management tools, companies can navigate from one competitive advantage to another in a systematic way.

Innovation Activity: Business Model Redesign

In our work with established companies we have developed a methodology to help them redesign their business models. We gather a cross-functional product team within the business for a full day workshop.

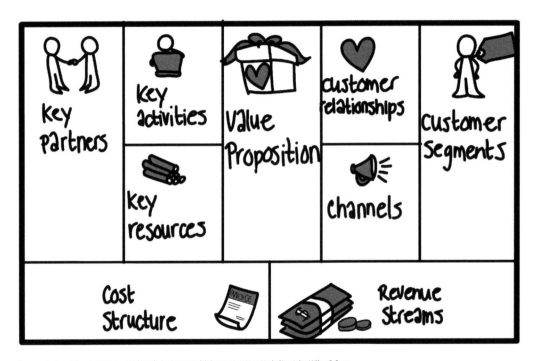

Source: Osterwalder, A. & Pigneur, Y. (2010). *Business Model Generation*. New York City: John Wiley & Sons.

Step 1 - Pre-Workshop: Prior to the main workshop, we host a one-hour pre-workshop in which we map the product's main business model. We use Osterwalder's Business Model Canvas for this.

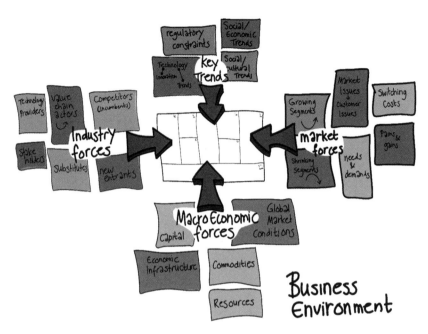

Source: Osterwalder, A. & Pigneur, Y. (2010). *Business Model Generation*. New York City: John Wiley & Sons.

Step 2 - Research: At the end of the workshop, we give the team A4 sized copies of the business environment canvas. They are then given two or three weeks to do the research necessary to be able to complete the categories on the business environment canvas (e.g. key trends). They are also encouraged to make a first pass at completing the environment canvas on their own.

Step 3 - Workshop: After the research period, we then reconvene the team for a full day's workshop. During this workshop we collaboratively map the key trends, market forces, industry forces and macro-economic forces impacting their business model.

Step 4 - Review: After mapping their business environment, we then have the team review their initial business model in terms of how adaptive it is to the business environment they have mapped. The point of the task is to identify key gaps and potential problem areas. The identified gaps are captured on a separate document.

Step 5 - Design: We then split the teams into two or three sub-groups and have each group redesign their business model to deal with the identified gaps.

Step 6 - Feedback: After designing business models in their sub-groups, we then have the whole team come together and give feedback on each other's redesigned models.

Step 7 - Combine: The team then use their best ideas to collaboratively work on one combined business model that they would like to test in order to renew their idea.

At the end of this workshop, there is follow-up work to do identifying risky assumptions and designing experiments. The redesigned business model forms the foundation for this work.

Innovation Activity: Key Partner Mapping

As we noted, most successful business models will depend on networks of key partners that fall beyond the control of the product team or company. Before a team begins working on renewing their business model, they may want to have to deeper review of their key partners and consider their potential impact on future success. So after completing their business model redesign session, we suggest that teams have a workshop focused on their networks of key partners.

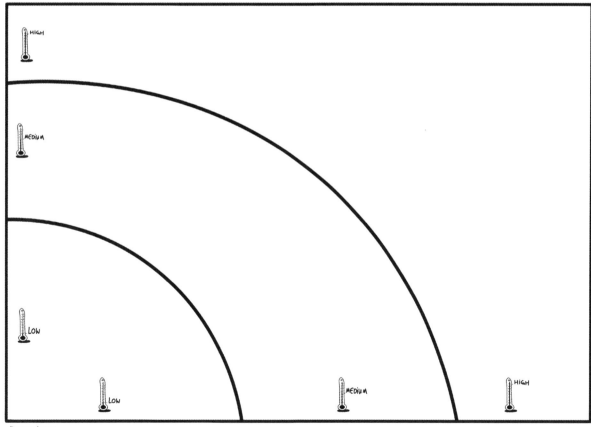

Reliability

Dependancy

This workshop lasts about sixty to ninety minutes, depending on the complexity of the partnership network. For the workshop, teams need the Key Partner Map, sticky notes in three different colors (e.g. yellow, blue and red) and Sharpie pens.

Step 1 - Research: Before the workshop, the team should spend at least a week researching their key partners. How dependent is the business model on each partner? How reliable is the partner? How easy is it to replace the partner?

Step 2 - Identify: After the research, the workshop can then take place. We often start by asking the team to list on individual sticky notes the names of all the key partners. We first ask them to put these names on the neutral colored sticky notes (i.e. yellow).

Step 3 - Reliability & Dependency: Once this activity is completed, the team is then asked to place each sticky note on the map based on each key partner's level of reliability and the degree of the business models dependency on them.

Step 4 - Replaceability: Once this is complete, we then have the team code each key partner for risk. We ask the team to color code the map using the blue and red sticky notes. The names of the key partners that are easy to replace are rewritten on the blue sticky notes and the names of the ones that are hard to replace are rewritten on the red sticky note. This exercise is done without changing their position on the map.

Step 5 - Review: We then have the team review the map and think about the key partners they need to manage most closely if their business model renewal efforts are to succeed. We encourage the team to make plans of how to manage these partners.

We complete the workshop by encouraging teams to revisit their map every now and again since the external environment can change and this can impact their ongoing relationships with key partners.

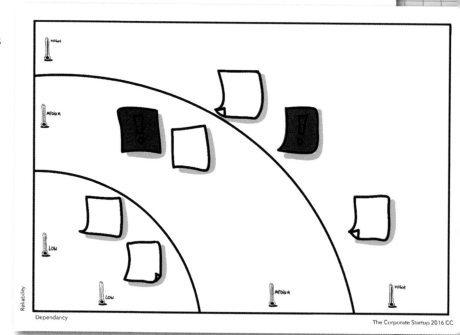

CONVERSATIONS ON INNOVATION
Peter DePauw

HEAD OF BUSINESS DEVELOP AND STRATEGY AT EANDIS

Peter DePauw is head of business development and strategy at Eandis. He is passionate about boosting innovation and intrapreneurship within the company. Eandis is a distribution system operator that is active in 239 municipalities in Belgium, servicing more than 2,6 million customers. The company offers network solutions for electricity, natural gas, heating and public lighting. The company also plays an important social role in achieving climate objectives, combating energy poverty and the independent management of energy data. Eandis is a relatively large company operating in a highly traditional and regulated industry. However, these constraints have not deterred their passion for innovation. With Peter's help, they have been working on renewing their business model and coming with new ideas for opportunities. They have developed an eight step process for business model renewal. We met with Peter to ask him about these steps, which he kindly outlined below.

CS: CAN YOU OUTLINE FOR OUR READERS THE EIGHT STEPS TOWARDS BUSINESS MODEL RENEWAL THAT WERE DEVELOPED WITHIN EANDIS.
PD: Preparing our company for the future is a journey we started at Eandis a couple of years ago. And looking back we can clearly see the eight different steps we followed:

STEP 1: BE AWARE
By studying the trends in the energy landscape, we discovered how fast the world around us was changing, and how these changes could have a big impact on our "stable, traditionally and high-

ly regulated business". The more and more we developed this "Outside-In" thinking, we became aware of the fact that these trends should be used as a guidepost for strategy and business development.

STEP 2: TAKE A BUSINESS MODEL VIEW

As a distribution system operator, "operational excellence" has been very much our focus. We need to take this approach in order to guarantee a reliable service. But we discovered that we needed to take another view that would allow us to evolve beyond our current day-to-day tasks. By using the business model canvas, we succeeded in adopting that other perspective. This business model view allowed to reformulate our company vision.

STEP 3: REALIZE WE CAN DO BETTER

We then used the trends in the energy business to review our current business model. This led us to realize that in order to sustain our company long-term, we have to do better. We therefore reformulated our company vision and communicated this to everyone as an invitation to let our company evolve.

STEP 4: BE AMBITIOUS

By realizing how we can do better, we were able to formulate our innovation ambitions. These ambitions were shared with all our managers and became concrete by formulating actions such as reducing or eliminating malfunctions, raising best practices and creating new opportunities. We were now ready to take our business to the next level.

STEP 5: FACE THE ROADBLOCKS

As we started doing our work, we also realized that we only could get to the next level by shattering some mental and organizational roadblocks that thwarted our company's progress. As such, we had a series of management meetings during which we addressed the question of why our strengths were not being used to realize our innovation potential. The answers to this question gave us an opportunity to improve. But it was important to have an open debate and make plans to take actions to remove these roadblocks.

STEP 6: FORMULATE INNOVATION THESIS AND INVITE FOR IDEAS

The action plans from step 4 and step 5 were communicated to the whole company, and employees were invited for ideas, focused on "renewing and revitalizing our business model by building on our strengths". With a lot of energy, new ideas were conceived by our teams and pitched to the management board. Management then invested in the most promising offerings that were in line with our innovation thesis.

STEP 7: EMPOWER YOUR INTRAPRENEURS

Before starting the design phase, we wanted to give our employees skills and resources. As such, all employees were invited to participate in the co-creation process. The chosen intrapreneurs were given space and support by the business developers, and a coalition of the willing was formed. Using a validated learning and iterative approach, teams worked on the initial ideas to turn them into viable businesses. After the business model validation process was complete, the management board then made the decision to create spin-in businesses that were managed by the intrapreneurs that co-created them.

STEP 8: KEEP DATING THE FUTURE

We are living in exciting times. Things are moving very fast, so we need to keep pace. Not only with evolving technology but also the big data tools that are changing our businesses very fast. In order to keep connect we created a disruption committee within Eandis. We called it DATE, because we want to keep on dating the future! We follow closely the disruptive changes within the domain of Data and Technology. Our goal is to keep tracking relevant trends and keep making changes to renew and revitalize our business model.

245

'It is not the critic who counts...
The credit belongs to the man who
is actually in the arena...'

Theodore Roosevelt, 26th President of the United States

CHAPTER TEN
Start Today

Every conference talk on innovation we have ever watched begins with the speaker lampooning some large company that just got disrupted. We are guilty of this ourselves in this book, and in our talks and workshops. And yet we wrote this book because we strongly feel that large established companies are poised to benefit the most from the lean startup movement. It is often taken as obvious that startups own the future in terms of creating breakthrough products and services. But this may not be as inevitable as the pundits claim.

Most of the major technologies we use today were developed in the R&D labs of large corporations such as Xerox's PARC and AT&T's Bell Labs. This trend continues today, with over 90% of the top 20 global R&D spending happening in large established companies such as Ford, Johnson & Johnson, Cisco and Roche.[19] It is correct to argue that R&D by itself does not represent innovation. Breakthrough technologies still have to be combined with viable business models in order to achieve commercial success.

But this is not a one-way street. R&D is still a key ingredient in the innovation formula. Without breakthrough technologies, well-designed business models cannot by themselves succeed. What most startups have been able to do over the last two decades is leverage existing technologies developed by large companies and apply great business models to them (e.g. Uber, Airbnb, Pinterest). This makes sense because startups often don't have the financial muscle needed to build a great R&D function. In contrast, large companies usually have the resources they need to succeed. They are usually more financially viable than startups; and within their ranks are some of the smartest researchers and scientists in world (e.g. Google X).

The Third Wave

This capacity to invest in R&D will put large companies at an advantage, as we enter a new age of technology and the internet. In the book *The Third Wave*, Steve Case identifies three waves of internet technology.[20] In the first wave (1985-1999), companies like Cisco, IBM, AOL and others were building the necessary technologies for the internet. Their work mostly involved laying the foundations of the online world that we have today. In the second wave (2000-2015), the app economy and mobile revolution took hold. Companies like Amazon, Google, Facebook, Twitter and others were able to leverage the foundations built in the first wave to create great products and services.

There is evidence that this second wave is peaking and the next technology wave is starting to take hold.[21] During the third wave (2016-), the internet will be fully integrated into everything we do and every product we use. In the era of *The Internet of Everything*, economic sectors that were hitherto only marginally affected by the internet will be facing disruption and change. Industries such as healthcare, education, transportation and food production will be impacted by the ubiquitous connectivity that visionary innovators will be able to leverage.

Building the Internet

App Economy & mobile revolution

Internet of everything

1985 – 1999

2000 – 2015

2016 →

1st wave

2nd wave

3rd wave

Source: Case, S. (2016). *The Third Wave*. New York City: Simon & Schuster.

According to Case, success in the third wave will require different ways of working. During the second wave, entrepreneurs
could create businesses based on niche applications and drive
adoption through online marketing and viral methodologies.
Indeed, some of the lean startup playbook was developed
during this era. Startup accelerators also took advantage of the
low barriers to entry, and invested relatively small amounts of
money to create high growth companies. In contrast, the third
wave will involve products and services that are much more
costly to create and distribute. The industry sectors will be
highly regulated by government and have powerful well established companies that are gatekeepers to the market.

To succeed in the third wave, innovators will have to make
large financial investments, form partnerships with other
companies and influence government policy. These requirements play well into the inbuilt advantages of large companies,
who have the resources to invest in the R&D required to create
third wave products (e.g. healthcare). Large companies also
have the muscle, knowledge and networks to form partnerships with other companies and influence policy decisions. All
these factors place startups at a slight disadvantage going into
the third wave.

Part of our goal with this book is to make sure that large companies do not fumble this emerging opportunity at the goal
line. It is critical to remember that the same factors for success
in the third wave of the internet were present during the first
wave of the internet. However, during that time established
companies like Xerox, IBM, GE and AT&T lost to young upstarts
like Cisco, AOL, Apple and Microsoft. Having advantages and
resources is not a guarantee of success. Without a well designed innovation process, large companies are just as likely to
lose to startups during the third wave.

249

What the lean startup movement has done is to reveal to the
business world how successful startups work. We now know
the difference between searching and executing. Codifying this
innovation best practice for large corporates is the goal of this
book. We have tried to show how innovation ecosystems help
companies connect the dots with strategy, innovation thesis, a
balanced portfolio, incremental investing, innovation accounting, R&D, business model design and iterative product development. Applying the principles and tools we outline in this
book, combined with advantages that they already possess, are
the reasons we feel strongly that large corporates will benefit
the most from the lean startup movement.

This final chapter is about how companies can start building their innovation ecosystems straight away. What factors do they need to consider? What are the building blocks for setting up an ecosystem? How do they build organizational support for the ecosystem? What innovation models and options are available to them? How do they incrementally and iteratively put the ecosystem in place? How do they measure success and track progress? Most established companies should have started building their innovation ecosystems yesterday. Better late than never - let's start today!

An Ecosystem Needs Support

In 2007, Yahoo set up an innovation studio in San Francisco called Brickhouse. This 'innovation lab' was physically separate from the main company and they were tasked with working like startups to create cool new products.[22] The studio developed some innovative products such as Yahoo! Live, Yahoo! Pipes and Bravo Nation. However, in 2008, after just two years, Brickhouse was shut down. It appears that there was a disconnect between the innovation studio and its corporate parent. This resulted in a revolving door of leadership at Brickhouse and nobody in the core company fighting to keep the studio running.[23] The Brickhouse story illustrates the importance of organizational alignment around innovation. It shows that when innovation is done in isolated pockets, it will not have sustainable success.

A well-designed innovation ecosystem can help create some organizational alignment. However, the design of the ecosystem itself has to allow alignment with the parent company's systems and processes. This means that innovators need to consider how other parts of the company will play a role in supporting their ecosystem. Below are five key factors that need to be considered as support for the innovation ecosystem:

- *Enabling Functions*: A key part of any innovation process is the level of support innovators get from the parent company's enabling functions. Even in a company with a divisional setup, there will be shared functions such as brand, legal, HR and finance. Support from these key functions is important for innovation to succeed. For example, help from finance is needed to set up innovation accounting and an incremental investment process. Legal and brand will be needed to create simple guidelines for innovation teams to be able to run experiments. The human resource function can help manage what happens to teams whose innovation projects fails. These teams will need to be assigned to other projects within the company on an ongoing basis. As such, innovation leaders have to work with enabling functions as a key part of developing any innovation ecosystem.

251

- *Tools and Resources*: The Corporate Startup represents new ways of working in most organizations. The tools that companies have traditionally used to manage their businesses are not well suited for innovation. As such, new tools have to be adopted or created for these companies. Throughout this book, we have presented some of the tools, practices and innovation activities that companies can use. Such methods need to be adopted and widely socialized within a company for product development best practices to thrive. But it's not only product teams that need to adopt new tools; executives also need to adopt new ways of managing their innovation teams. Tools and platforms to measure and track the right innovation metrics have to be put in place. This is what brings an innovation ecosystem to life and makes it practical.

- *Innovation Catalysts*: To help employees adopt new tools and ways of working, some training and coaching is necessary. Companies can run lean innovation training workshops. They can also create guides, toolkits and playbooks for teams to use. However, there will always be a need for real-time access to coaching and support when challenges arise. At Intuit, they were able to scale their Design for Delight (D4D) program by training a number of innovation catalysts who were coaches from all over the company, that worked with product teams to support their work. At Pearson, in addition to creating a playbook,[24] the Lean PLC team also trained a number of Product Lifecycle Coaches that support product teams with designing business models and running experiments.

- *Communities of Practice*: In addition to coaches, innovation ecosystems need the support of an engaged community of practitioners that interacts regularly. As we noted in Chapter 6, these communities can be created using virtual platforms where people write articles, host webinars and share knowledge, best practice and innovation tools. Companies can also host regular events for face-to-face interactions where employees can share their work, have conversations about challenges they are facing and share best practice. A well-managed community ensures that innovation principles and practices become a large part of the company's culture.

- *External Partnerships*: In order to keep up with global best practice, companies must be open to working with external partners, especially members of the startup community. External speakers, coaches and mentors can be invited to events that the company holds. Employees can also attend and speak at external events. As we describe below, companies can also engage more deeply with external partners through open innovation, working with startup accelerators and engaging in startup co-creation. All these activities foster a community of practice that extends beyond the walls of the organization.

Corporate managers often talk about creating a culture of innovation. But what is often put in place are artificial practices that have no real impact on the culture of the company (i.e. innovation theater). Culture is an intangible phenomenon that expresses itself through a company's structures and processes. Executives are often frustrated by the lack of innovation in their company. And yet they cling onto old management practices such as requiring business plans, or only calculating bonuses based on annual financial targets. These organizational instincts and incentives militate against the culture of innovation they are aspiring to create.

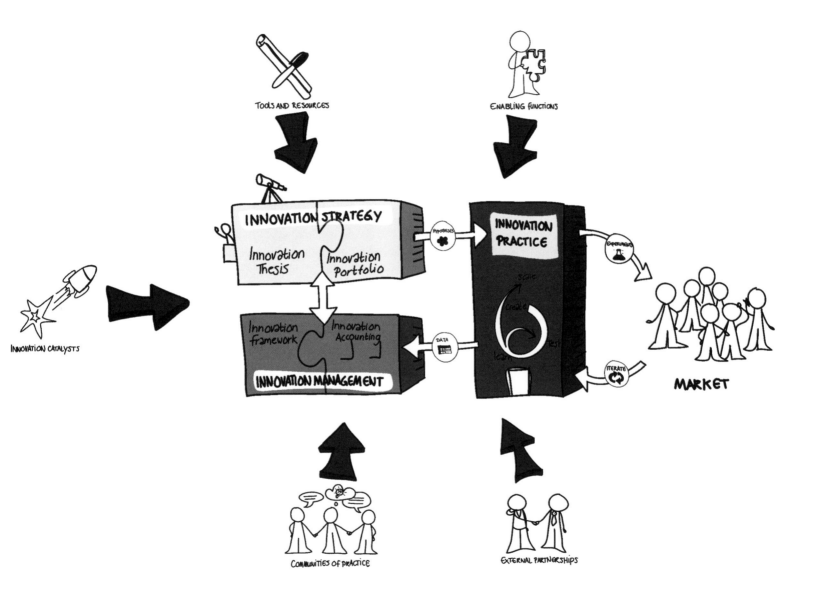

TOOLS AND RESOURCES

ENABLING FUNCTIONS

INNOVATION CATALYSTS

INNOVATION STRATEGY

Innovation Thesis

Innovation Portfolio

Innovation Framework

Innovation Accounting

INNOVATION MANAGEMENT

INNOVATION PRACTICE

Hypotheses

Experiment

Data

Iterate

scale

create

learn

test

MARKET

COMMUNITIES OF PRACTICE

EXTERNAL PARTNERSHIPS

The same applies to the innovation ecosystem. Any one of the five elements will not by itself transform your company.[25] An innovation thesis is just a theory if it is not supported by portfolio investments. Product development best practices will not work, unless they are supported by an investment management process that recognizes the stages in an innovation journey. Innovation accounting only works if product teams are running experiments, testing assumptions and tracking progress. The five elements of the ecosystem will also fail if they are not aligned with the rest of the organization's structures and processes. Enabling functions, tools and resources, innovation catalysts, communities of practice and external partners, are all an important part of the support system for innovation.

In fact, the innovation strategy of a company needs to be reflected in its human resource strategy. If the corporation needs more people that are better at searching for new business models than executing legacy models, the HR department needs to recruit accordingly. In a conversation Dan had with an executive from a blue chip financial services institution, the executive mentioned that HR were unwilling to hire the types of people that are needed to drive innovation. This was because such people often did not have the background the HR department was used to. The executive had found a workaround to ensure the right people were working on future growth initiatives; he hired freelancers. This was because the budget for hiring freelancers was not under HR. This practice is of course counterproductive for building the innovation capabilities of a company.

In building an ecosystem, there is a key role for leadership to play. Alexander Osterwalder recommends the appointment of a *Chief Entrepreneur* who is responsible for innovation, while the CEO runs the existing business.[26] Tushman and colleagues recommend appointing an *Ambidextrous CEO* who excels at both searching and executing.[27] Both options are practical depending on the company. But regardless of whether it is a *Chief Entrepreneur* or an *Ambidextrous CEO*, our conclusions remain the same. Innovation has to be an integral part of how a company runs its day-to-day business; and this can only be achieved with full leadership support.

Innovation Models

A fully implemented innovation ecosystem will have all five key elements (i.e. thesis, portfolio, framework, accounting and practice), and involve all five supporting factors (i.e. enabling functions, tools and resources, innovation catalysts, communities of practice and external partnerships). This is an ideal scenario that we are yet to find realized in any company. Most companies implement innovation models that contain some elements of the full ecosystem, but not others. We describe some common models below, along with their strengths and weaknesses.

INNOVATION INSTITUTE:

This is an institution that is set up to be open to all employees. Its main function is to develop innovation capabilities within the company. As such, the institute will design and run the company's innovation training programs. These include talks, seminars and workshops that cover topics such as design thinking, business models and experimentation. The institute can also develop innovation playbooks that serve as guides for product teams. A physical location is needed that can serve as both a training center and a co-working space for innovation teams. This physical location can easily become the cultural heartbeat of the company's innovation community; hosting events, meetups, hackathons and innovation weekends. These events can include external partners and speakers.

The innovation institute delivers on the innovation practice element of the ecosystem, as teams get training and coaching on lean innovation methods. It also provides support in terms of capability building and communities of practice. However, it has disadvantages with regard to the other key elements of the ecosystem. A training institute does not really help with innovation strategy (i.e. thesis and portfolio) or innovation management (i.e. framework and accounting). Although the institute can help train innovation catalysts, without the other ecosystem elements in place, these coaches would be getting deployed into an organization that is not ready for them.

INNOVATION COMPETITIONS:

To invest resources and spark activity around innovation, companies can host innovation competitions. In Chapter 6, we described open calls such as the Adobe's Kickbox and idea competitions, where winning ideas receive investment for further development. Innovation competitions can help create community and cultural excitement around innovation. They also provide support by giving teams the tools and resources they need for innovation (e.g. Adobe's Kickbox). In some way, competitions can support innovation strategy, if each call for ideas is rooted in a strategic theme.

However, if a company's innovation process in only based on idea competitions, there will be key weaknesses in its ecosystem. Just running competitions cannot deliver on innovation practice or the building of innovation skills. Competitions can also fail to transform how a company invests and manages innovation. We have seen idea competitions in which the winners are then expected to go and write business plans before they get investment. Without skills, capabilities or a clear innovation management process, a lot of ideas that are generated during competitions can fall through the cracks.

255

INNOVATION BOARD:

Some companies create a central fund that invests in innovation. The budget for the board is allocated and managed separately from the main business. This allows investment in innovation to be managed with different expectations in terms to ROI. Access to the fund can be open to all employees who have to go through some application process or win an innovation competition. The investment decisions of the board can be informed by an innovation thesis and the company's portfolio goals. Funding can also be released incrementally at certain stage gates. In this regard, an innovation board can deliver on innovation strategy and innovation management.

However, an innovation board by itself cannot create great innovation practice, build capabilities or develop communities. Its main priority is to manage investments in innovation and provide financial resources. Innovation boards are not responsible for developing innovation catalysts or provide innovation tools for teams. Given the seniority of its membership, the board cannot be involved in the day-to-day product development work of the teams. This often results in teams receiving funds for innovation, but using traditional waterfall methods to develop the products.

R&D LAB:

For companies that work on products with high levels of technical risk, an R&D lab can be a great investment to make. One of the key innovation questions for any product or service is: can it be done? Answering this question is particularly important for third wave industries such as healthcare and transportation. The work of the R&D lab can be informed by an innovation thesis and the company's balanced portfolio goals. The main limitation of a pure R&D lab is that it often fails to answer the second key question of innovation: i.e. should it be done? This means that business model validation work is often lacking. In this regard, the typical R&D lab does not help a company develop an innovation framework or innovation practice. R&D labs are also weak on developing innovation catalysts and creating communities of practice. The option most companies choose is to move promising technologies from the R&D lab into an innovation lab (e.g. Google's The Foundry).

INNOVATION LAB:

This is like an in-house startup accelerator. It combines elements of the institute, competitions and innovation board. Labs are often set up as separate institutions that are tasked with investing in ideas and managing innovation teams. The budget for the lab is allocated and managed separately from the main business. The lab is open to all employees who can apply to join on a cohort by cohort basis, although they do have to get permission from their line managers to join the lab if they are accepted. Competition for places is managed using application templates and an idea pitching process.

There are two options for managing an innovation lab. The company can manage the lab themselves with an internally hired staff or they can partner with an external accelerator such as Techstars or Startup Bootcamp. These external partners can bring their knowledge, expertise and networks to help the company with innovation. Teams that are chosen then spend a few months in the lab working on their ideas. The investment and acceleration process can be separated into two parts; a *seed stage* during which teams get an initial investment to test their ideas and validate their business models, and a *growth stage* during which teams get further investment to take their ideas to scale.

An innovation lab can be used to support innovation strategy and innovation management. Investments can be based on a clear innovation thesis and funding can be done incrementally with innovation accounting being used to track progress. The lab also delivers well on innovation practice as the teams can be trained and supported by innovation catalysts. Since the lab is often in a physical location, it can function like the institute in terms of community (e.g. hosting events). The major risk innovation labs face is isolation from the main business. This should be managed by making sure that there is strategic alignment between the parent company and the ideas that are being developed in the lab. A diplomat may also be needed to do the hard work of managing relationships between the lab and the parent company. The isolation of the lab can also mean that, while its own innovation culture might be great, this has very little impact on the innovation practices within the parent company.

257

THE ACCELERATOR:

This is similar to the innovation lab, except that the accelerator is set up to invest in external startups who can apply to join on a cohort by cohort basis. The company can manage the accelerator themselves but it might be more effective to partner with an external accelerator company (e.g. Techstars). The selected startups will then spend a few months in the accelerator working on their ideas. They can get *seed stage* or *growth stage* investments depending on their innovation stage. Some companies take stakes in each startup they invest in; while others fund startups on the agreement that they have rights of first refusal to acquire the startup should the idea succeed.

An accelerator is one way to manage the difficulty for employees in established company to find time to work on innovation. In this regard, innovation is being outsourced to startups. The accelerator can also deliver on innovation strategy by helping the company meet its innovation thesis and portfolio goals. However, because the accelerator only works with external startups, this can limit its impact on the overall company culture. The innovation management and product development practices of the parent company can remain traditional. This can cause a mindset and cultural rift between 'cool' people who work in the accelerator and those who work in the parent company.

STARTUP CO-CREATION:

In this model, the company collaborates with external partners to create new startups. First, the company can use its innovation thesis to identify markets it wants to enter, technologies it wants to develop or customer problems it wants to solve. They then work with a partner to identify external teams that are willing to work with the company to create new startups. This is better than investing in pre-formed startups because co-created startups are much more likely to be aligned with the parent company's strategic goals. At the end of the process, companies can choose to spin-in or spin-out the startups they have co-created. Ben Yoskovitz, who is featured in our *Conversations on Innovation*, co-founded Highline BETA to serve as a partner to large companies that are looking to identify startup founders.

Just like the accelerator, startup-co-creation is great for providing the space and resources for innovation. Companies get an opportunity to bet on the future by working with external partners to create products and services. The startups created can help the company achieve its innovation thesis and meet its portfolio goals. This process can also break the gridlock and inertia within most large companies. However, if a company uses only startup co-creation for innovation, then it will have weaknesses in other aspects of its ecosystem. For example, employees who are not involved in the co-creation process

may not be able to build their skills in terms of innovation practice. The company may also fail to create new tools and methods to manage innovation internally. As such, the overall company can only benefit from startup co-creation if the lessons learned from that work are applied to improving the rest of the company's innovation process.

OPEN INNOVATION:

No company, even with the best resources and talent, can innovate on its own. Open innovation breaks down traditional barriers between companies and the outside world. It allows ideas, intellectual property (IP), technology and people to move in and out of the company. The accelerator and startup co-creation models are versions of open innovation that allow outsiders to contribute to the company by creating new products and services (i.e. *outside-in open innovation*).[28] Companies can also use *inside-out open innovation* where they open up some of their assets, IP and technologies for outsiders to work on. For example, if companies have patents that are just sitting on the shelf, these can be licensed to outsiders. According to Chesbrough and Garman, many companies recover about 10%-20% of their R&D spend through such licensing.[29] Companies can also work with outsiders to develop non-strategic initiatives, create open platforms for others to have access to their technologies and create startups that become suppliers of key capabilities.

A great example of open innovation is Eli Lilly which has been using the method for new drug development.[30] Procter & Gamble, Philips, Unilever and Lucent have also used open innovation to develop new products and technologies. When managed well, open innovation can help a company meet its strategic goals around innovation. By working with outside partners, the company can develop its innovation thesis and

259

260 meet its balanced portfolio goals. The main limitations of open innovation are related to how much it can impact the overall innovation culture of the parent company. It is possible to manage a great open innovation platform, while the core business is still using traditional methods to create new products. As such, open innovation may need to be combined with other initiatives, if it is to have a broader impact on the company.

VENTURE CAPITAL:

This involves the creation of an investment fund that invests and takes stakes in early and later stage startups. The venture capital model also includes the acquisition of high potential startups. To be strategic, the fund should have an investment thesis that is based on the overall innovation thesis of the company. This can then serve as a filter for whether to acquire or invest in a particular startup. For early stage startups, investments can be made in a manner that allows the company to later acquire the startup, should it succeed.

Similar to open innovation, the main limitation of the venture capital model is related to how much it can impact the overall innovation culture of the company. Startup acquisitions often fail because of a mismatch between the culture of the acquired startup and the parent company.[31] It is often the acquired startup that struggles in its new environment, rather than the parent company culture changing. As such, more needs to be done beyond investing in startups to change a company's innovation culture. An innovation ecosystem can prepare the company to be able to absorb new startups as they get acquired.

These are some of the innovation model options that companies can deploy. The choice of a specific model can be based on company context and strategic goals. Simply implementing the latest vogue model may not produce the desired results. Furthermore, each innovation model, if implemented by itself, will result in some weakness in the overall ecosystem. An awareness of the relevant weakness can help executives develop ways to manage these. The best option may be to use two or more models simultaneously. Of course, we prefer that companies shoot for the moon and build a complete innovation ecosystem. This does not have to happen in one big bang. It can be done incrementally or iteratively. There are building blocks or steps that need to be followed in order to build an ecosystem.

261

The Innovation Ecosystem Elements & Innovation Models

Innovation Models	Innovation Thesis	Innovation Portfolio	Innovation Framework	Innovation Accounting	Innovation Practice	Enabling Functions	Tools and Resources	Innovation Catalyst	Communities of Practice	External Partners
Innovation Institute	Non existent	Non existent	Non existent	Non existent	Good	Minimal	Good	Good	Excellent	Minimal
Innovation Competitions	Minimal	Minimal	Non existent	Non existent	Non existent	Minimal	Good	Non existent	Excellent	Non existent
Innovation Board	Good	Good	Minimal	Minimal	Non existent	Good	Good	Non existent	Non existent	Non existent
R&D Lab	Good	Good	Non existent	Non existent	Minimal	Good	Minimal	Non existent	Non existent	Non existent
Innovation Lab	Good	Good	Good	Good	Excellent	Good	Excellent	Good	Good	Minimal
The Accelerator	Good	Good	Good	Good	Minimal	Good	Good	Minimal	Minimal	Excellent
Startup Co-Creation	Good	Good	Good	Good	Minimal	Good	Good	Non existent	Non existent	Excellent
Open Innovation	Good	Good	Non existent	Non existent	Minimal	Good	Minimal	Non existent	Non existent	Excellent
Venture Capital	Good	Good	Non existent	Non existent	Non existent	Minimal	Non existent	Non existent	Non existent	Excellent
Innovation Ecosystem	Excellent	Excellent	Excellent	Excellent	Excellent	Excellent	Excellent	Excellent	Excellent	Excellent

Legend: ☐ Non existent   ▣ Minimal   ▣ Good   ■ Excellent

262

Twelve Steps to the Epiphany

Building an innovation ecosystem is a systematic process. It cannot be done in one big bang. There are twelve interconnected building blocks that need to be deployed in a systematic way. These blocks can be viewed as a simple guide, pieces of a puzzle or points on a map. Deploying them is not necessarily a linear process, but each piece of the puzzle is important. Some companies will already have some of the building blocks we describe below in place. Others will prefer to start at a later step or work with a limited number of the blocks to begin with. There may also be other steps we have overlooked that some companies have to consider. Our goal is not to be prescriptive or provide an exhaustive list. We want to simply sign post a few key steps as a basic to-do-list for companies wanting to implement an innovation ecosystem.

264

1. EXPLORE YOUR CONTEXT:

We have found that innovation ecosystems cannot be built in a vacuum. They have to be developed and applied in context. As such, before designing and implementing an ecosystem, there is work to be done examining your company's current situation (i.e. *innovation audit*). How is innovation currently managed? What product development practices are in place? How are investment decisions made? Does the company have a strategy around innovation? This work also involves speaking to colleagues across the board to learn about the challenges they face. What are the barriers to innovation? What has worked well or failed in the past? What market and business pressures is the company facing? The main goal at this stage is to understand the lay of the land, so that the ecosystem is designed to suit the company's context.

2. GET EXECUTIVE BUY IN:

Innovators need aircover and support at the highest level of the organization. It is always worth it to spend time trying to get executive buy-in. Without such 'aircover', most innovation projects will suffer the fate of Yahoo's Brickhouse. Depending on your company, part of the work will involve diplomacy and cajoling. This is where finding a diplomat within the company can be useful. Bring in external speakers and influencers to help you convince your executives. In some companies, getting executive buy-in will be difficult and take a long time. In others, it will be relatively easy and the work will then involve helping them develop strategy, management frameworks and allocate resources to innovation.

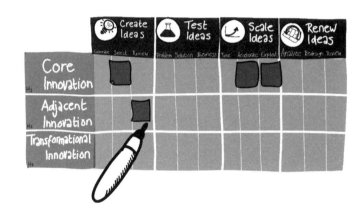

3. DEVELOP INNOVATION THESIS:

Executive buy-in creates the space and resources for innovators to work on new ideas. The excitement of getting such an opportunity can lull innovators into overlooking strategy development. However, developing new ideas without strategy can have the same consequences as not having executive 'aircover'. So it is important to spend time with the leadership developing an innovation thesis and developing strategic success criteria (see Chapter 2). This will provide the guardrails for future innovation projects.

4. MAP YOUR PORTFOLIO:

The ultimate goal of an innovation ecosystem is to help the company achieve a balanced portfolio. Therefore, it is important to map the current state of your company's portfolio or products and services (see Chapter 3). Each product within the portfolio should be mapped on the basis of its innovation type or horizon (i.e. core, adjacent, transformational). Each product should also be tagged with its innovation stage (i.e. create, test, scale, renew). Mapping a portfolio is a powerful way to identify gaps. This can then be used to inform strategy and resource allocation decisions. For example, if a portfolio is heavily biased towards core and adjacent products, then management can make the decision to allocate more resources to transformational innovation.

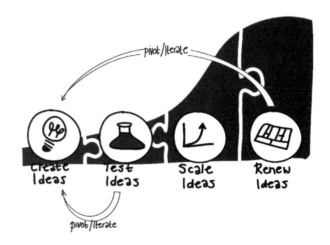

5. CHOOSE INNOVATION MODEL:

We have already described several models of innovation that can be put in place within a company (e.g. innovation institutes, internal accelerators or startup co-creation). Choosing a model is usually where most innovation leaders like to begin. However, the choice of an innovation model should be informed by an understanding of the company's context and innovation strategy. There are also pros and cons to consider for each model. As such, the choice of innovation model should be viewed as simply a starting point. There has to be a commitment from leaders to build on the chosen model with a more comprehensive ecosystem.

6. CREATE AN INNOVATION FRAMEWORK:

In this book, we presented a generic framework for innovation (i.e. create ideas, test ideas, scale ideas, renew ideas). There are other powerful frameworks such as Ash Maurya's Running Lean and Steve Blank's Customer Development Process. These frameworks, as well as ours, can be adopted as they are. However, we have found that it is more useful if a company develops its own bespoke framework based on the principles outlined in this book. For example, Intuit has their D4D framework, Adobe has the Kickbox and Pearson has the Lean Product Lifecycle. The development of an innovation framework can be based on the company's context, specific innovation challenges, strategic goals and the chosen innovation model. It is important to ensure that the framework is designed to embody both product development best practice and investment governance.

267

7. WORK WITH ENABLING FUNCTIONS:

As we argued earlier, an innovation ecosystem needs support from the rest of the organization. Enabling functions play a key role in the design of the innovation framework. They can help design what happens at each innovation stage and where product teams need to go for resources. Enabling functions can also help develop the innovation tools and platforms that the company will use. They can help ensure that these tools work well with other processes within the company. As such, they constitute an important building block in the development of the innovation ecosystem.

8. CREATE TOOLS AND PLATFORMS:

For innovation practice to succeed, companies need the right tools and platforms. As such, innovation leaders must develop or adopt key tools such as the business model canvas and experiment board. An innovation toolkit that contains all the key tools can be created both physically and virtually. Products teams can also be provided with playbooks or innovation guides. These can be based on the innovation framework and can make clear when and how each tool or method should be used.

9. DEVELOP INNOVATION CAPABILITIES:

Product teams also need training and coaching on lean innovation methods such as design thinking, business model design, customer discovery, experiment design, minimum viable products, iterations and pivots. Without the right skills in place, innovation practices will not flourish, even with great tools and methods. As such, companies must develop a training program for employees interested in innovation. This program can range from online webinars, full-day workshops or one-week design sprints. At Adobe, before people get the red Kickbox, they are encouraged to attend a workshop where they are trained on how to use it.[32]

10. SET UP INVESTMENT BOARDS:

Beyond product development practices, it is also important that the company manages its investments in innovation using the right methods. Setting up an investment board is one way to do that. At Pearson, these are called product councils and their job is to make incremental investment decisions at each innovation stage. Investment boards can be set up at different levels within the organization, depending on complexity and size. Their membership must be cross-functional and they must be given a clear mandate and budget to invest in innovation.

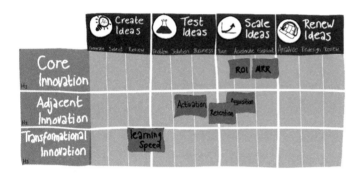

269

11. CHOOSE KEY METRICS:

To help investment boards make their decisions, companies need to replace the business case with new ways for teams to request investments in their ideas. These submission forms or presentation templates need to be aligned to the innovation framework. Each stage of the framework must have a submission template that is aligned to the requirements of that stage. These templates must allow members of the investment board to evaluate progress and make informed decisions. As such, key metrics and success criteria must be identified for each stage. Members of the investment board then need to be trained on how to make incremental investment decisions and use innovation accounting.

12. BUILD THE COMMUNITY:

The final piece of the puzzle is the community of practice. We will not repeat what we have already written about the role of the community in an innovation ecosystem. Suffice to say that the cultural impact of the ecosystem will be most clearly manifested in the strength and practices of its innovation community. This is part of what makes this a key building block when creating any innovation ecosystem.

These twelve building blocks are a lot for innovation leaders to put in place all at once. There will also be a lot of corporate politics to deal with. Organizations inevitably resist change. Some of the battles will be vicious and not easily won. This can often mean taking one step forward and two steps back. Some building blocks may need to be redone more than twice. It is enough to make innovators give up and walk away! Some innovation leaders we have worked with ended up leaving their jobs before the work is done. They were simply way too frustrated by the job. To build an innovation ecosystem in an established company, one has to be prepared for a long slog. As such, it is key to never try to do too much. The same practices of create-test-learn should be used to incrementally and iteratively build your ecosystem.

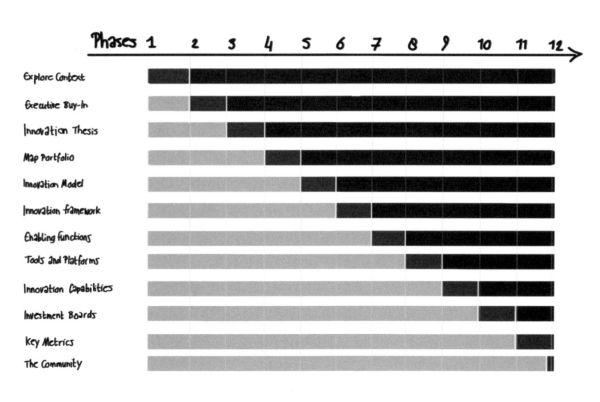

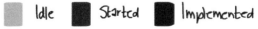

Minimum Viable Ecosystems

One way to build an innovation ecosystem is to take the company head-on. This can be done by following the steps above in an incremental way. Innovation leaders can start by assessing their business context and then get executive support. After that, they can then rollout the elements of the ecosystem one by one. They can work with executives to develop an innovation thesis, map the portfolio, develop an innovation framework and so on. Such an incremental method is extremely difficult to execute. This is because success takes a long time to show. The ecosystem has to be in place before its benefits are realized. At each incremental stage, people have to be convinced that they are doing the right thing. This act of faith is difficult to sustain in the day-to-day grind of running a large company. Of course executives can issue mandates and orders for employees to put the ecosystem in place. But we have found that things go better when people are truly bought into what their innovation leaders are trying to do.

We have found that innovation practices are easier to spread within a large company if we can get some early wins. Innovation leaders need to find places within the company where they can implement a minimum version of the innovation ecosystem and demonstrate early success. These early wins can then be celebrated publicly as great stories to inspire other parts of the business. They can also help galvanize executive support and provide a coat of armor for future battles with detractors. Innovation leaders can apply the adoption lifecycle here and start working with early adopters before targeting the rest of the company. Early adopters will be those parts of the business with leadership, that truly get the value of innovation. Early adopters can also be those parts of the business with products or brands that are struggling in the market and would be happy to receive help with innovation.

When Claudia Kotchka and her teams were trying to implement innovation best practices within P&G, they first worked with the Mr. Clean brand which had become stalled and stale.[33]

After examining customer needs, they helped launch Mr. Clean Magic Reach, which did well in the market. This success inspired other business units within P&G to take up some of the innovation practices that Kotchka and her team where advocating. If Kotchka had started by trying to convince parts of the business that were already doing well, the conversations would have been more difficult.

Sometimes even early adopter business units can find it hard to change their ways of working within the context of the parent company. An innovation lab can be used as a 'safe zone' for this. Rather than working only on new ideas generated by its staff, the lab can generate support within the main business by inviting early adopter product teams to use the labs resources and methods to solve their problems. In this way, the lab becomes a Trojan horse that slowly infiltrates its innovation practices into the main business. Over time the parts of the business that are most keen to use the lab can be encouraged to get their own staff trained as innovation catalysts. A minimum viable ecosystem is the smallest possible version of the full ecosystem that can be put in place with early

adopters. We can start by simply helping teams solve their problems using innovation best practice. Over time, this can be incrementally built-up to include innovation strategy and innovation management. At the end of our work with early adopters, we need to have had a chance to test an end-to-end version of the ecosystem. The lessons learned from that work can then inform the rollout of the ecosystem to the rest of the business. The challenge for innovation leaders is to not rest on their laurels after getting success with early adopters. The rest of the business still needs to be transformed. The twelve steps/building blocks must eventually all be completed. If this transformation fails, then the early adopter's business units will become innovation islands surrounded by the choppy waters of traditional business practices. It is difficult for such islands to sustain their innovation practices in the long-term.

The same applies to innovation labs (e.g. Yahoo's Brickhouse). Innovation leaders have to be very clear about their goals and measure their progress by how much they are changing their parent company's innovation culture. Such progress can be tracked through metrics, such as the number of employees that have received innovation training, the number of innovation catalysts in the business, the number of innovation events held (e.g. meetups and hackathons), the number of investment boards set up, the number of products that have been developed using lean innovation, changes in the balance of the portfolio and the number of products aligned to the innovation thesis. We have developed a measure for the maturity of an innovation ecosystem within any company (see innovation activity). This assessment scale can be used to track progress and identify areas that still need improvement.

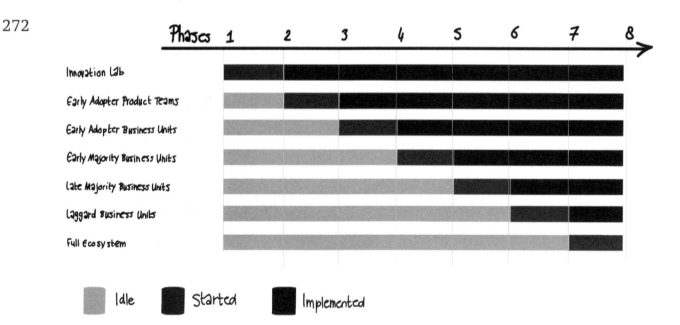

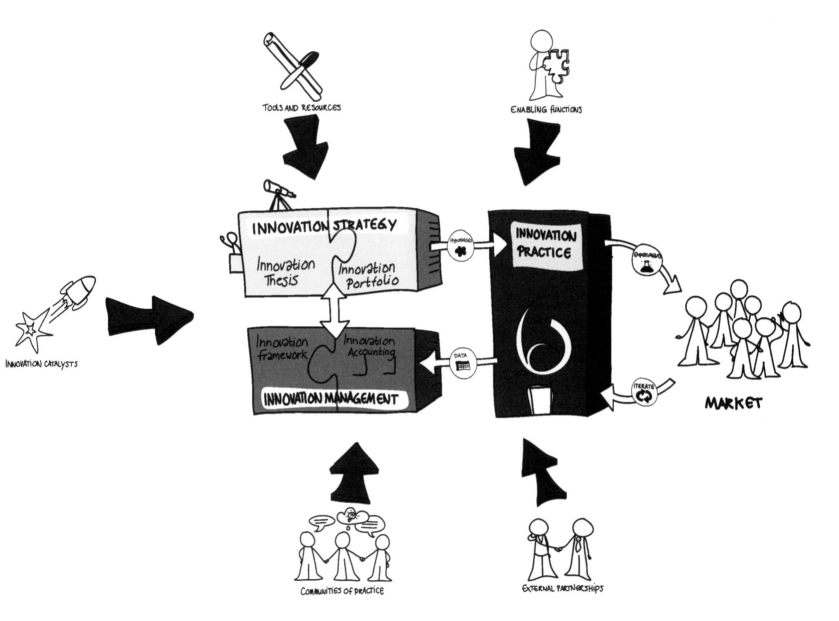

INNOVATION CATALYSTS

TOOLS AND RESOURCES

ENABLING FUNCTIONS

INNOVATION STRATEGY

Innovation Thesis

Innovation Portfolio

INNOVATION PRACTICE

Innovation Framework

Innovation Accounting

INNOVATION MANAGEMENT

Hypotheses

Experiment

DATA

ITERATE

MARKET

COMMUNITIES OF PRACTICE

EXTERNAL PARTNERSHIPS

Innovation Activity: Assessing Your Innovation Ecosystem

	ZERO	BASIC	GOOD	EXCELLENT
Within your company, is there alignment and support for innovation at the executive level?				
Does your company have a clearly articulated innovation strategy and/or innovation thesis?				
Are all employees in your company aware of the innovation thesis?				
Are all the innovation projects currently in-flight in your company, aligned to the innovation thesis?				
Does your company have a balanced portfolio of products/services?				
Is your company making investments across the three horizons in order to balance its portfolio?				
Does your company have an innovation framework?				
Do product teams use this framework as a guide for best practice?				
Does your company have an investment board for innovation?				
Does your company use incremental investing for innovation?				
Does your company protect its investments in innovation from budget cuts?				

Does your company have clear innovation KPIs, against which the success of new ventures is measured?				
Are your company's innovation KPIs aligned to the innovation stage of new ventures?				
Is your company's innovation framework aligned with and supported by the finance teams?				
Is there alignment with other key enabling functions with regards to innovation management (e.g. HR, Legal, Marketing, Sales)?				
Has your company adopted the right tools and methods for innovation?				
Does your company utilize cross-functional teams when doing innovation?				
Does your company have innovation catalysts that coach and work with product teams?				
When it occurs, is failure celebrated as learning within your company?				
Does your company continually monitor its environment for changes it needs to respond to?				

If any of your answers fall into the left two columns, then work still needs to be done to improve that aspect of your innovation ecosystem.

Ben Yoskovitz

CO-FOUNDER AT HIGHLINE BETA

Ben Yoskovitz is co-author of *Lean Analytics*. He is an experienced founder, investor and product manager. He has served as VP of Product at VarageSale and GoInstant (acq. $CRM); Co-Founder/CEO at Standout Jobs. He recently set up Highline BETA with Marcus Daniels, which is a company that helps large enterprises to innovate by co-creating startups.

CS: TELL US A LITTLE BIT ABOUT YOUR BACKGROUND AND HOW YOU CAME TO FORM HIGHLINE BETA?

BY: I've been in the digital and Web startup world for the last twenty years. In that timeframe I've started a few companies, worked as VP Product for others, made over fifteen angel investments and launched an early stage startup accelerator. I also co-authored a book, *Lean Analytics*, which brought together Lean Startup methodologies with an analytical approach. I feel like all of these efforts have led to Highline BETA, where I'll be leveraging a great deal of my past experience in building products, investing, mentorship and more.

I've started Highline BETA with a co-founder, Marcus Daniels. He has a similarly diverse background in startups as a founder, pre-seed investor, product person and more. We both came to a similar conclusion at the same time: we believe better startups can be created out of a collaboration with large companies.

CS: WHAT IS HIGHLINE BETA? WHAT DOES YOUR COMPANY DO?

BY: Highline BETA is a startup co-creation company. We essentially do two things. First, we work with large companies to identify areas of opportunity, disruption and growth within their own businesses. Second, we bring in founders to start new companies around those areas of opportunity and invest in those new companies. Our goal with large companies is to push forward their innovation agenda through external startups. To do that we need to understand their businesses and conduct early problem/solution validation work with their intrapreneurs. This work helps large companies understand their transformative opportunities more effectively, and helps Highline BETA make better decisions around where startups should exist. Once we've discovered a real opportunity where we believe a startup should exist, we recruit the founders, provide the initial pre-seed funding and then work with the startup to push them forward.

CS: IN YOUR EXPERIENCE, WHAT DO LARGE COMPANIES STRUGGLE WITH THE MOST WHEN IT COMES TO INNOVATION?

BY: Large companies can innovate internally but it's going to require a massive transformation from within. And that's an expensive and long process. Large companies have to go through this process, but the very process of transforming yourself (as a large company) and actually disrupting yourself before someone else does, is extremely challenging. Companies spend many millions of dollars trying to innovate internally with minimal results. The risk of change is often too overwhelming and the speed of change too slow.

277

CS: THE CONCEPT OF STARTUP CO-CREATION SOUNDS REALLY INTERESTING, CAN YOU TELL US MORE ABOUT THAT?

BY: Our hypothesis is that better startups will come out of the startup co-creation process, which involves bringing together large companies, venture-backable founders and pre-seed funding. Take any one (or two) of the pieces out of that equation (corporate customers + venture-backable founders + pre-seed funding) and it doesn't work. Our belief is that large companies are ready to work with startups in a new way, through the process of co-creation. Large companies, while working on massive transformations from within, can benefit from the speed of startup co-creation from the outside. And startups benefit from working with large companies too. Ideally the startups that emerge from the co-creation process have a fantastic customer, partner or even investor out of the gate. That's something that most startups don't have when they first start. Co-created startups will begin on day one with a huge advantage, having pulled ideas and insights from large companies, and having built a critical relationship.

CS: HOW DOES STARTUP CO-CREATION HELP ESTABLISHED COMPANIES WITH SOME OF THE INNOVATION CHALLENGES THEY FACE?

BY: Startup co-creation will give established companies a faster and less expensive way to see disruptive opportunities realized. It's important to note that in our model of startup co-creation, the startups are independent companies. But the initial spark for those co-created startups came from within a large company, and ideally there's a relationship established between the large company and co-created startup that's mutually beneficial. In absence of startup co-creation, we believe that too many large companies will move too slowly through their innovation processes and find themselves being disrupted too aggressively from the outside.

CS: DOES STARTUP CO-CREATION REPLACE OR COMPLEMENT OTHER INNOVATION ACTIVITIES THAT THE COMPANY MIGHT BE INVOLVED IN?

BY: Startup co-creation 100% complements other innovation activities. For example, Highline BETA isn't going to be the company that trains all employees on Lean Startup methodology and best practices. But we certainly benefit from companies that have gone through that type of training, because we work very closely with a small group of intrapreneurs to take opportunities, themes and ideas and validate them quickly in the market before deciding whether to co-create a startup or not. Highline BETA and the process of startup co-creation is an extension of existing innovation efforts going on inside companies. In fact, I believe we'll be more successful with companies that are already pushing aggressively on their innovation agenda versus those that are just getting started.

CS: IF HIGHLINE BETA IS NOT INVOLVED IN TRAINING THE COMPANY ON USING LEAN STARTUP METHODS, WHAT IF ANY IMPACT/BENEFIT DO YOU THINK STARTUP CO-CREATION CAN HAVE FOR A LARGE COMPANY'S ENTREPRENEURIAL/ INNOVATION CULTURE?

BY: While startup co-creation is about building external startups, I believe the co-creation process will have a positive impact on the large companies we work with. For starters, our programming/ process (while working with large companies) does involve training and education that a small group of intrapreneurs can take back into their organization. We'll be working with intrapreneurs on lean methodology, design thinking, product management/development and more. We may not transform an entire company, but the intrapreneurs we work with will be able to take the skills and experience they gain working with us (through the early validation process before a startup is co-created) back into their organizations.

Secondly, we see an opportunity for intrapreneurs to continue working with startups after they've been co-created, which I think will be a unique and interesting opportunity for those employees. For example, an intrapreneur that works with us through the process, may become an advisor or mentor to a co-created startup, maintaining a great relationship between the intrapreneur (and their company) and the startup. Finally, I think startup co-creation - because of the speed with which we can do things from the outside - will inspire and drive companies to push themselves further towards innovation and disrupting themselves successfully through multiple methods. Startup co-creation can be the catalyst that sparks more efforts within an organization.

CS: IF A COMPANY WANTED TO ENGAGE IN STARTUP CO-CREATION WHAT KEY THINGS SHOULD IT CONSIDER HAVING IN PLACE?

BY: In my mind the effort to get to startup co-creation is fairly minimal. Companies that are just starting out in terms of an innovation strategy may be too early for co-creation, because there's a certain "leap of faith" involved in recognizing that the best way to see disruptive ideas realized is on the outside. Our goal with startup co-creation is to help large companies disrupt themselves faster and innovate successfully, but to do it through external startups and not entirely from within.

CS: IS STARTUP CO-CREATION SOMETHING ANY COMPANY CAN DO? OR IS IT MORE SUITED TO CERTAIN TYPES OF COMPANIES?

BY: I believe all companies can benefit from startup co-creation. I think some will be more ready for it than others - specifically those companies that are already actively working to innovate from within and recognize the challenges of doing so. We know that startup co-creation is a relatively new concept and some companies may not be completely ready to see ideas move out of their organization and get executed elsewhere (through co-created startups). Marcus and I believe this is the key: the combination of large companies and external startups (not one or the other independently), along with the necessary funding, which Highline BETA provides, to make sure startups have the capital necessary to get to product/market fit.

279

We wish you the very best of luck on your innovation journey! There will be many detractors and critics. You will face several challenges and difficulties. In the business world, there are only a few things that are more difficult than transforming a large well-established company. It is gut-checking, difficult and grinding work every single day. But it is also very rewarding. Innovators should always remember that the credit goes to the person in the arena. Not the critics throwing stones on the sidelines.

Tendayi Viki   Dan Toma   Esther Gons

About the Authors

Tendayi Viki, PhD MBA

Dr Tendayi Viki is an author, speaker and advisor on the topic of corporate innovation. He helps companies of all sizes develop internal ecosystems so they can innovate for future while running their core business. He holds a PhD in Psychology and an MBA. He has worked with several companies including ABN AMRO, Airbus, Air France-KLM, American Express, The British Museum, Lufthansa-Airplus, Pearson, Salesforce, Standard Bank, Unilever and The World Bank. Dr Viki co-designed and helped implement Pearson's Product Lifecycle, which is an innovation framework that won Best Innovation Program 2015 at the Corporate Entrepreneur Awards in New York. He was nominated for the Thinkers50 2017 Innovation Award and listed on the Thinker50 2018 Radar List of emerging management thinkers to watch. He is also a Contributor at *Forbes Magazine*.

Dan Toma, MBA

Dan comes from an entrepreneurial background. He has been involved with Hi-Tech and internet start-ups across the world and is an entrepreneurship community leader in Europe. In recent years, he started focusing more on enterprise innovation management, specifically on the changes large organizations need to make to allow for disruptive new ventures to be built in a corporate setting. He has worked with companies like Deutsche Telekom, Bosch, Jaguar Land Rover and Allianz. A big proponent of the ecosystem approach to innovation, Dan has also worked with various government bodies in Asia and Europe, helping developing national innovation ecosystems and implement national innovation strategies. The work experience gathered from the public and private sector has been translated into various experiential courses that Dan has delivered for universities worldwide.

Esther Gons

Esther is co-founder and investor of NEXT.amsterdam, helping startups from ideas phase to a working business model. She has developed the entrepreneurship course for the Communication Multimedia and Design program at the Amsterdam University of Applied Sciences. She is also an international speaker who organized the first StartupBus Europe tour in 2011 and has acted as lead mentor at Rockstart Accelerator for the past six years. As a visual spatial thinker she was part of bringing the lean startup movement to the Netherlands. Esther has mentored over a hundred startups so far and still acts as advisor for many of them. Connecting corporates to the startup ecosystem is important to NEXT, so Esther is also frequently involved in corporate innovation.

Earlyvangelists

We would like to extend our deepest gratitude to our early adopters who supported our crowdfunding campaign and gave us early feedback on the book.

Alejandro Perez
Alessandra Correa
Alessandro Vigilante
Alexander Buddrick
Ali Tariq
Andelie Zeeman
Andrew Steele
Andre Knol
Annemette Reinholt Skou
Beetz Richard
Benjamin Yoskovitz
Bob Forgan
Bob Jansen
Bryonie Badcock
Carlos Rodriguez
Cedric Cuche
Chanade Murphy - Johnson
Charles Ward
Chris Locke
Christian Kramer
Christiane Gerigk
Consortia Adelwisa Paita
Corentin Cremet

Craig Strong
Dagmar Riess
Dan Koopman
David Trayford
David J. Bland
Diana Stepner
Duncan Brannan
Elia Morling
Elin Cathcart
Ephraim Viki
Erik Kongsvik-Ibsen
Erik Idzenga
Evelin Velev
Franck Debane
Gerhard Müller
Gillian Julius
Guillermo Rodriguez Lorbada
Guy Vincent
Guy Van Wijmeersch
Hans Balmaekers
Hans van Gent
Henry Warren
Jacob Hartstra

Jake Selvey
James Twigger
Jason Govender
Javid Jamae
Jean-Baptiste Theard
Jennifer Sutherland
Jeroen Tjepkema
Joanne Simpson
Joe Thomsett
Johan Schouwstra
Johan Vink
Johannes Mueller
John Elbing
Jordan Schlipf
Jorge Castellote
Jose Papo
Justin Coetsee
Justin Souter
Kees van Nunen
Kenny Nguyen
Klaas Jan Bolt
Klaus Wagner
Lee Constantine

Leon Pals
Leonard Giura
Liher Pillado
Lourens van der Kleij
Lu Jin
Lucia Meglio
Luis Fdo
Marcos Eguillor
Marielle van Bijsterveld
Marleen van Diest
Matthew Adendorff
Matthias Koller
Matthias Patz
Matthijs Scholten
Michael Bier
Michael Murphy
Michael Aechtler
Mike van Hoenselaar
Moritz Ackerhans
Nestor Gomez
Niall Smith
Nick Norea
Nick Stevens

Nina Angelo
Nestor Lombao
Otto Freijser
Paige Holroyd
Pascal Miserez
Paul Brown
Petar Stojanov
Peter Weichert
Peter Pascale
Peter O'Shaughnessy
Philipp Greiner
Raimon Rafols
Rasmus Vaupel
Rebecca Stephens
Reiner Walter
Rene Bastijans
Roberto Chaverri
Roberto Touza
Roland Hoekzema
Roland Merheb
Ronald Smulders
Rune Knudsen
Matthieu Salles

Sam Hysell
Sam Rye
Sebastian Palus
Serkan Unsal
Sjoerd Smink
Skot Carruth
Sonja Kresojevic
Startup Funding
Stefan Jungmayr
Steve Vosloo
Stuart Eccles
Suki Fuller
Tammo Ganders
Thoma Adrian
Thomas Hansen
Tim Kastelle
Tobias Fella
Tobias Brockow
Toby Cox
Trey Zagante
Tristan Kromer
Viktor Osum
Vincent Thamm

INDEX:
Keywords/Terms

286

Names/Organizations

291

293

Notes

Part One

1. Ulanoff, L (2015). 'In 2015, Microsoft got its groove back.' *Mashable*: http://mashable.com/2015/12/17/2015-microsoft-is-back/#9E7dahMO7mqn

2. Wingfield, N. (2015). 'A $7 Billion Charge at Microsoft Leads to Its Largest Loss Ever.' *New York Times*: http://www.nytimes.com/2015/07/22/technology/microsoft-earnings-q4.html?_r=0

3. Furr, N. & Dyer, J. (2014). *The Innovator's Method: Bringing the Lean Startup into Your Organization*. Boston: Harvard Business Review Press.

4. Foster, R. & Kaplan, S. (2011). *Creative Destruction: Why Companies That Are Built to Last Underperform the Market – and How to Successfully Transform Them*. New York City: Random House.

5. Stuart, T., Currie, B., Goodman, J. & Ives, G. (2014). 'Age of disruption: Are Canadian firms prepared?' *Deloitte Canada*: https://www2.deloitte.com/content/dam/Deloitte/ca/Documents/insights-and-issues/ca-en-insights-issues-future-of-productivity-2015.pdf

6. Metz, C. (2014). 'Tech Time Warp of the Week: Watch Steve Ballmer Laugh at the Original iPhone.' *Wired Magazine*: http://www.wired.com/2014/09/tech-time-warp-of-the-week-watch-steve-ballmer-laugh-at-the-original-iphone/

7. Wilhelm, A. (2013). 'Ballmer's Biggest Regret Is Missing Out On "The New Device Called The Phone".' *Techcrunch*: https://techcrunch.com/2013/09/19/ballmers-biggest-regret-is-missing-out-on-the-new-device-called-the-phone/

8. Statista (2016). Global market share held by Nokia smartphones from 1st quarter 2007 to 2nd quarter 2013: http://www.statista.com/statistics/263438/market-share-held-by-nokia-smartphones-since-2007/

9. Huy, Q. (2014). 'What Could Have Saved Nokia, and What Can Other Companies Learn?' *INSEAD Knowledge*: http://knowledge.insead.edu/strategy/what-could-have-saved-nokia-and-what-can-other-companies-learn-3220

10. Hesseldahl, A. (2012). 'How Garmin Failed to See the iPhone Threat.' *All Things D*: http://allthingsd.com/20120612/how-garmin-failed-to-see-the-iphone-threat/

11. Schumpeter, J.A. (1942). *Capitalism, Socialism and Democracy*. New York City: Harper & Brothers.

12. McGrath, R.G. (2013). *The End of Competitive Advantage: How to Keep Your Strategy Moving as Fast as Your Business*. Boston: Harvard Business Review Press.

13. March, J.G. (1991). 'Exploration and Exploitation in Organizational Learning.' *Organization Science*, 2(1), 71-87.

14. Marmer, M., Herrmann, B.L., Dogrultan, E. & Berman, R. 'Startup Genome Report.' https://s3.amazonaws.com/startupcompass-public/StartupGenomeReport1_Why_Startups_Succeed_v2.pdf

15. Bhide, A.V. (2000). *The Origin and Evolution of New Businesses*. Oxford: Oxford University Press.

16. Livingston, J. (2007). *Founders at Work: Stories of Startups' Early Days*. New York City: Apress.

17. Blank, S. & Dorf, B. (2012). *The Startup Owner's Manual: The Step-By-Step Guide for Building a Great Company*. California: K&S Ranch.

18. O'Reilly, C.A. & Tushman, M.L. (2004). 'The Ambidextrous Organization.' *Harvard Business Review*, 82, 74-83.

19. http://www.dictionary.com

20. Nielsen, T. (2015). 'Novelty is not Innovation.' *ThoughtWorks*: http://www.thoughtworks.com/insights/blog/enterprise-needs-lean-product-development

21. Smith, A. (2014). 'R&D spending unlinked to financial performance, study shows.' *The Financial Times*: https://www.ft.com/content/cdfe-1b2c-5abf-11e4-b449-00144feab7de#axzz3I5ez9PAL

22. Jaruzelski, B., Staack, V. & Goehle, B. (2014). 'The Global Innovation 1000: Proven Paths to Innovation Success.' *strategy+business*: http://www.strategy-business.com/article/00295

23. Jaruzelski, B., Loehr, J. & Holman, R. (2012). 'The Global Innovation 1000: Making Ideas Work.' *strategy+business*: http://www.strategy-business.com/article/00140

24. Nagji, B. & Tuff, G. (2012). 'Managing Your Innovation Portfolio.' *Harvard Business Review*, 90, 66-74.

25. See more at Tristan's blog: https://grasshopperherder.com/

26. Garud, R., Gehman, J. & Kumaraswamy, A. (2011). 'Complexity Arrangements for Sustained Innovation: Lessons from 3M Corporation.' *Organization Studies*, 32, 737-767.

27. Wilson, F. (2009). 'Thematic vs Thesis Driven Investing.' *AVC*: http://avc.com/2009/11/thematic-vs-thesis-driven-investing/

28. Maurya, A. (2012). *Running Lean: Iterate from Plan A to a Plan That Works*. Sebastopol: O'Reilly.

29. Blank, S. (2013). 'It's Time to Play Moneyball: The Investment Readiness Level.' *Steve Blank*: https://steveblank.com/2013/11/25/its-time-to-play-moneyball-the-investment-readiness-level/

30. Viki, T., Strong, C. & Kresojevic, S. (2017). *The Lean Product Lifecycle: A playbook for developing innovative and profitable new products*. London: Pearson.

31. McClure, D. (2010). 'MoneyBall for Startups: Invest Before Product/Market Fit, Double-Down After.' *Master of 500 Hats*: http://500hats.typepad.com/500blogs/2010/07/moneyball-for-startups.html

32. Viki, T., Strong, C. & Kresojevic, S. (2017). *The Lean Product Lifecycle: A playbook for developing innovative and profitable new products*. London: Pearson.

33. See here for Adobe's Kickbox: http://kickbox.adobe.com/

34. Anthony, S.D. (2012). *The Little Black Book of Innovation: How It Works, How to Do It*. Boston: Harvard Business Press.

35. De La Merced, M.J. (2012). 'Eastman Kodak Files for Bankruptcy.' *New York Times*: http://dealbook.nytimes.com/2012/01/19/eastman-kodak-files-for-bankruptcy/?_r=0

36. Stelfox, D. (2014). 'Last days of Kodak town: the decline and fall of the city photography built.' *The Guardian*: https://www.theguardian.com/artanddesign/2014/jun/25/kodaks-town-decline-and-fall-of-city-photography-built

37. Hardy, Q. (2015). 'At Kodak, Clinging to a Future Beyond Film.' *New York Times*: http://www.nytimes.com/2015/03/22/business/at-kodak-clinging-to-a-future-beyond-film.html

38. Deutsch, C.H. (2008). 'At Kodak, Some Old Things Are New Again.' *New York Times*: http://www.nytimes.com/2008/05/02/technology/02kodak.html?_r=0

39. McGrath, M. (2013). 'Kodak Is Back On The Big Board After Bankruptcy.' *Forbes*: http://www.forbes.com/sites/maggiemcgrath/2013/11/01/there-and-back-again-10-companies-that-returned-to-the-market-after-bankruptcy/

40. Hardy, Q. (2015). 'At Kodak, Clinging to a Future Beyond Film.' *New York Times*: http://www.nytimes.com/2015/03/22/business/at-kodak-clinging-to-a-future-beyond-film.html

41. Trefis Team (2015). 'BlackBerry's Software Business: Scenarios That Could Impact The Stock Price.' *Forbes*: http://www.forbes.com/sites/greatspeculations/2015/04/08/blackberrys-software-business-scenarios-that-could-impact-the-stock-price/

42. Ewing, A. (2015). 'Nokia to Return $4.4 Billion to Investors Amid Deal Savings.' *Bloomberg Business*: http://www.bloomberg.com/news/articles/2015-10-29/nokia-raises-networks-profitability-target-on-cost-savings

43. McCarthy, E. (2014). 'Garmin Profit Rises 5.5%, Beats Expectations.' *Wall Street Journal*: http://www.wsj.com/articles/garmin-profit-rises-5-5-beats-expectations-1406720452

44. Christensen, C.M. (2013). *The Innovator's Dilemma: When New Technologies Cause Great Firms to Fail*. Boston: Harvard Business Review Press.

45. Ireland, R.D., Hoskisson, R.E. & Hitt, M.A. (2011). *The Management of Strategy*. London: Cengage Learning.

46. McGrath, R G. (2013). *The End of Competitive Advantage: How to Keep Your Strategy Moving as Fast as Your Business*. Boston: Harvard Business Review Press.

47. Christensen, C.M. (2013). *The Innovator's Dilemma: When New Technologies Cause Great Firms to Fail*. Boston: Harvard Business Review Press.

48. O'Reilly, C.A. & Tushman, M. L. (2004). 'The Ambidextrous Organization.' *Harvard Business Review*, 82, 74-83.

49. O'Reilly, C.A. & Tushman, M. L. (2011). 'Organizational Ambidexterity in Action: How Managers Explore and Exploit.' *California Management Review*, 53(4), 5-22.

50. O'Reilly, C.A. & Tushman, M. L. (2011). 'Organizational Ambidexterity in Action: How Managers Explore and Exploit.' *California Management Review*, 53(4), 5-22.

51. McGrath, R.G. (2013). *The End of Competitive Advantage: How to Keep Your Strategy Moving as Fast as Your Business*. Boston: Harvard Business Review Press.

52. Anthony, S.D., Johnson, M.W. & Sinfield, J.V. (2008). 'Institutionalizing Innovation.' *MIT Sloan Management Review*, 49(2), 45.

53. Torres-Picon, P. (2015). 'How to Build an Investment Thesis.' *AVC*: http://avc.com/2015/04/video-of-the-week-how-to-build-an-investment-thesis/

54. McClure, D. (2010). 'MoneyBall for Startups: Invest Before Product/Market Fit, Double-Down After.' *Master of 500 Hats*: http://500hats.typepad.com/500blogs/2010/07/moneyball-for-startups.html

55. Burnham B. (2015). 'USV Thesis 2.0.' *Union Square Ventures*: https://www.usv.com/blog/usv-thesis-20

56. Wilson, F. (2009). 'Thematic vs Thesis Driven Investing.' *AVC*: http://avc.com/2009/11/thematic-vs-thesis-driven-investing/

57. These benefits are adapted from the talk by Torres-Picon, P. (2015). 'How to Build an Investment Thesis.' *AVC*: http://avc.com/2015/04/video-of-the-week-how-to-build-an-investment-thesis/

58. Wilson, F. (2009). 'Thematic vs Thesis Driven Investing.' *AVC*: http://avc.com/2009/11/thematic-vs-thesis-driven-investing/

59. Mintzberg, H. & Waters, J.A. (2006). 'Of strategies, deliberate and emergent.' *Strategic Management Journal*: http://onlinelibrary.wiley.com/doi/10.1002/smj.4250060306/abstract

60. Summer, D. (2008). 'No return to boom and bust: what Brown said when he was chancellor.' *The Guardian*: http://www.theguardian.com/politics/2008/sep/11/gordonbrown.economy

61. Osterwalder, A. & Pigneur, Y. (2010). *Business Model Generation: A Handbook for Visionaries, Game Changers, and Challengers.* New York City: John Wiley & Sons.

62. Christensen, C.M., Horn, M.B. & Johnson, C.W. (2008). *Disrupting Class: How Disruptive Innovation Will Change the Way the World Learns.* New York City: McGraw-Hill.

63. Carey, K. (2015). *The End of College: Creating the Future of Learning and the University of Everywhere.* London: Penguin.

64. CB Insights (2015). 'Funding To VC-Backed Education Technology Startups Grows 503% over 5 Years.' https://www.cbinsights.com/blog/ed-tech-funding-on-pace-record-year/

65. Mochari, I. (2015). '16 Startups Poised to Disrupt the Education Market.' *Inc. Magazine*: http://www.inc.com/ilan-mochari/16-startups-that-will-disrupt-the-education-market.html

66. Inc. Magazine (2016). 'Top Education Companies on the 2015 Inc. 5000.' http://www.inc.com/inc5000/list/2015/industry/education/

67. Christensen, C.M. (2013). *The Innovator's Dilemma: When New Technologies Cause Great Firms to Fail.* Boston: Harvard Business Review Press.

68. Nagji, B. & Tuff, G. (2012). 'Managing Your Innovation Portfolio.' *Harvard Business Review*, 90, 66-74.

69. Ansoff, H.I. & McDonnell, E.J. (1990). *Implanting Strategic Management.* New Jersey: Prentice Hall.

70. Bahgai, M., Coley, S. & White, D. (1999). *The Alchemy of Growth: Practical Insights for Building the Enduring Enterprise.* London: Orion Business.

71. Christensen, C.M. (2013). *The Innovator's Dilemma: When New Technologies Cause Great Firms to Fail.* Boston: Harvard Business Review Press.

72. Christensen, C.M., Raynor, M.E. & McDonald, R. (2015). 'What Is Disruptive Innovation?' *Harvard Business Review*: https://hbr.org/2015/12/what-is-disruptive-innovation

73. Bort, J. (2013). 'Hewlett Packard Could Have Been Apple If Not For 5 Bad Decisions.' *Business Insider*: http://www.businessinsider.com/woz-begged-hp-to-make-the-apple-pc-2013-2?IR=T

74. Christensen, C.M., Raynor, M.E. & McDonald, R. (2015). 'What Is Disruptive Innovation?' *Harvard Business Review*: https://hbr.org/2015/12/what-is-disruptive-innovation

75. Anthony, S. (2015). 'How Understanding Disruption Helps Strategists.' *Harvard Business Review*: https://hbr.org/2015/11/how-understanding-disruption-helps-strategists

76. Schmidt, E. & Rosenberg, J. (2014). *How Google Works.* London: Hachette.

77. Hern, A. (2016). 'How Alphabet became the biggest company in the world.' *The Guardian*: https://www.theguardian.com/technology/2016/feb/01/how-alphabet-made-google-biggest-company-in-the-world

78. Titcomb, J. (2015). 'Google and Alphabet: What does this all mean?' *The Telegraph*: http://www.telegraph.co.uk/technology/google/11796103/Google-and-Alphabet-What-does-this-all-mean.html

79. Page, L. (2015). Letter to the market on launching of Alphabet: 'G is for Google.' https://abc.xyz/

80. Lopez, N. (2016). 'Facebook's 10-year roadmap is basically lasers, bots and VR.' *The Next Web*: http://thenextweb.com/facebook/2016/04/12/facebook-reveals-10-year-roadmap/#gref

81. Howe, J. (2013). 'Clayton Christensen Wants to Transform Capitalism.' *Wired*: http://www.wired.com/2013/02/mf-clayton-christensen-wants-to-transform-capitalism/

82. Binns, A., Smith, W.K. & Tushman, M.L. (2011). 'The Ambidextrous CEO.' *Harvard Business Review*, 89, 74-80

83. Mathur, A. (2011). 'A Steve Jobs Landmark: The 1984 Apple Macintosh Launch Video.' *International Business Times*: http://www.ibtimes.com/steve-jobs-landmark-1984-apple-macintosh-launch-video-321860

84. Latson, J. (2015). 'Why the Computer Mouse's Inventor Isn't the Big Cheese.' *Time*: http://time.com/3831359/computer-mouse-history/

85. Gladwell, M. (2011). 'Creation Myth: Xerox PARC, Apple and the truth about innovation.' *The New Yorker*: http://www.newyorker.com/magazine/2011/05/16/creation-myth

86. Chesbrough, H. & Rosenbloom, R.S. (2002). 'The role of the business model in capturing value from innovation: Evidence from Xerox Corporation's technology spin-off companies.' *Industrial and Corporate Change*, 11(3), 529-555.

87. Osterwalder, A. & Pigneur, Y. (2010). *Business Model Generation: A Handbook for Visionaries, Game Changers, and Challengers.* New York City: John Wiley & Sons.

88. Wessel, M. (2012). 'Why Big Companies Can't Innovate.' *Harvard Business Review*: https://hbr.org/2012/09/why-big-companies-cant-innovate

89. Entrepreneurship World (2016). 'Lean Startup in the Enterprise – Prepare For A Bumpy Road.' https://intrapreneurship.world/lean-startup-in-the-enterprise-prepare-for-a-bumpy-road/

90. Dougherty, C. (2016). 'They Promised Us Jet Packs. They Promised the Bosses Profit.' *New York Times*: http://www.nytimes.com/2016/07/24/technology/they-promised-us-jet-packs-they-promised-the-bosses-profit.html?_r=0

91. Moore, G.A. (2006). 'To Succeed in the Long Term, Focus on the Middle Term.' *Harvard Business Review*, 85(7-8), 84-90.

92. Blank, S. & Dorf, B. (2012). *The Startup Owner's Manual: The Step-By-Step Guide for Building a Great Company*. California: K&S Ranch.

93. Ries, E. (2011). *The Lean Startup: How Today's Entrepreneurs Use Continuous Innovation to Create Radically Successful Businesses*. New York City: Crown Books.

94. Maurya, A. (2012). *Running Lean: Iterate from Plan A to a Plan That Works*. Sebastopol: O'Reilly.

95. Viki, T., Strong, C. & Kresojevic, S. (2017). *The Lean Product Lifecycle: A playbook for developing innovative and profitable new products*. London: Pearson.

96. Brown, T. (2009). *Change by Design. How Design Thinking Transforms Organizations and Inspires Innovation*. New York City: Harper Collins.

97. Gertner, J. (2013). *The Idea Factory: Bell Labs and the Great Age of American Innovation*. New York City: Penguin.

98. Livingston, J. (2016). 'Jessica Livingston's Pretty Complete List on How Not to Fail.' *Y Combinator*: http://www.themacro.com/articles/2016/06/how-not-to-fail/

99. Rogers, E.M. (1962). *Diffusion of Innovations*. Glencoe: Free Press.

100. Moore, G.A. (1999). *Crossing the Chasm: Marketing and Selling Disruptive Products to Mainstream Customers*. New York City: Harper Business.

101. Blank, S. & Dorf, B. (2012). *The Startup Owner's Manual: The Step-By-Step Guide for Building a Great Company*. California: K&S Ranch.

102. CIMA (2007). 'Theory of constraints and throughput accounting.' Topic Gateway Series No. 26. http://www.cimaglobal.com/Documents/ImportedDocuments/26_Theory_of_Constraints_and_Throughput_Accounting.pdf

103. Christensen, C. M., Allworth, J. & Dillon, K. (2012). *How Will You Measure Your Life?* New York City: Harper Business.

104. Ries, E. (2011). *The Lean Startup: How Today's Entrepreneurs Use Continuous Innovation to Create Radically Successful Businesses*. New York City: Crown Books.

105. Innovation Leader (2015). 'Untangling Innovation Metrics: What every innovation leader needs to know.' https://www.innovationleader.com/2015-metrics-report/

106. McClure, D. (2010). 'MoneyBall for Startups: Invest Before Product/Market Fit, Double-Down After.' *Master of 500 Hats*: http://500hats.typepad.com/500blogs/2010/07/moneyball-for-startups.html

107. Our create-test-learn loop is based on Eric Ries' Build-Measure-Learn loop for his 2010 book, *The Lean Startup*.

108. McClure D. (2007). 'Startup Metrics for Pirates: AARRR!' *Master of 500 Hats*: http://500hats.typepad.com/500blogs/2007/09/startup-metrics.html

109. McGrath, R. & MacMillan, I. (1995). 'Discovery-Driven Planning.' *Harvard Business Review*: https://hbr.org/1995/07/discovery-driven-planning

110. Hill, C.W.L., Schilling, M.A. & Jones, G.R. (2015). *Strategic Management: An Integrated Approach*. Boston: Cengage Learning.

Part Two

1. http://www.dictionary.com

2. Simonton, D. K. (2000). 'Creativity: Cognitive, Personal, Developmental, and Social Aspects.' *American Psychologist*, 55, 151–158.

3. Maddux, W.W. & Galinsky, A.D. (2009). 'Cultural Borders and Mental Barriers: The Relationship Between Living Abroad and Creativity.' *Journal of Personality and Social Psychology*, 96(5),1047-1061.

4. Maddux, W.W., Adam, H. & Galinsky, A.D. (2010). 'When in Rome… Learn Why the Romans Do What They Do: How Multicultural Learning Experiences Enhance Creativity.' *Personality and Social Psychology Bulletin, 36*(6), 731-741.

5. Tadmor, C., Galinsky, A.D. & Maddux, W.W. (2012). 'Getting the Most Out of Living Abroad: Biculturalism and Integrative Complexity as Key Drivers of Creative and Professional Success.' *Journal of Personality and Social Psychology*, 103(3), 520-542.

6. http://www.dictionary.com/

7. Fry, A. (1987). 'The Post-it Note: An Intrapreneurial Success.' *SAM Advanced Management Journal*, 52(3), 4.

8. Garud, R., Gehman, J. & Kumaraswamy, A. (2011). 'Complexity Arrangements for Sustained Innovation: Lessons from 3M Corporation.' *Organization Studies, 32*, 737-767.

9. Millard, A.J. (1990). *Edison and the Business of Innovation*. Baltimore: Johns Hopkins University Press.

10. Gertner, J. (2013). *The Idea Factory: Bell Labs and the Great Age of American Innovation*. New York City: Penguin.

11. Johnson, L.A. (2006). 'Bell Labs' history of inventions.' *USA Today*: http://usatoday30.usatoday.com/tech/news/2006-12-01-bell-research_x.htm

12. Foremski, T. (2011). 'How The "Traitorous Eight" Created Silicon Valley...' *Silicon Valley Watcher*: http://www.siliconvalleywatcher.com/mt/archives/2011/05/how_the_traitor.php

13. Isaacson, W. (2012). 'Inventing the Future – "The Idea Factory", by Jon Gertner.' *New York Times*: http://www.nytimes.com/2012/04/08/books/review/the-idea-factory-by-jon-gertner.html

14. Gertner, J. (2013). *The Idea Factory: Bell Labs and the Great Age of American Innovation*. New York City: Penguin.

15. Wikipedia: https://en.wikipedia.org/wiki/Telstar

16. Kelley, T. (2007). *The Art of Innovation: Lessons in Creativity from IDEO*. London: Crown Business.

17. Choi, J. (2014). 'The Science Behind Why Jeff Bezos's Two-Pizza Team Rule Works.' *I Done This Blog*: http://blog.idonethis.com/two-pizza-team/

18. Kniberg, K. & Ivarsson, A. (2012). 'Scaling Agile @ Spotify with Tribes, Squads, Chapters & Guilds.' https://dl.dropboxusercontent.com/u/1018963/Articles/SpotifyScaling.pdf

19. Hargadon, A.B. & Bechky, B.A. (2006). 'When Collections of Creatives Become Creative Collectives: A Field Study of Problem Solving at Work.' *Organization Science*, *17*(4), 484-500.

20. Leancamp was founded by Salim Virani as an unconference for people from different disciplines to share learnings about innovation and entrepreneurship.

21. Jain, R., Triandis, H.C. & Weick, C.W. (2010). *Managing Research, Development and Innovation: Managing the Unmanageable*. New York City: John Wiley & Sons.

22. Grant, A. M. (2016). *Originals: How Non-Conformists Move the World*. New York City: Viking.

23. Kelley, T. (2007). *The Art of Innovation: Lessons in Creativity from IDEO*. London: Crown Business.

24. Knapp, J., Zeratsky, J. & Kowitz, B. (2016). *Sprint: How to Solve Big Problems and Test New Ideas in Just Five Days*. New York City: Simon & Schuster.

25. Burkus, D. (2015). 'Inside Adobe's Innovation Kit.' *Harvard Business Review*: https://hbr.org/2015/02/inside-adobes-innovation-kit

26. Wilson, M. (2015). 'Adobe's Kickbox: The Kit To Launch Your Next Big Idea.' *Fast Company*: https://www.fastcodesign.com/3042128/adobes-kickbox-the-kit-to-launch-your-next-big-idea

27. Goetz, K. (2011). 'How 3M Gave Everyone Days Off and Created an Innovation Dynamo.' *Fast Company*: https://www.fastcodesign.com/1663137/how-3m-gave-everyone-days-off-and-created-an-innovation-dynamo

28. Upbin, B. (2012). 'Four Ways Intuit Keeps New Ideas Flowing.' *Forbes*: http://www.forbes.com/sites/bruceupbin/2012/09/05/four-ways-intuit-keeps-new-ideas-flowing/

29. Truong, A (2013). 'Why Google Axed Its "20% Time" Policy.' *Fast Company*: https://www.fastcompany.com/3015877/fast-feed/why-google-axed-its-20-policy

30. Hill, C.W.L., Schilling, M.A. & Jones, G.R. (2015). *Strategic Management: An Integrated Approach*. Boston: Cengage Learning.

31. Ross, A (2015). 'Why did Google abandon 20% time for innovation?' *HRZone*: http://www.hrzone.com/lead/culture/why-did-google-abandon-20-time-for-innovation

32. Livingston, J. (2007). *Founders at Work: Stories of Startups' Early Days*. New York City: Apress.

33. Hoffman, R. & Casnocha, B. (2012). *The Start-up of You: Adapt to the Future, Invest in Yourself, and Transform Your Career*. New York City: Crown Business.

34. Nieva, R. (2016). 'YouTube started as an online dating site.' *CNET*: http://www.cnet.com/uk/news/youtube-started-as-an-online-dating-site/

35. Garber, M. (2014). 'Instagram was first called "Burbn" Yes, after the drink.' *The Atlantic*: http://www.theatlantic.com/technology/archive/2014/07/instagram-used-to-be-called-brbn/373815/

36. Sarasvathy, S.D. (2009). *Effectuation: Elements of Entrepreneurial Expertise*. Cheltenham: Edward Elgar.

37. Popper, K.R. (2005). *The Logic of Scientific Discovery*. Oxford: Routledge.

38. Kromer, T. (2016). 'The Real Startup Book.' *Trikro*: http://www.trikro.com/downloads/playbook

39. Based on the Experiment Map by Moves The Needle: http://www.movestheneedle.com/resources/lean-innovation-experiment-map/

40. Tristan Kromer has written a great post on this: https://grasshopperherder.com/assumption-vs-hypothesis-to-the-death/

41. Gilbert, D. (2006). *Stumbling on Happiness*. New York City: Random House.

42. Gross, D. (2003). 'Lies, Damn Lies, and Focus Groups.' *Slate*: http://www.slate.com/articles/business/moneybox/2003/10/lies_damn_lies_and_focus_groups.html

43. Fitzpatrick, R. (2014). *The Mom Test: How to talk to customers & learn if your business is a good idea when everyone is lying to you*. Amazon CreateSpace.

Note on page 178. Adapted from Fitzpatrick, R. (2014). *The Mom Test: How to talk to customers & learn if your business is a good idea when everyone is lying to you*. Amazon CreateSpace.

44. Liker, J.K. (2004). *The Toyota Way: 14 Management Principles from the World's Greatest Manufacturer*. New York City: McGraw-Hill.

45. Tim Bajarin (2014). 'Why the Maker Movement Is Important to America's Future.' *Time*: http://time.com/104210/maker-faire-maker-movement/

46. Christopher, M. (2000). 'The Agile Supply Chain: Competing in Volatile Markets'. *Industrial Marketing Management*, 29, 37-44.

47. Sorescu, A., Frambach, R.T., Singh, J., Rangaswamy, A. & Bridges, C. (2011). 'Innovations in Retail Business Models.' *Journal of Retailing*, 87, S3-S16.

48. Leonard, D. & Clough, R. (2016). 'How GE Exorcised the Ghost of Jack Welch to Become a 124-Year-Old Startup'. *Bloomberg Businessweek*: http://www.bloomberg.com/news/articles/2016-03-17/how-ge-exorcised-the-ghost-of-jack-welch-to-become-a-124-year-old-startup

49. Power, B. (2014). 'How GE Applies Lean Startup Practices.' *Harvard Business Review*: https://hbr.org/2014/04/how-ge-applies-lean-startup-practices

50. For the Segway story see Grant, A. M. (2016). *Originals: How Non-Conformists Move the World*. New York City: Viking.

51. Olson, P. (2016). 'Samsung Officially Scraps The Galaxy Note 7.' *Forbes*: http://www.forbes.com/sites/parmyolson/2016/10/11/samsung-ending-production-galaxy-note-7/

52. Knapp, J., Zeratsky, J. & Kowitz, B. (2016). *Sprint: How to Solve Big Problems and Test New Ideas in Just Five Days*. New York City: Simon & Schuster.

53. Coleman, K. (2009). 'Gmail leaves beta, launches "Back to Beta" Labs feature.' *Google Blog*: https://gmail.googleblog.com/2009/07/gmail-leaves-beta-launches-back-to-beta.html

54. Bland, D.J. (2015). 'Lean Startup Comes Home.' *Medium*: https://medium.com/@davidjbland/lean-startup-comes-home-8f205993da40#.likbps46e

55. On the difference between the divisional and functional organization, check out Ben Thompson's 2013 article 'Why Microsoft's Reorganization Is a Bad Idea.': https://stratechery.com/2013/why-microsofts-reorganization-is-a-bad-idea/

56. Apple is the only notable exception to this rule. It is a functional organization that is highly innovative.

57. Thompson, B. (2013). 'Why Microsoft's Reorganization Is a Bad Idea.' *Stratechery*: https://stratechery.com/2013/why-microsofts-reorganization-is-a-bad-idea/

58. Gray, D. & Vander Wal, T. (2014). *The Connected Company*. Sebastopol: O'Reilly.

59. Brat, I. (2016). 'Whole Foods Works to Reduce Costs and Boost Clout With Suppliers.' *Wall Street Journal:* http://www.wsj.com/articles/whole-foods-works-to-reduce-costs-and-boost-clout-with-suppliers-1455445803

60. Haden, J. (2013). 'Best Way to Track Customer Retention.' *Inc. Magazine*: http://www.inc.com/jeff-haden/best-way-to-calculate-customer-retention-rate.html

61. Donelly, K. (2016). 'Why Customer Lifetime Value Matters (and How to Calculate It for Your Business).' *Shopify Blogs*: https://www.shopify.co.uk/blog/customer-lifetime-value

62. Gotham, E. (2016). 'Calculating customer lifetime value (CLV) in e-commerce.' *Ometria*: https://www.ometria.com/blog/how-to-calculate-customer-lifetime-value-clv-in-ecommerce

63. Maurya, A. (2016). *Scaling Lean: Mastering the Key Metrics for Startup Growth*. New York City: Penguin.

64. Sutton, R.I. & Rao, H. (2014). *Scaling Up Excellence: Getting to More Without Settling for Less*. New York City: Crown Business.

65. Sutton, R.I. & Rao, H. (2014). *Scaling Up Excellence: Getting to More Without Settling for Less*. New York City: Crown Business.

66. These steps have been adapted from Maurya, A. (2016) *Scaling Lean*. New York City: Penguin.

67. Patel, N. & Taylor, B. (2016). 'The Definitive Guide to Growth Hacking.' *Quicksprout*: https://www.quicksprout.com/the-definitive-guide-to-growth-hacking/

68. For a great book on pricing check out Neil Davidson's 2009 *Don't Just Roll The Dice: A usefully short guide to software pricing*: http://neildavidson.com/downloads/dont-just-roll-the-dice-2.0.0.pdf

69. Collier, P.M. (2015). *Accounting for Managers: Interpreting Accounting Information for Decision Making*. New York City: John Wiley & Sons.

70. Howard Schultz's Starbucks memo (Feb 23, 2007). *Financial Times*: https://www.ft.com/content/dc5099ac-c391-11db-9047-000b5df10621

71. Buchanan, L. (2014). 'How to Grow Without Losing What Makes You Great.' *Inc Magazine*: http://www.inc.com/magazine/201403/leigh-buchanan/how-to-scale-your-company.html

72. Feloni, R. (2015). 'Zappos' sneaky strategy for hiring the best people involves a van ride from the airport to the interview.' *Business Insider*: http://www.businessinsider.com/zappos-sneaky-strategy-for-hiring-the-best-people-2015-12

Part Three

1. Evans, B. (2013). 'The Irrelevance of Microsoft.' http://ben-evans.com/benedictevans/2013/7/20/the-irrelevance-of-microsoft

2. Blank, S. (2016). 'Why Visionary CEOs Never Have Visionary Successors.' *Harvard Business Review*: https://hbr.org/2016/10/why-visionary-ceos-never-have-visionary-successors

3. McLean, B. (2014). 'The Empire Reboots.' *Vanity Fair*: http://www.vanityfair.com/news/business/2014/11/satya-nadella-bill-gates-steve-ballmer-microsoft

4. McLean, B. (2014). The Empire Reboots. *Vanity Fair*: http://www.vanityfair.com/news/business/2014/11/satya-nadella-bill-gates-steve-ballmer-microsoft

5. Ulanoff, L (2015). 'In 2015, Microsoft got its groove back.' *Mashable*: http://mashable.com/2015/12/17/2015-microsoft-is-back/#9E7dahMO7mqn

6. Siberzahn, P. (2010). 'Nespresso: when the simplicity of the product hides the complexity of the innovation process.' https://philippesilberzahneng.wordpress.com/2010/03/18/nespresso-complexity-innovation-process/

7. Wikipedia: https://en.wikipedia.org/wiki/Nespresso

8. Osterwalder, A., Pigneur, Y., Bernarda, G. & Smith, A. (2015). *Value Proposition Design: How to Create Products and Services Customers Want*. New York City: John Wiley & Sons.

9. Della-Santa, L. (2013). 'Thinking Again... The Future of Coffee Pod Machines.' *Euromonitor International*: http://blog.euromonitor.com/2013/05/thinking-again-the-future-of-coffee-pod-machines.html

10. Osterwalder, A. (2015). Nespresso Today. *Strategyzer Academy*: https://strategyzer.com/platform/training/courses/business-models-that-work-and-value-propositions-that-sell/1/1/4

11. Osterwalder, A. (2015). Nespresso Today. *Strategyzer Academy*: https://strategyzer.com/platform/training/courses/business-models-that-work-and-value-propositions-that-sell/1/1/4

12. Christensen, C.M., Hall, T., Dillon, K. & Duncan, D.S. (2016). *Competing Against Luck: The Story of Innovation and Customer Choice*. New York City: Harper Business.

13. Sandström, C. & Osborne, R.G. (2011). 'Managing business model renewal.' *International Journal of Business and Systems Research*, 5(5), 461-474.

14. Wee, H.M. & Wu, S. (2009). 'Lean supply chain and its effect on product cost and quality: a case study on Ford Motor Company.' *Supply Chain Management: An International Journal*, 14, 335-341.

15. Osterwalder, A. (2014). 'Navigating Your Business Model Environment.' *Strategyzer Blog*: http://blog.strategyzer.com/posts/2014/7/26/your-business-model-environment

16. Klein, G. (2007). 'Performing a Project Premortem.' *Harvard Business Review*, 85, 18-19.

17. Frankish, J.S., Roberts, R.G., Coad, A., Spears, T.C. & Storey, D.J. (2012). 'Do entrepreneurs really learn? Or do they just tell us that they do?' *Industrial and Corporate Change*, dts016.

18. McGrath, R.G. (2013). *The End of Competitive Advantage: How to Keep Your Strategy Moving as Fast as Your Business*. Boston: Harvard Business Review Press.

19. Jaruzelski, B., Staack, V. & Shinozaki, A. (2016). 'Software-as-a-Catalyst.' *strategy + business*: http://www.strategy-business.com/feature/Software-as-a-Catalyst?gko=7a1a

20. Case, S. (2016). *The Third Wave. An Entrepreneur's Vision of the Future*. New York City: Simon & Schuster.

21. Lessin, S. (2016). 'Era of Lean Startups Nears an End.' *The Information*: https://www.theinformation.com/era-of-lean-startups-nears-an-end

22. Gray, D. & Vander Wal, T. (2014). *The Connected Company*. Sebastopol: O'Reilly.

23. Arrington, M. (2008). 'Yahoo To Close Brickhouse By End Of Year.' *TechCrunch*: http://techcrunch.com/2008/12/09/yahoo-to-close-brickhouse-by-end-of-year/

24. Viki, T., Strong, C. & Kresojevic, S. (2017). *The Lean Product Lifecycle: A playbook for developing innovative and profitable new products*. London: Pearson.

25. This is also connected to the Anna Karenina principle which is an important principle in ecology. https://en.wikipedia.org/wiki/Anna_Karenina_principle

26. Osterwalder, A. (2015). 'The C-Suite Needs a Chief Entrepreneur.' *Harvard Business Review*. https://hbr.org/2015/06/the-c-suite-needs-a-chief-entrepreneur

27. Binns, A., Smith, W.K. & Tushman, M.L. (2011). 'The Ambidextrous CEO.' *Harvard Business Review*, 89, 74-80

28. Chesbrough, H.W. (2011). 'Everything You Need to Know About Open Innovation.' *Forbes*: http://www.forbes.com/sites/henrychesbrough/2011/03/21/everything-you-need-to-know-about-open-innovation/

29. Chesbrough, H.W. & Garman, A.R. (2009). 'How Open Innovation Can Help You Cope in Lean Times.' *Harvard Business Review*, 87(12), 68-76.

30. Raja, B.H. & Sambandan, P. (2015). *Open Innovation in Pharmaceutical Industry: A case study of Eli Lilly*. Master of Science Thesis. Stockholm: Department of Industrial Economics and Management.

31. Ingram, M. (2011). 'Why Most Startup Acquisitions Fail, and Always Will.' *Gigaom*: https://gigaom.com/2011/02/23/why-most-startup-acquisitions-fail-and-always-will/

32. Zhang, M. (2016). 'Adobe Kickbox Gives Employees $1000 Credit Cards And Freedom to Pursue Ideas.' *Forbes*: http://www.forbes.com/sites/mzhang/2015/08/19/adobe-kickbox-gives-employees-1000-credit-cards-and-freedom-to-pursue-ideas/

33. Sutton, R. I. & Rao, H. (2014). *Scaling Up Excellence: Getting to More Without Settling for Less*. New York City: Crown Business.